JOHN BETJEMAN

John Betjeman was born in 1906 and educated at Marlborough and Magdalen College, Oxford. His gave his first radio talk in 1932; future appearances made him into a national celebrity. He was knighted in 1969 and appointed Poet Laureate in 1972. He died in 1984.

STEPHEN GAMES

Stephen Games writes on architecture and language. He was educated at Magdalene College, Cambridge. He has made documentaries for BBC Radio 3, worked for the *Independent*, *Guardian* and *Los Angeles Times*, and was deputy editor of the *RIBA Journal*. He has edited the radio talks of Nikolaus Pevsner and, most recently, *Tennis Whites and Teacakes*, an anthology celebrating Betjeman's England.

TRAINS AND BUTTERED TOAST

Selected Radio Talks

JOHN BETJEMAN

Edited and introduced by
STEPHEN GAMES

JOHN MURRAY

Preface, Introduction and Selection © Stephen Games 2006
Broadcasts © The Estate of John Betjeman 2006

First published in Great Britain in 2006 by John Murray (Publishers)
A division of Hodder Headline

Paperback edition 2007

A CIP catalogue record for this title is available from the British Library

ISBN 978-0-7195-6127-6

Typeset in Monotype Bembo by Servis Filmsetting Ltd, Manchester

Printed and bound by Clays Ltd, St Ives plc

Hodder Headline's policy is to use papers that are natural, renewable and recyclable
products and made from wood grown in sustainable forests. The logging and
manufacturing processes are expected to conform to the environmental regulations of
the country of origin.

John Murray (Publishers)
338 Euston Road
London NW1 3BH

Contents

CONTENTS

ECCENTRICS

CHRISTIAN SOLDIERS

THE COMFORT OF CHURCHES

HOLIDAY ESCAPES

ESSENTIAL VIEWING

AUTOBIOGRAPHY

Preface

The book that follows includes most of the best of Betjeman's radio talks for the BBC but it is not comprehensive. It does not include eight of the seventeen 'Coast and Country' talks (from the 1949 and 1950 series) or his remarkable talk on Aberdeen (1947), all of which were published in *First and Last Loves* in 1952. With one exception only, it misses out all his religious talks from the 1970s, though these may appear in a future volume, and all those broadcasts in which Betjeman appeared alongside other speakers, such as his 'Built to Last' series of 1939.

Space was one of the factors determining what to put in. A sound portrait of the poet William Lisle Bowles deserved to be published but was too long for the space available. On the other hand, three talks that appeared in truncated form in *First and Last Loves* – on a number of West Country churches (1948) – have been included so that they can be appreciated in something closer to their original glory. The other determining factor was quality and this screened out several topical talks, such as Betjeman's assessment of the Festival of Britain exhibition on the South Bank, a number of book reviews and two short stories.

A word needs to be said about the editing. Unlike Betjeman's poetry, very few recordings exist of Betjeman's talks. That this book is as large as it is owes much to the fact that numerous typescripts (and microfilms of typescripts) have survived. These reside in two locations: the BBC's Written Archives Centre in Caversham and the Special Collections Library of the University of Victoria in British Columbia. But this material is a definitive guide neither to what was broadcast nor to what deserves reprinting. A few scripts – especially those in Canada – are Betjeman's original drafts or versions retyped either by his own secretaries or by BBC secretaries. Some are transcriptions made after a broadcast had aired. Others – especially those in Caversham – are copies of studio scripts. The latter invariably have annotations and deletions, sometimes by Betjeman, sometimes by his producers. These may be factual corrections, stylistic changes or edits caused by pressure of time. Even then, errors occur – spellings, place names, dates – as well as grammatical and other inconsistencies.

As editor, I have tried to be as faithful as possible to what I imagine were Betjeman's intentions while saving him from solecisms. In the end, in view of the range and uncertain status of the scripts, I have tended to act as I would have done had this been a new book. I have reincorporated material that seems to have been cut for time, I have corrected simple mistakes and I have standardized – and sometimes updated – spellings, especially where place names have changed or where we no longer use hyphens or apostrophes ('to-day' has become 'today', for example; ''buses' has become 'buses'). In a very few places I have taken the liberty of actually rewording sentences that would otherwise have been confusing. Because of the nature of this book, I have not indicated where these changes have occurred. In that sense, this is not a scholarly edition; but I hope that it is a responsible and respectful one.

This book is none the less made up of archive material, and I therefore need to sound one other warning: many of the places that Betjeman described enthusiastically have changed out of all recognition. His six 'Town Tours' of 1937, for example, were conducted at a time when familiar West Country landmarks were already starting to be demolished. 'As I speak, the Theatre Royal is white powder and broken bricks,' Betjeman lamented on a visit to Plymouth; and that destruction was quickly accelerated by German bombing in the war and the depredations of planners in the 1950s and '60s. Topographical talks in this book should therefore be regarded not as a guide to what can now be seen and enjoyed but as a memorial to what set Betjeman's pulses racing and what he feared the loss of.

When I started hunting for Betjeman's talks, the BBC was able to identify some ninety talks and almost eighty other radio appearances. As this book goes to press, my tally of talks has now topped three hundred, and I want to thank Terry Tuey, working long-distance from Canada, who has helped me in my quest. I also acknowledge the great help given me by the BBC's staff in Caversham. (Researchers should note, however, that neither institution possesses a comprehensive list of Betjeman's radio work; they are welcome to contact me for further information.)

As for other sources, Bevis Hillier's three-volume biography proved invaluable as did Candida Lycett Green's *John Betjeman Letters*. I must also thank David Winter for sharing his memories and allowing me to quote from his autobiography, *Winter's Tale* (Lion, 2001); Peter Newbolt for his help with the poetry and prose of his grandfather Sir Henry Newbolt; R. M. Healey, co-editor of *My Rebellious and Imperfect Eye: Observing Geoffrey Grigson* (Rodopi, 2002) for his advice about Geoffrey Grigson; Virginia Murray at 50 Albemarle Street for access to John Murray's publishing records; the Highgate Literary and Scientific Institution for access to its Betjeman archives; and numerous others including Ann Crawford (Swell), Jane Harding (Ilfracombe), David Harrison (Marzials), Hazel Harvey (Exeter), Michael Howarth (Exeter); David McConkey (St Mark's, Swindon), Angela Nutbrown (Bristol), Stuart Moverly (Plymouth), Tony Rouse (N. T. Carrington), Win Scutt (Plymouth); Ilona Soane-Sands (Alderney), and Caroline Steel and David Trayhurn (Swindon Town). I also wish to express my gratitude to Candida Lycett Green and to Justin Gowers at Gillon Aitken Associates Ltd for wholeheartedly supporting this publication; to Caroline Knox at John Murray, who liked the idea; to my editor Rowan Yapp, who saw it through to completion with unfailing good judgement, and to those other members of John Murray's staff who helped it on its way; to Douglas Mathews for his indexing; to Angela Judd for her typing; and to Bracha Nemeth for her sensible advice at all times.

Finally, every effort has been made to clear permissions. If permission has not been granted please contact the publisher who will include a credit in subsequent printings and editions.

Stephen Games
Muswell Hill, 2005

INTRODUCTION

From trains to buttered toast, John Betjeman's enthusiasms have made him one of the keystones of England's common culture. Associations that we normally discount as sentimentality and nostalgia exercised a powerful grip over him throughout his life and he was rebellious enough to stand his ground and insist that they mattered not just to himself but to his audience. Against all odds, he made his case. Thanks to his determination, his memories and loves are now an intrinsic part of our literary heritage and have reawoken the English to their past to an extent without parallel anywhere else in Europe or America.

The chances of Betjeman's becoming a national icon seem slight when one looks back on his career. Although the product of Oxford University and an intimate of some of its most brilliant minds, he was eccentric and homespun and passionately at odds with the received wisdom of his day. He was a stubborn and self-taught amateur in the English tradition and even his admirers found him odd. His field of expertise was wayward: he visited the unvisited, read the unread and learned piecemeal from other one-offs like himself. And yet he was able to turn the tide of history, rescue nineteenth-century architecture from being written off and win the affection of some of his most doubting onlookers.

How he did this is evident in the collection of radio talks that follows. Now brought together for the first time, these essays beautifully reflect Betjeman's blend of wit, whimsy, nostalgia and criticism. Their themes, touching on everything from people and poetry to places and publishing, testify to his own remarkable scope and combine his fervent pleas for provincial preservation with a unique capacity for enjoyment. They also reveal very clearly the arc of his career from a bare-knuckle fighter against mock-Tudor bungalows to Britain's national romancer for whom nothing was ugly.

Betjeman began his broadcasting career in what is generally regarded as the BBC's golden age. At the time, radio broadcasting was divided into two services, one national and one regional. With the war, it was reorganized into the more formal Home Service and the more entertaining Forces Programme, with the intellectually ambitious Third Programme being added in 1946. This segregating of output meant that Betjeman, who in 1937 had described himself on air as a '*semi*-intellectual', could easily have been pigeonholed as Home and Third material. In fact he broadcast across all the networks and it was this flexibility that enabled him to reach all sections of the population.

His breakthrough, in terms of mass appeal, came with his appearances during the war in 'The Brains Trust', broadcast on the Home Service and repeated on the Forces Programme, in which a panel of experts answered listeners' questions on political and philosophical subjects. After the war the Light Programme replaced the Forces Programme and Betjeman became a welcome guest on two other popular talk programmes: 'Any Questions', the Friday-night current-affairs programme, from 1949, and 'Woman's Hour', from 1952. In modern terms, he had acquired the rare distinction of multi-channel appeal.

'The Brains Trust' and 'Any Questions' established Betjeman as a knowledgeable and provocative sceptic and his contrarian opinions and self-deprecation found fans not just among his listeners but with BBC producers and fellow panellists, at a time when public manners were still marked by deference and a stiff upper lip. 'Woman's Hour' extended his reach by turning him into a personality of special appeal to female listeners. He also benefited from radio's growing interest in poetry during and after the war, which led to his being used as a reader both of other poets' work (his first reading was of Tennyson's 'Audley Court' in 1943) and later of his own.

Betjeman's versatility was evident immediately the Corporation relaxed its habit of pre-scripting all output. Once speakers were free to talk *extempore*, a new sort of broadcasting emerged, creating opportunities for more instinctive performers. Betjeman made the transition easily, proving to be a natural ad-libber and satirist. Over the course of nearly fifty years he made more than three hundred appearances on radio, conducting interviews, taking part in and chairing discussions, reviewing books and reading short stories. Few of these broadcasts have survived in audio form. There are, however, two large archives of his talks scripts – at the BBC Written Archives Centre in Caversham, England, and at the University of Victoria in British Columbia, Canada – and it is from these sources that this book has managed to resurrect Betjeman as a radio personality.

The range of the talks is distinctive. Having begun his career as a writer on architecture, Betjeman was naturally drawn to buildings but, encouraged and inspired by his friend the artist John Piper, he came to write about them in terms of topography and townscape. Many of his most brilliant talks concern the way in which places are seen. He spoke about the impact of light and shade, the effect of rain, the view from a train window, the profound emotion of suddenly seeing the sea. He also insisted, in defiance of the new profession of architectural historians, that buildings were inseparable from those who lived in them.

He was equally intrigued by people and their worlds. An inveterate gossip, he relished the minutiae of lives overlooked and wrote a number of very amusing talks about West Country poets and hymn-writing vicars. Throughout his writing, one feels his deep sense of identification with eccentricity and the urgent need to defend individuality. In one characteristic talk, he broached the unlikely topic of Tennyson as a humorist; in another he spoke about a parish priest who, at the age of twenty-one, had swum out to a rock off the coast of Bude and sat in the moonlight like a mermaid, naked but for an oilskin wrap, combing a wig of seaweed.

In any study of popular culture in the twentieth century, it is impossible to miss the drift from the earnest at the start of the century to the lightweight at the end. That move can be seen in miniature in Betjeman's engagement with the BBC. His later talks – from the 1940s – seem more winsome but it was seriousness of purpose that first led him to knock on the BBC's door in 1929.

The BBC's first Director-General, John Reith, had wanted radio to elevate the masses but most listeners tuned in for its popular music. Highbrows were horrified; so was Betjeman. In his famously angry poem about Slough, he only excused the town's 'bald young clerks' for not knowing 'the birdsong from the radio' because their existence on what he called the Great Worst Road meant that they had 'tasted Hell'. And in a satire that he broadcast in 1938, he sympathized with Colonel Cabbage, a stereotypical seaside resident, whose afternoon nap was disturbed when 'a confounded wireless set somewhere or other started blarin' out one of those wretched croonin' songs'.

Betjeman's antipathy to popular broadcasting was part of an overall snobbery about the masses and mass culture. In 1949, while watching day-trippers on a ferry, he complained that

> In one horrible car like a sausage made of black plastic, a fleshy couple had the wireless on and read newspapers. They represent a type of visitor who'll not be listening to this talk. They represent those unseeing ones who swirl round the Isle of Wight in luxury coaches and never go off the beaten track. For them this western and remoter part of the island, for which we are bound, will be dull indeed.

But, although he associated the radio with vulgarity, he also imagined that radio could be used to attack mass culture. To do this, it had to offer a higher quality of aspiration and that meant two things: making people aware of what he later called 'the repulsiveness of their surroundings' and introducing them to modern architecture.

To begin with, he directed himself not at the public but at officialdom. In his very first talk, in 1932, on the proposed demolition of Waterloo Bridge, he confessed to feeling 'rather alarmed by experiments in steel and concrete' but went on to acknowledge that the introduction of these materials into architecture 'has shown that new proportions must be made'. It was no longer enough to festoon Georgian decorations on fine steel structures like flowers around a maypole, he suggested: a new bridge for Waterloo must be 'the first great work of a new age'.

As assistant editor on the *Architectural Review* between 1930 and 1935, Betjeman repeated the line that any young enthusiast for architecture would have taken at the time. He went on to try to persuade the BBC to broadcast talks that would raise the profile of the architectural profession and move the government to create jobs in areas where architectural preservation was needed. Almost without exception, the BBC's Talks Department found his ideas unconvincing. 'What is all this bilge?' wrote one producer to another in response to the latest of his ideas. 'We had a whole thumping series on architecture from every point of view and it bored listeners excessively.'

As his efforts continued, he gained the reputation inside the BBC's Broadcasting House headquarters as a crank. When in 1937 the spy and BBC producer Guy Burgess asked him to give a talk in a series called 'Eccentrics', Burgess did so with the words 'I said to myself who more suitable than you to talk about one of the others?' Betjeman's appearance did not help. Wilhelmine Cresswell, to whom he was briefly engaged in 1933, recalled years later that 'he was a sort of joke we all knew. His hair was like last year's bird's nest. And his teeth were covered in green slime.'

Betjeman must have hoped for a warmer reception from the handful of BBC insiders he had known at Oxford or met subsequently. In its absence he was buoyed up by his own bubbling enthusiasm. In 1932, having just received his second commission to broadcast, he wrote a confirmation note brimming with confidence that read, 'Three o-clock will be splendid, Old Boy. Sorry not to have replied before. Yours til death, J. Betjeman' and jokily added a rubber stamp at the bottom saying, 'Statements in these letters cannot be guaranteed by the medical officers.'

As it became evident that what thrilled architects about architecture thrilled no one else, Betjeman found himself forced to try other approaches to becoming a broadcaster. In 1934 he attempted to lever himself out of his new appointment as film critic of the *Evening Standard* and into an equivalent position at the BBC:

> I get damn'd well paid here but I'd rather have less pay and more congenial hours. Writing to please the stinking advertisers and inane stuff about whether Garbo wears silk or linen stockings are not in my line – for long. I have told the *Evening Standard* this and I would have no difficulty in changing over to you . . . On the BBC I should be able to say what I like.

His gushing manner was counter-productive. 'I think I had better be quite frank with you,' came the damning reply. 'I doubt very much whether you are "a master of the microphone". I think your writing is admirable but that's quite a different thing, and particularly in the case of film criticism, where we want someone who will ring the bell every time.' In 1935 an overture of renewed friendship to another talks producer, whom he had known at Oxford, received polite encouragement but nothing more tangible.

Betjeman had emerged from university as a bright young thing, an urban sophisticate and an unashamed social climber. In a studio discussion in London about the movie industry in 1937, he was introduced light-heartedly as having 'learned to speak with the voice of authority at about the same age as Napoleon'. He was also a cynic. When the film-maker Sidney Bernstein asked of Betjeman in the same programme 'Why does he sneer . . .?', the chairman, the laconic Irish barrister and wine expert Maurice Healy, had to come riding to the rescue: 'I don't think Mr Betjeman was really sneering – I think it was only his natural expression.'

In some ways Betjeman was not a natural broadcaster. When it was suggested in 1943 that Winifred Salmon, the Acting Director of Talks, produce him in a talk on war-weariness, she replied that 'his particular voice and manner (no offence intended) might make a good many people think he was weary before the war began. He must contrive to sound entirely sincere so that if he doesn't convince people he may at least sound like a man who believes in his own values.' David Winter, the last producer to work with him in the mid-1970s, commented that 'his voice was technically unexciting, lacking in dynamic range and trapped in a slightly camp Oxbridge accent.' Winter continued, however, that Betjeman had 'a completely distinctive broadcasting style' and that his voice 'was undeniably arresting to the ear. The listener was invited to share his boyish enthusiasms and fascinations. And there was, of course, that quite wicked sense of humour, made all the more mischievous by the artless way in which the barbs were delivered.'

What changed the manner and scope of Betjeman's public utterances was the interest taken in him by the BBC's newly launched West of England service. Early in 1934 he had moved from London to Uffington, on the borders of Oxfordshire and Berkshire. Just sixty miles from his new home was the new Bristol studio that the BBC had opened three years earlier in a converted Victorian villa in Whiteladies

Road. 'It wasn't too big and it wasn't an appendage of London,' Betjeman recalled in 1970. 'It looked rather like a dentist's house in a provincial town. The dentist's waiting-room was the studio, and his surgery in the front was where the staff worked who were grand enough to be on the ground floor. The rest were up in the bedrooms.'

Betjeman always loved Bristol and thought of it as a happy place. He later described it as 'the liveliest part of the BBC'. 'Engineers, producers, artistes – I like that final "e" in "artiste", which is what I think I am – knew each other and ate and drank together – the natural-history people, mostly in tweeds; the industrial correspondents in serge; the sprucely dressed announcers . . .'

It was here that Betjeman met J. C. Pennethorne Hughes, whom he had known very slightly at Oxford and who became a Talks producer in Bristol in 1935. Pennethorne Hughes was a year younger than Betjeman, had worked briefly for the railways after leaving Oxford and later became a writer on witchcraft, topography and local lore. A troubled soul, he was also the great-grandson of the architect Sir James Pennethorne, who had laid out Carlton House Terrace for John Nash and married the illegitimate daughter of Mrs Nash and the Prince Regent – a pedigree that delighted Betjeman. The poet Geoffrey Grigson believed that Pennethorne Hughes gravitated to the BBC as a compromise between teaching and the cloth and found a role for himself talent-spotting for broadcasters. In Grigson's words, 'More than anyone except Betjeman himself Jim Hughes was responsible for establishing the cult of Betjemania in broadcasting.'

Betjeman's first commission from Bristol was a diversion. In 1936 Pennethorne Hughes invited Betjeman to cover three West of England spring festivals: the parading of the Padstow and Minehead hobby horses, on May Day, and the Helston Furry Dance, usually held on 8 May. Part of the ensuing programme contained the following surrealistic exchange with a local speaker:

BETJEMAN:
What's the origin of all this dancing? I've heard a story about it. Somebody told me that a fiery dragon sailed across the town one day and I certainly did notice this morning somebody dressed up as St George with a fire helmet on.

LOCAL:
Well now, fancy that! I see the twinkle in your eye and sparkling like a good one, so I know you've got that all right. I could see that in a minute.

BETJEMAN:
Oh, yes. I'm clever!

LOCAL:
Yes. I thought so too when I seen you –
Betjeman giggles . . .

LOCAL:
Now this is a little secret that I'm going to tell you before you go, and that's this. Suppose there's in a great crowd in Australia, say, there was a man there with one leg. Well, he'd have a stump for the t'other, wouldn't uh?

BETJEMAN:
Yes, yes. I agree there.

LOCAL:
Very good. Now, little band start up 'Helston Floral Dance' and you see that stump wiggle and twitch, and he'd be beating time with that stump. I say in a minute, 'That's a Helston man. He was born in Helston and was reared there, I'll swear.'
Betjeman chuckles . . .

LOCAL:
Well, anybody can tell that. Well, you can see that yourself, can't thee? Now, look, be honest.

BETJEMAN:
Oh yes, I can see that. I've started moving about myself.

LOCAL:
I know – I can see you all of a jiggle now. I want you to stay quiet a minute and 'ark to the story!

What followed was rather more substantial. Pennethorne Hughes quickly established that what lay at the core of Betjeman's soul was not a passion for modern architecture but a wistful longing for an age just out of reach. This realization resulted in a complete turnabout in Betjeman's broadcasting. Out of this, he and Pennethorne Hughes created programmes that introduced a wholly novel conception of a nostalgia rooted not in the long ago but in the relatively shallow soil of recent decades.

In the course of two important series – 'Town Tours' and 'Built to Last' – in the late 1930s, Betjeman made twelve programmes that established his reputation as a broadcaster. He looked at threats to Georgian and Regency townscapes, which few then valued, in Bristol, Plymouth, Exeter and other towns in the south-west of England. He also raged against the fashion for the inauthentic – especially fake 'municipal Renaissance' and 'mock-Tudor' buildings – and hit out at the conversion of genuine old buildings into vulgar tourist attractions. Most controversially, Betjeman linked the devastation of townscapes to the planning decisions of elected councillors, accusing them loosely of incompetence, apathy, corruption and self-interest, and charging the speculative builders who kept them busy with bribery and aesthetic ignorance.

In one of his hardest-hitting talks, in 1937, he described the railway town of Swindon as 'a blot on the earth', floundering about 'like a helpless octopus, spreading its horrid tentacles into quiet untroubled places, waiting no doubt till one long and loathsome tentacle shall twine with that of the vile octopus London'. In a talk two years later he wondered why the offence of common littering carried a fine of £5 while the litter of ugly bungalows generated a hefty reward for those who built them.

Two years after the war a sympathetic BBC producer would advise Betjeman to make his talks more temperate if he hoped to turn enemies into friends. At the time, however, Pennethorne Hughes found the talks arresting and persuasive and set out to promote them unconditionally. He was doubly successful. From 1938 he managed to get London to rebroadcast all Betjeman's Bristol programmes nationwide; and in so doing he made topography and architecture into two of Bristol's enduring concerns. Thanks to Pennethorne

Hughes, Betjeman not only presented far more talks from Bristol than from London but also presented more talks on his core interests. It was with some prescience that Betjeman described Bristol, in the first of his 1937 talks, as 'always a pioneer city in movements that sweep the rest of the country'.

Betjeman could easily have turned into a provincial West Country phenomenon. In his Bristol talks of the late 1930s, he talks of loathing what London was turning into. What brought him back to the capital was the war. Early in 1940 Betjeman got a full-time job at the Ministry of Information, then quartered inside London University in Malet Street. This move, coupled with the introduction of petrol rationing, meant that he could no longer travel to Bristol as easily as before. Broadcasting House in London now had to take over the business of rehearsing him and producing him in programmes that Bristol was originating. It also had to liaise more closely on his scripts, not just because he was now being broadcast nationally but because, with the outbreak of hostilities, all broadcasts were having to be approved by a government censor.

As a consequence Betjeman started to come in contact with BBC staff who had known of him only at a distance before – in particular with the powerful figure of George Barnes, the new Director of Talks, who found him amusing and became a firm friend. This gave him a patron at the very hub of the BBC's operation. It was from this base that his status as a celebrity began to grow.

Betjeman's job at the Ministry involved him in vetting propaganda films and this reinforced his growing awareness that in order to persuade people of anything it was usually necessary to identify with them. He had first learned of the need to do so following his uncomplimentary remarks about Swindon in 1937. He immediately received a letter from a local listener objecting to what he had said. It was an epiphany: the first time that Betjeman had had to face the fact that the public consisted of real individuals with real feelings, rather than a stereotypical mass. For years afterwards he was tortured by guilt. A brief explanation in a subsequent programme was not enough; nor was an apology in a talk in 1940. But eleven years later he ended the third of three talks on West Country churches by praising the honesty of Swindon's 'red-brick' rash of ugly buildings and admiring its architecturally undistinguished main church for the saintliness of those who worshipped in it. He then made the following act of public contrition:

> I know that the people of Swindon first taught me not to be so la-di-da and architectural, not to judge people by the houses they live in, nor churches only by their architecture. I would sooner be on my knees within the wooden walls of St Saviour's [Swindon] than leaning elegantly forward in a cushioned pew in an Oxford college chapel.

His first attempt to reach all rather than just some of his audience came in March 1940. In a talk about the need to use trains rather than cars, he imagined himself sitting in a crowded carriage and getting drawn into conversation with other passengers. It was a symbolic moment. From then on, Betjeman's relationship with the public was inclusive rather than superior. He openly beat his breast about his pre-war snobberies and gave a sentimental embrace to 'the average man'. In the next of his talks, four months later, he acknowledged his sneers of a few years earlier and found himself able to say:

> I *like* suburbs; nothing is ugly. Bicycling in the suburbs of a great city, I see a strange beauty in those quiet deserted evenings with the few remaining children showing off in the evening sunlight, laburnums and lilac weeping over the front gate, father smoking his pipe and rolling the lawn, mother knitting at the open window.

Subsequent broadcasts found him speaking of having made new friends as a result of billeting and of having been touched by the kindnesses that the war had brought out in people.

In the main, this new generosity of spirit carried through into all his post-war work. When he had spoken about the British holiday-maker in 1938, what he had seen was a caricature:

> Which are you? I don't know which you are.
> Probably you are of the biggest lot of all – those who want cinemas, dance halls, theatres, fun, noise, splendour, sand stretching for miles, bathing machines, mixed bathing, lights, winkles, rock as opposed to rocks, souvenirs, postcards, funfairs. Probably you've seen enough of the country all the rest of the year and want a contrast now. More

probably you like the town – country frightens you – and you want
more of it, and some sea and bathing chucked in as well.

But when he reported at first hand on the tourist industry in the Isle
of Man eleven years later, he saw real people:

> A small and perfect dance band strikes up – ah, the dance bands of the
> Isle of Man! Soon a thousand couples are moving beautifully, the
> cotton dresses of the girls like vivid tulips in all this pale cream and
> pink, the sports coats and dark suits of the men acting as a background
> to so much airy colour. The rhythmic dance is almost tribal so that
> even this middle-aged spectator is caught up in mass excitement, pure
> and thrilling and exalting.

In personalizing the public, Betjeman also personalized himself.
Having been an outsider and an unknown quantity, he now turned
into an Everyman, confessing to his own loves and hates in an effort
to clear the slate and lay the groundwork for the post-war world. He
also set about introducing the public to his pre-war themes as if they
were newly discovered.

The same change occurred in his poetry. With the war, he
warmed to characters who were 'common' only by virtue of their
social class and cooled to those who were cheap because of what they
stood for: the woman at prayer who begged God to bomb the
Germans but to take special care of 189 Cadogan Square, for example. He also warmed to places he had previously sniffed at and
began introducing into his verses the names of commercial products
– Craven A and Kia-Ora and Selfridge's and Meccano – for the sheer
pleasure of their rhythm, their associations and, in spite of himself,
their modernity. This sense that the war promoted of participating in
a new democracy transformed him.

Betjeman was aware that his embrace of sentimentality confused listeners who continued to hear in his voice the satirist that he had been
before the war. Many assumed he was mocking what he now professed to love – something he denied some years later when giving a
public poetry reading at the Stratford-upon-Avon Festival. Even
close friends wondered if his professed affection for the suburbs was
not a double bluff, a private joke rather than the raw material of an

aesthetic revolution. At a time of massive public support for a modern, better world, it was also strange to hear Betjeman calling for the clock to be turned back to a time before cars and cinemas.

How did he reconcile his new openness to popular culture with his passion for the past? Partly by suggesting that the two were connected – a concept that since the late 1960s has been encapsulated into the word 'heritage', meaning those national assets 'bequeathed by the people' to the next generation. The historical texture of towns and villages should be preserved, he said in a talk in 1943; rather than converting slums and cottages into blocks of flats (with multi-denominational worship rooms on their roofs), they should simply be brought up to modern habitable standards. Most contemporaries thought such an idea ridiculous. As late as 1948 Evelyn Gibbs, then editor of 'Woman's Hour', found herself mystified by Betjeman's modest suggestion that remote homesteads in Cornwall should be fitted with toilets.

The bond between people and past became a central part of Betjeman's philosophy and set him against anyone who threatened the status quo. Academics, politicians and businessmen were a long-standing threat; foreigners were a new one – especially clever refugee architects with their love of Bauhaus design. This thought reflected a fear that would come to dominate conservative thinking: that the new rational architecture of the left, once it was adopted universally, would be as oppressive to England as the politics of the extreme right and as damaging to the spirit as to the landscape. In a talk in 1943 Betjeman spoke of Nazis and modern, progressive town planners as if they had a shared agenda:

> Are all roads to be straight and all wild-rose hedges to be swept away? All trees except quick-growing conifers to be cut down? . . . I do not believe we are fighting for the privilege of living in a highly de-veloped community of ants. That is what the Nazis want. For me, at any rate, England stands for the Church of England, eccentric incum-bents, oil-lit churches, Women's Institutes . . .

To protect his vision, he set about giving talks that proposed a new pantheon of popular heroes – unknown individualists, eccentrics, nonconformists, people who refused to bow to the normal canon of accepted beliefs – and evoked an old England that would prove a model for the new one: 'I know the England I want to come home to is not very different from that in which you want to live. If it were some efficient ant heap which the glass-and-steel, flat-roof, straight-road boys want to make it, then how could we love it as we do?'

This wartime realignment steeled Betjeman for his fight against philistinism. Having started off as a flibbertigibbet at the BBC, he suddenly became quite remarkably focused. He now had a subject to which he could return again and again. Looking back on the talks that followed, we may misread them as genial appreciations of England's heritage; but in the context of their times they were the product not of the 'teddy bear to the nation', which is how *The Times* saw him years later, but of a young firebrand moved not by mellowness and old age but by anxiety and alienation.

His England was in peril; he saw fifth columnists taking over from inside. His only weapon was an alternative vision. And so when he resorted to nostalgia, or marvelled at polished oak pews and rusty croquet hoops on rectory lawns, he did so not just as a lament but as a provocation. In spite of the bullying he had endured at school and his subsequent struggle to raise his social status, he was delighted by Mrs F. M. Alexander's line about 'the rich man in his castle' and wallowed in the reverence that he thought had once attached to the traditional English squirearchy. In a talk about the poet William Lisle Bowles (not included in this collection), he even quoted with relish:

> How false the charge, how foul the calumny
> On England's generous aristocracy,
> That, wrapped in sordid selfish apathy,
> They feel not for the poor!
>   Ask is it true?
> Lord of the whirling wheels, the charge is false!

Unlike those architectural historians whom he regarded as rivals and pedants, Betjeman liked to present himself as a practical man. He was self-taught rather than academic. He knew how things worked and could make programmes that gave advice ('How to Look at a

Church', 'How to Look at Books', 'How to Look at a Town'). He
travelled, he conducted his research on location rather than just in
libraries and he knew his English churches: in one talk he claimed to
have visited five thousand of the twenty thousand that then existed.
He knew his Victorian railway companies as if they were old friends.
He knew his Victorian poets: he had really read them. And he knew
his plants – the mesembryanthemums and cotoneasters and other
regulars of Victorian plantsmen.

He also loved the sound of words. Barely a talk passed without reference to an ilex tree – 'holly or holm oak' to most other people –
and to feather-grey slate roofs. Thinking about what gave him comfort when away from England in the war, he rattled off a list of places,
as delicious in his mouth as chocolate. 'To think of the names is to
feel better,' he said: 'Huish Episcopi, Whitchurch Canonicorum,
Willingale Spain, Tickencote, Bourton-on-the-Hill, Iwerne Minster,
Piddletrenthide, South Molton, Wotton, Norton, Evenlode, Fairford,
Canons Ashby, Bag Enderby, Kingston Bagpuize.'

The lyricism of his prose has a very evident poetic root. Two of
his later talks begin with sentences in iambic pentameter:

> We came to Looe by unimportant lanes.

and

> Safe and wide and sheltered Weymouth Bay!

His prose style was indirectly influenced by the watercolour tech-
nique that he had learned from his art master at Marlborough school
('Wet the whole surface for sky, apply cobalt blue and ultramarine
but no prussian blue, and if you want a grey cloud add light red to
the ultramarine while the surface is still wet. Now apply blotting
paper or a handkerchief to get the patchy effect of clouds . . .'). The
following example from 1948, with its rhetorical inversions of
speech, perfectly illustrates the dabbing of Betjeman's brush as he
enjoys the use of mechanical coloration, of list and repetition as
rhythmic devices and of favourite words for detail and highlight:

> Down what lanes, across how many farmyards, resting in how many
> valleys, topping what hills and suddenly appearing round the corners
> of what ancient city streets are the churches of England? The many

pinnacles in Somerset, of rough granite from the moors in Devon and Cornwall, of slate by the sea coasts, brushed with lichen, spotted with saffron, their rings of five and six bells pouring music among the windy elm trees as they have poured their sound for centuries, still they stand, the towers and spires of the West.

Betjeman's innovative adaptations of the poetic, with their collo-quialisms and Tennysonian apostrophes, were regarded in their day as modern and witty hybrids, particularly striking at a time when most other radio performers were striving to be succinct. An affectionate *Punch* parody captured his tone perfectly in 1954:

> Ah, Smoggy Fields! Victim of Progress and the Welfare State! Yet your ragged elms and stuccoed railway-station (Sancton Wood, 1848, but ruined by British Railways of course) recall to me a bright morning on which I set out with my great-uncle to see the opening of the White City. What art-nouveau panes may not still lurk in your Ladies' Waiting Room? What sets of tennis may not be played out in the dusk on your Municipal Courts? What etc.? Ah! etc., etc.*

Betjeman's talks revel in gossip and speculation; accuracy was his paramount concern less often. After making a programme in the mid-1970s about the hymn-writing author of 'Onward, Christian sol-diers', Sabine Baring-Gould, he was taken to task for claiming that, as a young curate, Baring-Gould had lined up all the virgins from the village mill and chosen the most fertile-looking to be his wife. When his producer put it to him that the story was malicious invention, Betjeman apparently sucked in his teeth and then muttered that he was sure he had heard the story somewhere and that anyway it was charming rather than malicious.

The BBC forgave him. More than thirty years earlier he had talked about the blood-and-thunder poet Sir Henry Newbolt, by then hopelessly out of fashion, claiming wrongly that Newbolt's only son had died in the First World War. (Betjeman may have been confusing Newbolt with Kipling, whose son was killed at eighteen, six weeks after reaching the front.) Newbolt's son was surprised to learn of his own death and wrote to the BBC to say so. Pennethorne Hughes,

---

* Peter Clarke, 'Non-Stopography', *Punch*, 13 October 1954.

who had produced the programme, ran to Betjeman's defence. The son was, after all, very nearly killed in the war and had suffered shell concussion, 'which may, I suggest without facetiousness, be a reason for his being touchy'. 'What is really infuriating', Pennethorne Hughes continued, in a letter to George Barnes, then the Acting Director of Talks, 'is that we should have been lucky enough to discover anyone who would talk about Newbolt without laughing at him, and then through his making this one silly mistake should have it implied that there are other admirers who would have done better.' The Newbolt family should have been grateful; accuracy aside, 'the talk seems to have been a very successful one.'

The next proposal for a Betjeman talk was prefaced by a promise by Pennethorne Hughes that 'Humbled by Newbolt, [Betjeman] should not do anything dangerous.' Later in the year, Barnes sent Betjeman a whimsical note that read, 'Once again I shoulder my cross and offer to rehearse you for your talk on Thursday 4th July . . . I wonder which family you will offend this time.'

Betjeman made his last talks for Pennethorne Hughes in 1940. The following year he was posted to Dublin to become the UK's press attaché. When he came back thirty months later in the summer of 1943, he found that Pennethorne Hughes had been sent to Cairo as Egypt's Director of Broadcasting.

Pennethorne Hughes's vacancy was filled by Geoffrey Grigson, one of England's great cultural entrepreneurs and a man with a well-deserved reputation for bringing out new talent and forging helpful introductions. He and Betjeman were birds of a very different feather. They had known each at Oxford, often fell out over poetry and politics and Betjeman's snobberies but saw each other socially. Betjeman respected Grigson as a critic, asked him to read a book proposal, sent him proofs of his poetry and invited him to write a propaganda film for the Ministry. Grigson, although he found Betjeman's verse too lightweight with its regular metre and neat rhymes, wrote generously about it in public and even recommended that Betjeman be erected in Piccadilly Circus or bought for the nation.

Grigson had joined the BBC in late 1942, working for the Talks Department, which operated out of Bristol for much of the war.

He admired Betjeman as a broadcaster and did all he could to promote him on the air. He complimented Betjeman on his 'marvellous ability to be on the listeners' side' and assured a fellow producer that Betjeman was 'a kindly and engaging broadcaster' who 'doesn't set himself a low standard, or one too far from the centre of common taste'. When the Acting Director of Talks wondered whether Betjeman was capable of sympathizing with public attitudes to wartime privations ('I wish I cared more about the war,' Betjeman wrote in a private letter to John Piper and his wife in 1941), Grigson insisted that 'Whatever one may know about him oneself, I find that he sounds sincere, convinced and rigorous. The fact remains that we get a bigger correspondence after his talks down here than we get after talks by any other speaker, and that correspondence is always 99% appreciative.'

Jenifer Wayne, a Features producer at Bristol, recalled in her autobiography* in 1979 how 'Occasionally, [Grigson] brought in his friend, the then young and just up-and-coming John Betjeman and they would stir their tea with the communal teaspoon, kept on a chain at the end of the counter, and retire to a side table, where they enjoyed their own company and jokes.'

Under Grigson's influence, Betjeman gave five talks not on planning or topography but on the publishing trade, a field dear to them both. The results represent the most journalistic of all Betjeman's talks, though not necessarily the most successful. Grigson wanted Betjeman to look at how paper rationing was affecting what publishers chose to print and how this in turn was affecting the public's reading and book-buying habits. Betjeman, by contrast, wanted to persuade listeners that, with the wartime shortage of cheap new fiction, they should revert, as he did, to Edwardian classics and second-hand bookshops. This discrepancy between Grigson's objectivity and Betjeman's advocacy was matched by a discrepancy in tone between the need for critical intelligence and a preference for anecdotes and plot lines.

Betjeman craved security – social and financial – but also needed to feel independent. These two drives collided in his relationship

---

* *The Purple Dress*, Jenifer Wayne, Victor Gollancz, 1979.

with George Barnes, an empire-builder and, from 1946, the first Controller of the Third Programme. Two years earlier, with the prospect that Grigson would soon be giving up his BBC job, Barnes took over the baton of Betjemania and made Betjeman his protégé, keeping a fatherly eye on him. For several years Barnes's house, near Tenterden in Kent, was a virtual second home for Betjeman and their two families spent several happy summer holidays together in France. Betjeman called Barnes 'The Commander', became a close friend but struggled at the same time not to be subsumed by him.

As Director of Talks, Barnes had warmed to Betjeman ever since the Newbolt faux pas. He had also warmed to the idea of putting Betjeman on the Talks Department's payroll and had persuaded himself that Betjeman liked the idea too. When a vacancy came up in March 1944, Barnes lunched Betjeman at his club and triumphantly unveiled his proposal. To his surprise, Betjeman turned the offer down in favour of an unlikely posting with the Admiralty in Bath, in a department that dealt with the prioritization of supplies. Soon regretting this mysterious transfer, Betjeman went back to Barnes in despair. Barnes found another vacancy for him four months later only to have Betjeman turn him down a second time.

Betjeman also resisted Barnes's programme ideas. Barnes constantly tried to capitalize on their energetic conversations about Victoriana but could rarely stir Betjeman into action. In December 1944 Barnes wrote to him to try and pin him down:

> I wish you would do some work in addition to expressing willingness. For instance, the idea which I put to you some time ago that some kind of broadcast series might be devised to illustrate the great clashes of thought in this country in recent years . . . What about the Oxford Movement? . . . Other subjects which I have in mind are: the controversy over Darwin's theories on evolution, and the first impact of Wesleyanism. Of course you will want to do the Gothic revival. That might come later, but is too visual and too narrow to start with.

Barnes was more successful when, in 1947, he, Grigson (now freelance) and the Talks Department concocted a series that would enable Betjeman and other presenters to visit and speak about places that had inspired earlier writers. 'We all agreed that you would be our first choice,' Barnes told him. Grigson had recommended 'some immense Gothic fantasy in the Midlands called Grace Dieu, or some such foreign name; or does Fingal's Cave or Godmanchester appeal more?' This time Betjeman agreed to take part and chose Aberdeen.

Betjeman's invariable truculence reflected his awareness of his dependence on Barnes. He did not want to be a hired hand and did not want to be beholden to anyone's good intentions for him. At the same time, he needed more income. He was so embarrassed by this conflict that when his *Selected Poems* came out in 1948 he sent a begging letter to Barnes, cheekily signing it 'Tambimuttu', the name of the Sinhalese poet who had founded *Poetry London* in 1939 and edited it throughout the war: 'The BBC hasn't been particularly friendly lately, but as I know we can count on you as a sympathizer, we expect better things . . . Incidentally it is about time you broadcast some of my poems. I am having my book sent to your private address by registered post. Please return . . .'

The solution to Betjeman's financial problems was to give more broadcasts. Up until the late 1940s his output for the BBC had been modest. Since 1936, allowing for peaks in 1937 (ten appearances), 1939 (nine) and 1944 (fourteen), he had appeared on air only about five times a year. In 1949 his workload suddenly shot up, perhaps at the instigation of Barnes, and took in fifty appearances, including twenty-three talks, in two years. Under the producership of Gilbert Phelps, he presented three studies of West of England churches, the last of which the new Controller of the Third Programme, Harman Grisewood, an Oxford friend, regarded as a model of its kind and preserved on a Telediphone disc. Betjeman also made seventeen journeys to West Country towns for Bristol's 'Coast and Country' series for Rupert Annand, his new Pennethorne Hughes.

Meanwhile, in London, he started doing one-off talks for Eileen Molony, two of which she published in a series of anthologies that she later compiled on the wonders of Britain. He tried to flirt with the young art historian and producer Basil Taylor while doing a programme for him on the mythical history of Padstow. (Taylor resisted.) He also gave three talks in a nine-part series on houses produced by Richard (R. E.) Keen.

Confirmation that Betjeman had arrived as a radio personality came in April 1949 when the first of many charitable organizations asked him to present the weekly appeal on its behalf in the Home Service's 'The Week's Good Cause'. He was such a success that between 1956 and 1972 he presented an average of one appeal a year, mostly for church-related causes, which represents a rationing of his use by the Appeals producers. He was also so compelling a radio personality that in 1954 he satisfied the Tom Stoppard test of celebrity by appearing on 'Desert Island Discs'. A year later he took part in what the Controller of the Light Programme called a 'delightful' interview with Gilbert Harding.

Betjeman was now fully in command and his talks expressed his confidence in a profusion of superlatives about the world around him. Glasgow Cathedral was 'the most satisfying mediaeval cathedral in these islands'; the Georgian architecture of Devon was 'the simplest, gayest, lightest, creamiest Georgian of all'; Ilfracombe Museum was 'quite the nicest and most old-fashioned provincial museum I've ever seen'; Lyndhurst parish church by William White was in 'the most fanciful, fantastic Gothic style that ever I have seen'; the five-and-a-half miles of railway into Padstow was 'the most beautiful train journey I know'. He brought the same gusto to people. In 1956, interviewing the architect Professor Sir Albert Richardson, who was by then universally regarded as a silly old duffer, Betjeman drooled with hammy but unfeigned deference.

To present an average of one talk a month, however, involved a greater commitment of time than he was prepared to sustain, especially when he knew that the BBC's Talks Department was paying him far less than it paid to other radio celebrities such as Malcolm Muggeridge and J. B. Priestley, whom Betjeman ridiculed as 'Eeh Bah Goom Priestley'. That knowledge and the greater ease of unscripted broadcasting began to dissuade him from doing talks, but not before he had waged a ten-year campaign of ever more baroque complaints about BBC parsimony.

His first letter, addressed to the Talks Contracts Manager Ronald Boswell in March 1944, had been modest enough: 'BE GENEROUS to a starving poet.' Subsequent pleas turned financial protest into a literary form. In September 1944, having estimated that, after

expenses and tax, he would be left with just £1. 16s. 5d. from a
fee of seven guineas for a poetry reading in Bristol, he wrote, 'On
no account pay any attention to this letter if it is going to cause
difficulties or ill-feeling. Money is not that important. But when
I hear of "workers" getting £25 a week for turning a handle in factories in Slough, I feel that the *illustrious* slaves of the state like you
and me should assert ourselves.'

Two years later, Betjeman sent Boswell a four-page letter explain-
ing what was involved in preparing a talk about Evelyn Waugh. It had
taken four days to review all Waugh's books, a day and a half to meet
him and chat with him, two more days to write 2,500 words and
a further day to travel to and from Bristol for the broadcast: eight-
and-a-half days in all, for just fifteen guineas, of which the 'slave state'
took about half. At best, he would be left with ten guineas: 'You do
see, don't you, that it would be cheaper to go out char-ing?' He had
had to turn down an offer from Gilbert Phelps to write again about
Newbolt, 'because I cannot afford to do so . . . If I get paid fifteen
guineas for talking badly and without having to write a script on the
Brains Trust and BBC food thrown in, why do I get the same fee for
ten times so much work?' On the other hand, if the BBC insisted on
paying him its standard fee,

> then I can only accept future broadcasts when
> (1) I am a famous writer like J. B. Priestley – an unlikely event – and
>   can afford low fees owing to immense royalties
> (2) I have a manual job
> (3) the broadcast is one I can write out of my head like the ghost
>   story I'm doing for Mr Lewin ['Seeking Whom He May Devour',
>   a December 1946 Christmas special].

Boswell replied, thanking him for his 'amusing letter' and agreeing to
up his fee from fifteen to twenty guineas.

In addition to his campaign against the BBC's meanness, Betjeman
opened up a second front against its bureaucracy, invariably by
indulging himself at the BBC's expense. He would either ignore
requests to sign and return contractual documents promptly or return
them late with facetious apologies. Accounts of travelling expenses

were embellished with anecdotes – of journeys taken, hardships suffered and, in place of actual receipts, loose guesswork about money actually spent.

One of his most outrageous performances, in the late 1940s, followed a programme he had made about the Isle of Man. Instead of listing his costs, Betjeman told the full story of how they might have been incurred, on the grounds that Boswell's work 'must be very dull, dealing with people's expenses and with contracts' and that Betjeman's doings would 'put some colour' into Boswell's life:

> There was only one bathroom and the queue for this in the morning was extraordinary . . . There was no hot water and only one closet. All that is very Manx and explains why there are so many hundreds of public wash houses in every town on the island. On the other hand, the food was excellent – two eggs and three sausages for breakfast and heaps of butter and marmalade and toast and tea at a table with a nice large Lancashire family, three generations of it. High tea with Manx kippers cured in woodsmoke at six o'clock. Then off to the dance halls of Douglas by luxury coach or narrow gauge railway . . .
>
> I do not know how you would like to assess all these peregrinations. I have kept no accurate account. It would be a mass of sixpences and shillings and one-and-sixpences paid out about every hour of every day . . . I think if you gave me the usual allowance I would not lose very much on it . . .

As his confidence and celebrity grew, his playfulness became more exotic. Doodles became a recurring feature on letters typed for him by his secretaries after 1950. He also resorted to the ecclesiastical calendar to date his correspondence, displayed an almost Tourette's-like keenness for anyone and anything Irish (including the use of pidgin Irish to sign his name: Seán O'Betjeméan), fabricated a love affair with Eileen Molony and harassed the long-suffering Boswell with references to Boswell's career, school and stinginess.

The fabricated love affair began when Betjeman received a note from Molony announcing that she was moving from the BBC's Bristol studios to those in London. In his reply, he compared her to a large-bosomed character with voluptuous eyes in a Thomas Hardy poem. This became office gossip in November 1945, as Molony duly reported:

> Your letter beginning 'Ah my darling dark yellow-stockinged
> Amazon', not being marked Personal, bounced its way merrily from
> hand to hand through the BBC Registry, and eventually ran me to
> Earth in the Talks Department. Little did you know what a cham-
> pagne bottle you were breaking across my bows as I was launched into
> London life. The whole organization is humming with interest and
> speculation as a result.

Subsequent letters (in both directions) began with 'Darling' and
ended with 'love and kisses'. His were further decorated with Xs,
fantastic signatures and jokey non-sequiturs ('I have been given some
yellow socks').

Molony responded in kind, partly for fun but also because she felt
manipulated into doing so, especially when Betjeman let her down.
In 1949, during the planning of his programme about the Isle of
Man, she received what she called a 'highly irreverent postcard' and
had to appeal to Boswell: 'I am afraid he doesn't take me very seriously and he is a terribly vague person so I think . . . perhaps a
formal letter from you . . . would be more effective than if I were to
write.' After that, Molony was a little more detached in her dealings
with Betjeman but often had to fall back on professions of devotion
to get him to perform.

The battles with the Talks Department made Betjeman increasingly
stubborn in his relations with the BBC and increasingly selective
about what he did. In search of a good Christmas talk from Betjeman
in 1950, Harman Grisewood sent a memo to one of his staff observing that Betjeman 'could be made to turn in something very good if
he was bullied a bit'. He received the reply that 'Miss Molony usually manages to bully John Betjeman to some purpose.' A year later,
however, Molony confided that her attempt to get Betjeman to give
'a satirical talk "to end all talks"' had failed because 'I could not get
Betjeman to come up to scratch.'

Those talks he did agree to give started to suffer from a lack of
effort. He conducted a disastrous interview with Rose Macaulay that
had to be re-recorded and heavily edited before it was suitable for
broadcast. A musical entertainment based around the eccentric poet
Theo Marzials just before Christmas in 1950 and a short story two

weeks later about a man who got off an Underground train at an abandoned station were both editorially unbalanced. The second of his three talks for Richard Keen's nine-part series 'Landscapes with Houses', was no more than a room-by-room tour of Syon House. Even his exceptional 'Coast and Country' series ended with a whimper rather than a bang.

By 1950 his nostalgia was beginning to look a little over-performed. He found it too easy; it no longer asked enough of him. A talk on the awfulness of children's parties in 1951 seemed cribbed from Richmal Crompton or Joyce Grenfell. Other talks relied too heavily on his own mannerisms; and some, with their perennial ilex trees and slatey-grey roofs, approached self-parody. There was also the question of his judgement as a lobbyist. In late 1948 D. F. Boyd, the man who wrote the *Manchester Guardian*'s editorial style book, had had to alert a fellow producer to the dangers of Betjeman's scatter-gun approach to invective in a discussion on new and old books. Some of Betjeman's remarks, though 'admirable as abuse', were not justified by facts, said Boyd. 'Age and beauty are not hated by all Council officials and Whitehall. It isn't age and beauty that makes cottages condemned.' In addition, many listeners might be town councillors: 'Why so grossly attack them? We need ardent converts surely?'

Although Betjeman's falling-off was triggered by an overwhelming frustration about the BBC, the Corporation was not solely to blame. He had started to play himself out. His Victorian mission was still vital to him but he had spoken about it on radio too often, and with too little variation, to be able to draw anything new from it. He needed a fresh challenge and could not generate it from within.

Fortunately, an ever larger number of producers wanted to co-opt him for programmes of their own. Normally they would ask him to talk about conservation, art and literature. Occasionally he would get invitations for more marginal topics. In early 1955, for example, at the age of forty-eight, he was invited to quiz token foreigners on the reality of British preconceptions about their countries for a series of four programmes wisely billed as 'experimental'. To Dr Faher Iz of London University's School of Oriental and African Studies he shot remarks such as 'You don't look at all Turkish. You've got a fair skin and dark hair and I expected you to be wearing a fez' and

'Are your baths entirely of steam?' Some months later he observed to the chef Ken Lo, 'We always imagine in this country that if you just stick a double "e" on to "me no likee soupee" and things, any person from China who's Chinese will be able to understand what that means.'

The one area of interest to which Betjeman did remain committed was religion. Whenever possible, he contributed to the West of England's 'The Faith in the West' series on Sunday evenings and was uncharacteristically accepting of the section's frugality. In 1968, while in the middle of another wearying dispute about rates of pay, he sent an unexpectedly accommodating letter to BBC management saying that past dealings with the BBC had 'left me with the impression that if I was to work for the West Region, I must do it largely for the love of the thing. There is no doubt that it is a very pleasant region in which to work, particularly when one has got to know, as I have done over the years, the crews.'

'I was sent down from Oxford for failing in Holy Scripture,' he had recalled in the *Daily Telegraph* some years earlier; he seemed to spend the latter part of his life in an extended struggle for redemption. Religious broadcasts became his acts of grace. During the early 1950s, at the request of the Revd Martin Willson, the West's Director of Religious Broadcasting, he composed and recited a number of verse monologues for a strand within 'The Faith in the West' called 'Poems in the Porch' and was happy to be paid three guineas a time. In August 1952, when asked by Religious Broadcasting's J. Ormerod Greenwood whether he still wished to give a religious talk in view of the lower fees that the department paid, he replied, 'O Lord yes. Six guineas is jolly good for what is anyhow a duty.'

In 1955 commercial television was launched, ending a monopoly that the BBC had enjoyed since its inception. The BBC responded by trying to sign its star performers into exclusive deals. Aware of this, Betjeman let it be known that he was available. What followed was a rerun of 1944. Barnes, now head of Television, put in a bid and Betjeman turned him down, twice. The next year Betjeman changed his mind and tried to reopen negotiations. This time it was the BBC that passed. 'Betjeman is good value but not such good value as a television performer as we first thought,' wrote a television executive in a memo; 'a talk by Betjeman is no longer such a good proposition as he will not take sufficient trouble,' a radio executive agreed. Both were sure that Betjeman would continue to work for the BBC without being tied in to an exclusive deal and that commercial television was no threat.

They were right. After a brief sulk, Betjeman continued to do live entertainment on radio and television, though he dropped the Talks Department for ever. Religious Broadcasting was luckier. In the winter of 1965–6, it persuaded him to contribute a few minutes of architectural commentary to a weekly series called 'Britain's Cathedrals and their Music'. A year later he took part in a series called 'Church and Collegiate Choirs'. His contribution to both series was none the less lacklustre. Perhaps recognizing this, he gave no more radio talks about buildings.

Nine years later, however, he got the opportunity to concentrate specifically on religion when Religious Broadcasting's David Winter asked him out of the blue to record a thirteen-part series on hymn writers in a Sunday-evening series called 'Sweet Songs of Zion'. He leaped at the chance, requesting help with his research but also amazing his production team with his wide knowledge of historical and foreign hymns and his fund of comic stories about various hymnists, some too scurrilous to broadcast. Though he was by then suffering from Parkinson's disease and morbid depression, these talks had more energy and spark than anything he had written for the BBC since 1952 and enjoyed an exceptional mailbag from listeners, giving rise to a second series in 1976 and a third in 1978.

The style of 'Sweet Songs of Zion' was simpler than that of his earlier work. In conformity with the conventions of religious broadcasting, the programmes were less mannered and more direct and yet full of insight. They were also punctuated with frequent shafts of humour, many delivered off-the-cuff. His first talk – on Isaac Watts, included in this collection – began 'Hymns are the poems of the people' and suggested a powerful personal identification that was echoed in those subsequent talks that dealt with hymns as an expression of personal torment. The last, in September 1978, was as assured as the first. It was recorded, however, only with the help of a considerable quantity of champagne that Betjeman had apparently had flown in the same morning from France, which improved his own performance but impaired that of his producer and editor. He appeared on radio only once after that: in 1979, in an interview on the John Dunn Show about the founding of the National Piers Society. He died in 1984, three months before his seventy-eighth birthday.

By the time that Betjeman refused to go on working for the Talks Department in 1956, radio had taken him as far as it could. It had made him into a media celebrity and helped him to become Britain's most popular twentieth-century poet. How popular? In 1959, the year after his *Collected Poems* came out in the UK, his earnings from poetry-book sales and publication rights alone came to almost £13,500 – equivalent to fifteen times the annual average white-collar wage for men. He himself ascribed his success to his guest appearances on television in light-hearted panel games and chat shows but it was radio that had brought him to public attention long before his poetry was widely read or television was widely available.

Of all his radio work, talks were not the format that delivered him his largest audiences; nor were they necessarily a wholly faithful representation of his literary skills, for Betjeman always gave his producers carte blanche to rewrite them as they saw fit. Nevertheless, talks commanded the highest status of all his contributions to radio and represented the most considered of his performances. For a quarter of a century they also provided an uninterrupted backdrop to his own metamorphosis and how he saw the world.

They reveal, to sum up, his change of emphasis from zealotry for the architectural profession in the early 1930s to an increasing rage about speculative building and modern town planning in the later 1930s. They reveal the development of his rhapsodic style during the war and his struggle to attune himself to the national mood. They reveal his post-war fondness for unearthing the unconventional and unregarded from England's literary and architectural past. They reveal in his last years his shift of allegiance from topographical to religious concerns.

Finally, they reveal something of the inner life of a man of rich humanity and deep feeling who was troubled by inner demons.

George Barnes had spoken of Betjeman's 'extraordinary visual sense and the ability to translate it into words'; Geoffrey Grigson would call him 'kindly and forgiving'. In Betjeman's own mind he was a man in pain – pained not just by the aesthetic abuses that he saw around him but by his abstract feelings of guilt and religious doubt, by his intense self-scrutiny, by his baldness and what he regarded as his unusual skin colour (once 'yellow', then 'green') and by what he saw as his repugnance or invisibility to pretty girls who made him feel the passing of the years.

Talks were his plea for our sympathy and understanding; they were also a momentary respite. When he conjured up railway journeys and teatimes and his various other madeleines, he was not just evoking a childhood world of innocence or throwing down the gauntlet to the barbarians, he was also constructing a haven from the agonies that haunted him. What he wanted, as he said in his autobiographical poem *Summoned by Bells*, was to be

> Safe, in a world of trains and buttered toast
> Where things inanimate could feel and think . . .

VICTORIANA

VICTORIAN PROVINCIAL LIFE

From the series 'The West in England's Story'

West of England Home Service
Tuesday 24 May 1949
Producer: Gilbert Phelps

• • •

Let us walk down a village street in the sun-soaked silence of a summer morning ninety years ago. It looks like one of those coloured folding plates we used to find in that delightful West Country publication *Doidge's Annual*. Poultry is scratching in the dust of the unmetalled road. The clink of the forge can be heard at the crossroads and a carthorse stands outside the smithy waiting to be shod. Huge lollipops, many of them home-made, melt in bottles in the post-office window. The sweet smell of bread baking comes from an open cottage door. Even by afternoon, the village reprobate will be hopelessly drunk, for farmhouse cider is strong and so is home-made wine and the beer at the inn has hops and malt in it.

Few people have heard a train, much less seen one. The parish is the orbit of most people's lives and a visit by farm cart, gig or jingle, between high hedges, down steep hills where we all get out and walk, to cross by footbridge the stream at the bottom while the horse and cart splash through the ford – a visit to a town so small as South Molton or Callington – is an adventure. As for a trip to Exeter, Plymouth or Truro, that is an event that happens only two or three times in many a remote cottager's life, for these are capital cities, as distant-seeming, nay *more* distant-seeming, than London is today. To go to London itself is like going to Brazil today, a rare distinction worthy of a lecture in the village on one's return. And of course there is the joke, time-honoured even then, about the farmer and his wife who thought all London was under glass since they went no further than Paddington Station.

Here and there in the village are signs of the new middle class that rose in the Victorian age. Old-fashioned farmers look askance at those younger farmers who are having their daughters taught to play the piano and whose wives give tea parties in parlours stuffed with gimcrack furniture, screens and painted fans and steel engravings. The old men think that a farm woman's place is in the kitchen and that farmers' daughters should learn cooking and preserving, instead of strumming *Moore's Melodies* on a newfangled instrument.

But stay! What is the activity outside the parish church? Mr St Aubyn, the London architect, has just been here; the old box pews and three-decker pulpit have been cut down at his command and taken away for panelling or firewood. Bright new pitch-pine pews replace them. The old, uneven roof has been tiled afresh and neatly guttered. The old stone walls have been repointed with cement so that they look quite new. The clear glass windows that buzzed with bluebottles and gave a view of elmy slopes are to be filled with greenish glass, which gives no view at all. The village instrumental choir has been disbanded and its old west gallery demolished. Instead, we are to have a slap-up new chancel with an organ and shiny tiles and stained glass windows, a cross on the 'altar' and those old choir members who are not permanently offended or who are in mortal fear of the parson and squire (who are paying for these improvements) will be clothed in white samite – mystic, wonderful – and will 'process' from the vestry into their stalls.

This is a time of religious controversy, fiercer and more full of hate even than modern politics. For example, that great man Henry Philpotts, Bishop of Exeter, was an old-fashioned High Churchman. He ruled the diocese, which then included Cornwall, from 1830 to 1869 with a rod of iron. He was a loyal friend of the Church, courageous and uncompromising. No one could have called the see of Exeter 'the Dead See'. In Philpotts' reign, while the Church entrenched itself in impregnable walls of doctrine, chapels sprang up like coloured mushrooms at its feet. A glance at *Kelly's Directory* will show you how over Devon and Cornwall the Free Churches and particularly the Methodist followers of Wesley either enlarged their existing chapels or built new preaching houses in towns and villages. The church for the squire and parson and their retainers; the chapel for the smaller farmers and the merchants and tradesmen and those of the poorer people. The division was often as much social as theological, though we must not forget that the doctrines of the Plymouth Brethren also swept over all ranks of Devon people in Queen Victoria's day.

But now let us step from such troubled waters, up the curving drive to the Hall. Here there is every sign of prosperity. Gardeners clip the lawns around the house with shears. The walled garden has acres of glass, with a vinery, an orchid house and a house for leaved plants to be carried from when at their stripiest and spottiest, to decorate the entrance hall and drawing room of the Big House. In winter there are coal fires in every bedroom. Maidservants wear mobcaps and scuttle away into corridors when anyone from the family approaches, for servants are neither heard nor seen, except for the butler and his hierarchy of footmen. And of course the house-keeper and the lady's maid see their mistresses.

Sport is the occupation of most of the men. The libraries of almost all country houses stop at about 1820 and thereafter we find in them just a few sporting books. Gun rooms and billiard rooms are built on to stately houses; stables are enlarged; plate-glass windows, then an expensive luxury, replaced the old leaded lights or Georgian sash windows, giving the old houses a bombed and hollow aspect. By the laws of primogeniture, eldest sons inherited the house and estate, younger sons went into the services – in Devon and Cornwall it was as often the navy as the army – and others into the Church. The son who went into the Church usually inherited the family living. The Revd S. Baring-Gould of Lew Trenchard was a Devon squarson in this tradition. But these laws of inheritance had their unwritten laws of obligation. Poor relations of the family paid annual visits to the house and stayed sometimes for weeks. They were welcomed and expected. Indeed, there's no question that a village with a rich and benevolent landowner – a resident one, not an absentee – was a more compact and law-abiding unit than some remoter hamlets given over to magic, cruelty, drunkenness and small farmers of which we may read in Hawker's letters and essays and Fortescue's books. (It is also hard to believe that a public institution or a government office in a country house is so friendly and personal as a landowner. And, except on those estates where absentee landlords left their affairs in the hands of a grasping agent, the farm workers, gardeners, gamekeepers and small farmers of the Victorian period were kindly treated.)

A happy village was like a family, with the squire as father and his wife as mother, the latter with her daughters bringing round soup and jellies to cottagers who were ill, the father with his sons as keen on sport (except of course poaching) as his tenants, and providing work for the men. Of course this feudal family, like all big families, had its rebels among the children. But read any stories or novels of the Victorian West Country – Henry Kingsley, Charlotte M. Yonge, Hardy, Eden Phillpotts, 'Q', Baring-Gould, Fortescue – and you will find that those words of Hymn 573, *Hymns Ancient and Modern*, 'All Things Bright and Beautiful' –

> The rich man in his castle,
> The poor man at his gate,
> God made them, high or lowly,
> And order'd their estate

– that those words expressed what was generally accepted*. It occurred to few to question the settled social order. The squire was still temporal lord of the village, just as the parson was spiritual lord.

Victorian towns of Devon and Cornwall I have left till last, because when one thinks of the West one thinks of country first and town second.

Seaside resorts were a Georgian creation. Sidmouth, Teignmouth and Torquay still have neat stucco villas of the late Georgian age with wide verandahs, broad eaves and an ilex tree on the lawn. And of course Devon had long been popular for holidays – Torquay, for example, with its palms, myrtles and blue sea and its Italianate buildings – because Torquay was thought to resemble Italy. But in Victoria's reign these modest places were transformed out of recognition. And the transformation, of course, was brought about by the railways. In the 1850s, railways had reached Plymouth from London

---

* The above verse is generally omitted from modern editions.

via Bristol and Exeter. In '59, Brunel's great bridge across the Tamar at Saltash was finished and Cornwall was connected with England by steam. The London & South Western soon came hurrying down to Exeter from Waterloo by a shorter though more difficult route and filled in the gaps in North Devon and North Cornwall left by the Great Western, buying up local lines and opening branch railways with gay abandon.

From the 1860s onwards, seaside places flourished. Then the rows of lodging houses appeared all the way from the station to the front; then the Gothic suburban churches were built from designs by R. Medley Fulford; then the circulating libraries did a roaring trade in the season and shell boxes appeared at the fancy-goods shops and piers jutted out into the water and local marbles were worked up into souvenirs and bathing machines lined the shore.

Later, a more sophisticated taste, inspired by the Morris movement and a love of the simple life, turned from these seaside resorts and left them to the crowds and to retired colonial officials and found solace instead in coves and quaint nooks and uneven cobbles and smelly lobster pots and the rugged fishermen of Cornwall. By the end of the century, St Ives, Polperro and Looe, Boscastle and Clovelly drew the artistic and discriminating, who sketched, etched and painted the scenes we know so well, finding in Cornwall and North Devon a second Brittany.

As for Exeter, Plymouth and Truro, they by the eighties had ceased to be capitals and become provincial towns. County families gave up their town houses in these places and bought houses in the newly built squares of London or, hit by the agricultural depression of '79, gave up having a town house at all. Though county families withdrew, hotels and suburbs increased. Once again the old square-paned Georgian shop windows were supplanted by ones with acres of plate-glass window. Big drapers opened (often owned by Welshmen); overhead miniature railways carrying change whizzed in and out of pennants of Nottingham lace and lengths of silk and satin. The beautiful broad Union Street between Plymouth and Devonport was no longer broad, for greedy commerce ordained that the front gardens of its houses should be covered with shops. (Similar spoliation may be seen in the streets of most other towns.) We stood so high in the world's esteem, our trade was so thriving, our industrial North was hammering away so late into the night, that our shops were stocked with wonderful things. Competition was vigorous, visitors increased and so did the town's population (generally at the expense of the small market towns without railways or only with branch lines). In Plymouth, Exeter, Truro and Redruth, everything seemed to be getting better and better. Then it was that people seriously thought bigger was better, and more was merrier, and a material paradise on earth was approaching. Mayors glowed in their chairs. Municipal enterprise increased. Streets were lighted with gas lamps. Town halls were built bigger than the biggest churches — like Norman and Hine's now bombed Guildhall of 1870 at Plymouth. Enormous cemeteries were opened on hill slopes; new spires pricked the skyline of hills serrated with suburbs. Elementary schools rose out of asphalt playgrounds.

Merchants and councillors were men of consequence and lived in large villas on the outskirts of the towns with an entrance drive in front and coach house at the back. Public libraries, institutes and reading rooms disseminated culture. Electric tramways spread the towns out into the country. But the West Country was not so badly hit by what was then called 'progress' as most other parts of England. Still the country remained and agriculture and fishing held their own. Still county differences survived.

Thus it is that Devon and Cornwall remain, to this day, like another country within our island, as yet not quite suburbanized, not quite given over to the chain store and the farming syndicate, the local-government official and his ally in Whitehall. The sins of the Victorians in the West were of a gentler kind than in the North and in the Midlands, though they ruined many old churches with their 'restorations', spoiled many old high streets and sprinkled the outskirts of towns with more mean houses than magnificent ones. In spite of its worship of 'progress', it was not the Victorian but our own age that ruined the wild west coast with bungalows and strung the sky with wires, littered the roadside with shacks and hoardings, turned old inns into glittering pretension and floodlit the whole with fluorescent light.

A HUNDRED YEARS OF
ARCHITECTURE IN WESSEX

West of England Home Service
Monday 17 April 1950
Producer: Rupert Annand

• • •

This is really about Victorian architecture. If you say you like Victorian architecture today you are considered affected or ignorant. Victorian, so far as most people are concerned, is another word for jerry-built, ugly, over-decorated, hypocritical and all that goes with what is known as 'bad taste'. I cannot understand why people take this attitude to Victorian building. For instance, in literature, Victorians come out almost as high as Elizabethans – Dickens, Thackeray, Tennyson, Swinburne, to name a few – and in art the Pre-Raphaelites are coming into their own – Millais, Holman Hunt, Arthur Hughes, and there is always Alfred Stevens of Hunsford, and we have those later painters like Whistler and Conder.

And can it be that an age that produced Mendelssohn, Wagner and Brahms produced no architecture? If all the other ages had their great men, surely the art of building produced some too. And of course it did. So what I have decided to do in this talk is first to give you some things to look for in Victorian architecture and then to quote a few examples from the different counties of the West.

I think one of the reasons why people dislike Victorian buildings is that they are all so keen on Georgian ones. Certainly it is very difficult if you like, as everybody must, such beautiful sweeps of simplicity in golden ashlar as the Crescent of Bath and the terraces of Clifton or such cheerful stucco dignity as the seaside Georgian houses of Teignmouth, Sidmouth, Brighton and Weymouth. If you like a

well-planned spa such as Cheltenham, I can see that Victorian buildings, with their turrets and pointed windows, their spikes and uneven
skylines, their conifers and rhododendron bushes, must seem very
ugly, or if not ugly just mad. Georgians and Victorians looked on
architecture, or at any rate on public architecture, from different
points of view. The Georgians bothered about the outside of the
house, keeping it trim and regular and obeying Palladian rules of
proportion that had been handed down from the late seventeenth
century. The Victorians were interested in the plan of a house: they
planned it first and let the inside determine the outside appearance.
The Georgian architects followed rules; the Victorians invented
theories, especially about church architecture.

Now I am not trying to defend all Victorian buildings. There are,
of course, acres of slums and miles of gimcrack pretensions in the
way of shopping arcades and town halls. Also, the Victorians had one
persistent quality now regarded as a fault: they were not very interested in texture.

Railways made it possible for Welsh slate and hideous tiles and ter-
racotta from the Midlands to be available to builders in London and
Somerset, where such strident materials had never been seen before.
People thought that because they were new, they must therefore be
good. We still sometimes think new means good. Again, Victorian
theorizing did infinite damage to our old churches. Forty-nine out
of every fifty churches throughout the West Country have been
restored by the Victorians – plaster knocked off the walls, new roofs,
sticky pews, cocked-up chancels – and hard tracery in the Decorated
style of Northamptonshire has been let into the windows. In fact, if
you like old churches, it is very hard to like Victorian architecture.

Now we have admitted all that. But when Victorians were good
and interesting – far more interesting and romantic and original and
sensitive than most people ever believe – when they *were* like this was
when they started from scratch: a large country house for some
manufacturer wishing to set himself up as the squire; a new church
in a classy suburb, or where some rich landlord inspired by the
Tractarian movement wished to build something worthy of the
Creator of cliffs and hills and trees and rolling sky. Then Victorian
architects came into their own.

Bristol, always a pioneer city in movements that sweep the rest of the country, is a pioneer at the moment. The Art Gallery and the Bristol Society of Architects have organized an exhibition of photographs of Victorian architecture in Bristol and neighbourhood. It is the first such exhibition to be held in England but I am sure it will not be the last. As soon as people start to use their eyes they will be able to discriminate good from bad Victorian, and that is half the fun of the thing.

But be careful to know what you mean by good and what by bad, what you mean by ugly and what you mean by beautiful. I think a building is successful, whatever its age, if it shows good craftsmanship (that is to say, a delight in the use of materials, well-cut ashlar, neat joinery, delicate ironwork, good masonry and brickwork) and a suitable practical plan (and, mind you, what was practical fifty years ago is not practical today and one must not blame the Victorians for building for their own time). And above these two qualities that make a building good, there is that additional one that makes it beautiful: the genius of the designer. I think that the men of genius in Victorian architecture were William Butterfield, Henry Woodyer, G. E. Street, William White, J. L. Pearson, Norman Shaw, Philip Webb, J. D. Sedding, Temple Moore and G. F. Bodley. All have left examples of their work in Wessex except, I think, Temple Moore. The successors to these great men, who were the Tennysons, Dickenses and Wagners of their art, were F. C. Eden, Sir George Oatley, Sir Giles Gilbert Scott, Sir Edwin Lutyens and Sir Ninian Comper. They too have left examples of their work in the West.

I mentioned all those names then deliberately. The point about the last hundred years of architecture is that until lately it was a matter of names of great men and their imitators. In Georgian times it was a matter of districts and local styles, like a local accent − a charming, countrified thing. For instance, anyone can tell the sort of Georgian that you get in Devon from the kind you get in Bath. The Devon style is squarer and flatter − that criss-cross ironwork on verandahs with rosettes at the intersections; those broad eaves of stucco houses; those ilex trees which seem always to have been planted beside a new Georgian house. Local styles depended on local builders, and builders were their own architects in those days when architecture had not yet become a profession. Very often, as with the Patys of Bristol, an architect was also a monumental mason and designed those beautiful marble urns and well-lettered inscriptions that may be seen incised on veined white marble on chancel walls or by the squire's pew in country churches.

But the Victorians mostly did their work from London, and employed quantities of clerks to carry out their plans. Thomas Hardy, you will remember, came down to restore St Juliet's on behalf of his master from London, Mr John Norton. Sometimes, especially where Sir George Gilbert Scott – Giles Gilbert Scott's grandfather – was at work, the clerk did more than the master. In other places, as with Street and Butterfield, the master would allow the clerk to design nothing on his own. Sir George Gilbert Scott, indeed, who restored churches all over the country, had so much work to do that there is the story about him going up to a town in the Midlands and the office, slackly assembling the next morning, receiving a telegram from him saying, 'Why am I here?' Butterfield was the opposite extreme. He was a very austere man who looked and dressed like Mr Gladstone. He never went into his drawing office and his clerks would bring him their drawings – which he would correct in ink, so that they had to do them all over again. When Mr Butterfield went down to his jobs, the builder had to dust the scaffolding and everything had to be trim before the great man ascended the ladder. He was an ardent Tractarian and his severe and practical buildings are an expression of the severity and sincerity of his beliefs. Butterfield said to himself, 'Gothic is the Christian style but this is an age when stone masonry is almost forgotten and most builders can use brick, so I will build in brick. Now, since I cannot cut decorations in brick like I could have done in stone, I shall make my decorations with coloured bricks, increasing the elaboration of my colour scheme the higher I get up my building.' That is the origin of the polychromatic brick Victorian style to which so many people object. Yet if you want to see how simple and straightforward Butterfield could be when he found local craftsmen who *could* use the local materials, look at Salisbury Theological College on The Close, where he has used most harmoniously brick and flint and stone; or look at the Crimean block of Winchester College or his superb restoration of Ottery St Mary church, surely the best and least obtrusive of all Victorian restorations. The font there certainly is obtrusive – it is Butterfield at his most original, making full use of every kind of Devon marble.

But I am forgetting, in my enthusiasm for the mighty Butterfield, to do what I intended to do when I started this talk, which is to give you a list of what I think are some of the great buildings of the last 100 years in the West. Of course, it is utterly inadequate and I have, I am sure, left out even more original work.

In Cornwall, Truro Cathedral by J. L. Pearson, 1887. The building has been designed to rise up out of the houses that cluster closely round it, just as the old French cathedrals do. It is built of local stone in a thirteenth-century Pointed style unknown to Cornwall but well known to Pearson, who uses it with consummate skill. Why I prefer Truro to that other great modern cathedral, Liverpool, is that its interior is mysterious. A Gothic building, I think, should create vista beyond vista and seem never to end. When you go into Liverpool Cathedral, that magnificent vastness of its exterior seems quite small because the whole building is revealed at once. But Truro is full of vistas. Pearson seemed to delight in them and he has deliberately set the nave of Truro on a different axis from that of the choir so that wherever you stand you glimpse vaulting crossing vaulting in a forest of intersecting stone.

I ought to say here that the most successful of all Pearson's churches – and, I venture to think, the most beautiful Victorian church in the South-West – is St Stephen's, at Bournemouth. The inside of this church seems never to end and each time I go into it I see more ingenious beauties in the construction of its vaulted roof, its aisles and side chapels.

In Devon I choose the house of Knightshayes near Tiverton, which was built from designs by William Burges in 1869. He used a reddish local stone, massive walls, bold gables, stout mullions nearly half the width of the light that they divide, large and solid-looking chimney shafts and high-pitched roofs. Then Norman Shaw designed Flete near Ivybridge in a vast and bold late-Tudor style. I don't know whether it is still there. And the other great house of the century is Castle Drogo, Drewsteignton, by Lutyens. Its outline all Devonians will know: a solid cliff upon the Dartmoor skyscape. It is Lutyens at his most daring, original and imaginative. For churches, I put St David's,

Exeter, very high – designed by W. D. Caröe in 1897–1900. It is in an Art-Nouveau Tudor style in stone, a sort of church equivalent of the old Deller's Café at Exeter. There is also that strange and thrilling church of St Peter, Shaldon, by Edmund Sedding.

In Somerset there is Goodridge's Percy Chapel in Bath, now being turned into a youth centre I think, and there is the College of Art at Taunton by Samson and Cottam, 1904, and there are the Bristol houses by Henry Dare Bryan. These houses are forerunners of the snug modern cottage building of the garden suburbs of today. In Bristol public buildings you have Colston Hall by Wood and Foster, a stalwart, simple building in contrasting bricks. (I wish they would take that ugly modern lettering off it.) There is the Granary on Welsh Back by Archibald Ponton, the abandoned church of St Raphael by Henry Woodyer, the work of Bodley and Sedding in the Sisterhood building at Knowle, and, lastly, Sir George Oatley's great tower of Bristol University, set three-corner-wise, as a Gothic tower should be, to the place from which it is most seen – the steep climb of Park Street. All these are to be seen in photographs in the exhibition in the Art Gallery at Bristol.

In Dorset there is Street's church of Kingston. He said of it, 'On the whole I think this is my jolliest church.' Victorians by 'jolly' meant beautiful. It was a sort of William Morrisy phrase. Kingston church is built of local Purbeck stone and within it is a wonder of ironwork and masonry. Viewed externally it stands proudly on a steep slope. I must not forget in Dorset Norman Shaw's great house at Bryanston, an exercise in brick and stone in the Renaissance style – a predecessor of the work of Lutyens. I do not think one can appreciate Bryanston fully without going into it and noticing the grand scale of everything – the size of mouldings and of arches and doors in relation to the human body. Bryanston is what one means by noble. It was built in 1890. And I must not forget the little early-Victorian church of Sutton Waldron near Blandford, so beautifully proportioned inside and so delicately coloured with blues and reds and pinks that it is as satisfying, soaring, graceful and mysterious within as many a better-known mediaeval church.

In Gloucestershire there is Woodyer's church at Highnam, and in Hampshire William White's amazing brick church at Lyndhurst, with its paintings by Lord Leighton, its carved stone capitals and its Pre-Raphaelite glass. I am not sure that this is not the most original of all the churches of the South-West, if you can call Lyndhurst 'West'. Then there are the houses by Tugwell and the churches by Sedding and Sir Giles Gilbert Scott and Harold Gibbons in Bournemouth and there is Philip Webb's house called Clouds in Wiltshire, if it still stands. Indeed, there seems no end to good Victorian buildings. As fast as elm trees now, we are pulling them down. The Ministry of Town and Country Planning employs antiquarians to make lists of Georgian buildings; sometimes, as a great favour, they allow buildings to be put on its list that date as late as 1850. What the point of the list is I do not know, for more old buildings are being destroyed by flashy shopfronts now than were destroyed before the war. But why I mention them is, you see, that art is supposed officially to stop at 1850.

Few of the great buildings I have mentioned stand any chance of survival. No minister will recommend them. Only your affection and your looking at them and finding out new ones that I have omitted – and I have omitted hundreds – only you can help to save Victorian architecture.

One final word: we are always told it is the Victorians who destroyed England with their ugly buildings. The Victorians did not string the sky with wires and turn old villages into Canadian lumber camps with forests of upright poles. The Victorians did not plant cathedral cities and old country towns with lamp-posts of concrete that look like boa constrictors leaning over with corpse lights in their mouths. No, Salisbury was the pioneer of this particular form of vandalism, which has now spread to Winchester, Abingdon, Hungerford, Wokingham, and I have no doubt will soon ruin the streets and skyline of every old city in the country. The Victorians did not ruin market squares with flashy façades of chain stores – particularly tailoring establishments – whose black glass and glittering vulgarity have no reference to the old brick houses above them. The Victorians did not spread new villas in lines along all the main roads. They did not construct huge building estates on the outskirts of towns, far from shops and with inadequate bus services. No, all this glorious work was done by our own age, not by the Victorians.

URBAN CAMPAIGNS

WATERLOO BRIDGE IS
FALLING DOWN

National Programme
Wednesday 17 February 1932
Producer: Unknown

• • •

I have in my hand today's paper. The headings read, 'Old Waterloo
Bridge Doomed – To be pulled down this summer – LCC
Decision'. Eight years ago the cracks were noticed by the *Architect's
Journal* and the agitation started. Mr Herbert Morrison, a late Minister
of Transport, said, according to my paper, that before the agitation
started ninety-nine people out of every hundred had not noticed the
beauty of the bridge, which is a debatable point. I will not contradict
him although it was Canova, the great sculptor, who said that it was the
finest bridge in Europe; I shall leave Mr Herbert Morrison to quarrel
with Canova. At any rate, probably that one person out of every hundred who sees architecture will have noticed those regular arches of
white Cornish granite, with pairs of white plain Doric columns
between them. If he throws himself off the bridge, having heard now
that it is doomed, I will beg him to notice the enormous blocks of granite from which it is made, as he passes. Should he care to try death
another way, he can stand by where the trams come out on to the
Embankment. There are no other opportunities of seeing the bridge in
detail to advantage, for no other important building has such inadequate
approaches. The new one will doubtless have long avenues approaching it from South London and through the Strand. Perhaps they will
have to clear away Somerset House to make way for such avenues.

But it is by those large blocks of granite that there hangs the history of the bridge. In 1811 John Rennie, a Scot and an engineer, was

called in after other plans for the bridge had proved unsatisfactory. No one had heard of such enormous blocks being carried before but to Rennie all things were possible. He has left some amusing notes on the construction of the bridge, which are well worth reading. 'It is singular,' he says,

> that nearly the whole of the stone for the bridge should have been drawn by one horse familiarly termed by the workmen 'Old Jack', who was a most sensible animal, and did his duty in a most exemplary manner, being always in good trim and ready. Tom, his master, used to call at a public house. On one occasion he remained there longer than usual. At length, the horse put his head in at the door and, taking Tom by the sleeve, pulled him out of the house. Tom took the hint and was never afterwards found loitering during working hours.

In 1817 the nine arches were completed and the Prince Regent, that splendid patron of architecture, opened the bridge with great ceremony. Though privately owned by a company that had been bold enough to put its trust in John Rennie, it was decided to name the bridge after the victory of Waterloo. But the history of the bridge was not over then. First came phaetons and market wagons over it; then came the steam vehicles and new lorries and six-ton sentinels and six-wheel buses, and the bridge stood firm – for it was a bold feat of engineering and Rennie was a bold engineer.

Then in 1923 a subsidence was noticed in one of the piers – known to most engineers as Pier Number Four. In little over a year after this, it sank another eleven-and-a-half inches. Why was there this sudden collapse? It was the result of experiments in the river bed, whose nature I am not allowed to disclose. But people began to notice Waterloo Bridge. A report was made by Mr Dalrymple Hay, the famous engineer, at the request of the Society for the Protection of Ancient Buildings about the reconditioning of the structure. It is to Mr Dalrymple Hay that several million Londoners yearly owe their lives. He built all the tunnels under the Thames, the new Piccadilly Circus Station and all the Underground stations. He knows London underneath better than he knows it above. When the report was published, Mr Dalrymple Hay showed that the bridge could be reconditioned for £650,000. Three contractors separately offered to undertake the job. But the London County Council engineers, with their formidable experience and greater numbers, decided that the whole fabric was rotten and must be taken down. There was a deadlock. So a Royal Commission was appointed by Mr Baldwin.

There are those who say that English architects should have the courage to pull down Waterloo Bridge at once and build something even finer – a task that Sir Reginald Blomfield, the architect of the new Regent Street, refused to do. Now that we are the subjects not of single autocrats but committees of them, this is impossible. Anyhow, I do not think an architect would have had much chance of displaying any natural genius if he were to carry out the orders of this Royal Commission, for the Commission adopted a compromise. It said that half the bridge was to be left standing and the other half to be pulled down and rebuilt. Again there was a deadlock. And now we know the fate of the bridge – unless a bill for its removal has to pass through Parliament, and then we aren't quite sure. The new structure will cost £1,295,000.

Meanwhile, *what* of the new bridge and *why* is it to be? We must remember that Rennie's structure seen from the other side of the river – seen from the draught and thunder of Hungerford Railway Bridge – is designed to look like an arched façade along the bottom of Somerset House! Somerset House and Waterloo Bridge are one piece of architecture. And Somerset House is in a severe Classical manner in Portland stone. Of course hitherto, Sir Giles Gilbert Scott, who is to build the new Waterloo Bridge, has done buildings mostly in the Gothic style, like Liverpool Cathedral, or the Romanesque, and then generally in brick. We must now wait and see what he is going to do with the difficult task of fitting in with Sir William Chambers' Classical and stone façade. He is a well-known architect and he will be severely tried.

I am not going to suggest that it is unwise to build a new bridge. I know we have plenty of architectural talent and, although we may be getting rather tired of the monumental Queen Anne style – magnified editions of the garden front of Hampton Court or Chelsea Hospital – we are rather alarmed by experiments in steel and concrete. We are not convinced about what we ought to do. In fact I doubt whether we have any convictions. But it will be hard for the new Waterloo Bridge to lack conviction – there is bound to be so much of it. But it is purposeless to worry about what the new bridge is going to look like. The great question is: What is it going to be for? At the present moment, the old bridge, with that unpleasant-looking steel caterpillar – the public footbridge – crawling along one side of it, is said to be inadequate for London traffic. I don't doubt it. But so is the Strand. Dr Raymond Unwin's theory of road traffic is not too technical for everyone to understand and I hope not too boring. He says that if you have four ways of traffic down a road with no turnings off and no obstruction save the termination at either end, and if all traffic moves continuously down it at 30 m.p.h., you will be able to put twice as much traffic on that road as there is, say, on a crowded day in Holborn. The present Waterloo Bridge has three ways for traffic and if the present bridge were widened on one side, as was done at Kingston, four ways could be got in. The new bridge is to have six ways, so that an almost unimaginable amount of traffic will be able to pour down it. But what will happen to it at the bottleneck by the Strand and opposite Wellington Street? And what will happen at that fearful roaring mass of carts and lorries a little way down the Waterloo Road? I do not know, but doubtless the London County Council has replanned that part of the Strand and is going to remove some streets opposite or sink a tunnel for buses or even trams. On the Surrey side of the river there is more room to play about, for the streets of South London by Walworth, Waterloo, the Elephant and Castle, and Kennington and Lambeth are still a model for town planners. They are as broad and handsome as the last two Georges in whose reigns they were most of them built. Most of these will have to be remodelled if Charing Cross Station is removed to the other side of the river, as more traffic will be needed in London still and probably even more bridges. For it is the planning of towns that comes first and the carrying of workers from where they live to where they sleep that comes afterwards. Traffic depends on town planning. It may seem a little like putting the cart before the horse to build the bridge first and then plan the town afterwards, but as we do not know which is the cart and which the horse, since the future planning of London has not been altered much or any report been published for the benefit of the public, it is not for us to criticize.

The greatest question of all that arises from the destruction of Waterloo Bridge is how much an architect ought to be an engineer. Rennie is not well known to everybody. He is frequently confused by people who want to be funny or ignorant with Wren and the Renaissance. His chief work is Waterloo Bridge, if we except his magnificent docks at Stonehouse in Plymouth, and in both the bridge and docks he showed himself to be an architect and an engineer at once. In the eighteenth century these two qualities were generally combined, but with the coming of factories in the last century there was too much to learn and not enough time for an architect to learn it. Engineering and architecture got divorced and we have the result in the St Pancras Station and hotel: that magnificent steel roof which is pure architecture and engineering, with that fantastic Baronial palace of a hotel appended to it.★ King's Cross Station, built in 1851, next door to it, is a fine example of engineering and architecture in one. It is so hidden by huts and litter in front that no one notices it. But now that we have had about eighty years wherein these two great sciences have been divorced, there is a chance for them to come together again. The introduction of steel and concrete into architecture has shown that new proportions must be made and new and vaster scales on which flats, offices and halls are to be built. A bridge is a wonderful opportunity. An architect must be an engineer and a town planner at once. We have shown in the Crystal Palace, which is steel and glass, and in King's Cross that we in England were the first modern architects and that Germany and the Continent only copied us.

I do not want to suggest that the new Waterloo Bridge must be something inappropriate in those materials but I think that since Sir Frederick Palmer, the engineer, and Sir Giles Gilbert Scott, the architect, are two separate persons, the combination of them both

★ Betjeman's enthusiasm for St Pancras's Midland Grand Hotel was written out of his talk, presumably at the behest of his producer, and he was made to say instead, 'That magnificent steel roof, which is architecture and engineering combined, has a ridiculous-looking hotel, half cathedral and half Baronial hall and like neither, obscuring it from the street.'

will have to be wonderfully harmonious if a fine design is to be the result. We are no longer impressed by fine steel structures on which Georgian decorations are festooned like flowers around a maypole. Waterloo Bridge is a great chance for an architectural engineer – or both working as one. But what will be the result? Since one of the last great works of a great age is being destroyed (for Waterloo Bridge has more admirers abroad than in England), we must not ask questions. We must be content with hoping that the first great work of a new age will take its place.

BRISTOL

From the series 'Town Tours'

West of England Programme
Monday 12 April 1937
Producer: J. C. Pennethorne Hughes

• • •

I feel a bit of an insult, coming here as a non–Bristolian to talk about the good and bad of Bristol. What right have I, a green–faced, bald–headed semi–intellectual, to say something that will make a city father wince or some kind–hearted housewife sitting in the ugliest villa between here and Weston, listening in to a wireless set whose fretwork case looks like a cross between a bonded warehouse and the Taj Mahal – what right have I to criticize? The idea of this talk, and of the subsequent ones I hope to give on West Country towns, is to help you to look about you when you are in a town. If people took as much trouble to preserve decent simple houses in towns as they do to preserve views and downs and woods in the country, if people were as anxious to have abolished vulgar buildings covered with beams and whatnots in various repulsive shades of red brick, if people were as anxious to abolish these as they are anxious to preserve the bluebell and the lesser stitchwort, England might even yet have a chance of being as beautiful as it was before the war.

Bikers, motorists, railway travellers see the villages they loved pulled down by local councils and built up by speculators; they see the familiar skyline strung with wires as though some dear old lady on her flight to heaven had left her knitting behind and it had stayed in mid-air. Tinned food, tinned brains, tinned souls – we are just beginning to look about us and see that 'progress' is not to be measured in terms of scientific invention. We are beginning to see that the people who lived a hundred years ago were perhaps wiser than we are today, just because they had more time to think and use their eyes, and fewer blatant trivialities to distract them.

So I have come to talk about Bristol without any axe to grind. I see advertisements in the railway trains about PROGRESSIVE BRISTOL, showing various factories illustrated in repulsive oranges and greens and giving such odd information as that there are 232 telephone kiosks in Bristol. I remain unnerved because I know Bristol is not yet painted such hideous colours as orange and green and because I don't care how many telephone kiosks there are. I am not preservation-mad and entirely wrapped up in the past. I only share with most of you an intense distaste for the way in which English towns and country are being spoiled today and I hope, by making you look at all buildings – painful as that often is, especially in some 'recently developed' estates – to make you see that Bristol is still the most beautiful big city of England: far finer than London, which must a hundred years ago have been the loveliest city in Europe. But London has pulled down its best domestic buildings – 'domestic', by the way, is the architectural word for houses in which we have to live – and erected instead huge blocks of unwanted flats in a commercial Renaissance style as ugly as your own office blocks built in the last twenty years. Bristol has been spared much of this sort of 'progress'. London has not solved its traffic problem but instead is continually hacking chunks out of the centre of itself, building huge bridges (such as the new Waterloo Bridge) where they are not wanted in a feeble attempt to stave off the increasing flood of motors on the road. And all the time London goes on building blocks of flats and offices where the traffic is thickest and where there should be open spaces – so the traffic gets worse and worse.

Bristol has no such difficult traffic problems as London. What problem there is will be partially solved by the four ring roads which I am told are being built round Bristol. One of them, the inner one, runs right across Queen Square. This is unfortunate but unavoidable. If we have many motor cars, we must pay the price not only in tax and the cost of the car but also in the scenery that motors are intended to take us to see. The road through Queen Square is part of a circle round the inner part of Bristol which, it is intended, will divert that most unpleasant rush of traffic on to Bristol Bridge. I am happy to say that this circular road will have very few houses or offices actually on it. So it will be a really useful through-road instead of a main street with a succession of traffic blocks.

London once had the most beautiful Georgian estates, laid out in the days when people really knew about vistas, proportions and handsome living rooms. London has destroyed or is destroying all of these. But Bristol is still in possession of Clifton, a place of quiet terraces where perhaps this very evening retired colonels and admirals are putting down the newspapers to look for a moment across the trees and garden beds, lit up by the lamplight, now that evening has closed in, and watching the Avon Gorge, perhaps, with the Clifton Suspension Bridge floating across it. Terrace after terrace, crescent and square: stately houses, some of them turned into flats, but still preserving their outward beauty. In Clifton, as impressive in its way as Bath, Bristol has a suburb that is better than anything that has been spared to London, unless it be those fine terraces round the Regent's Park. I could go on making comparisons favourable to Bristol with London until this talk is over but I am told that it is bad form to create bad feeling. So let's start something quite different. Let's think of Bristol.

And now, I am sorry to say, I have got to say something that may make Bristolians wince. I have never heard of anyone – recently at any rate – coming to Bristol to see it. They come for business, with bowler hats on their heads in small saloon cars, and they hurry away. Or they come to die among the ilex- and plane-shaded terraces of Clifton, but they do not think Bristol is a show place. People go to Canterbury to see the cathedral, they go to Stratford-upon-Avon and see so much half-timber that they don't know what's Elizabethan and what's 1923, but they never go to Bristol to see the most unspoiled large city left in England. I should think Bristol Cathedral is one of the least known in England. Yet it is, now that it has been cleaned up and painted inside, one of the most beautiful. I should think Clifton, with that amazingly delicate suspension bridge, is *almost* – I say 'almost', for it isn't quite – as lovely as Bath. The main streets of Bristol certainly are none too lovely, but once you get out of them you come across row after row of exquisite Georgian houses. You climb up hills by steps and look back on a forest of towers, spires and the masts of vessels that have threaded up the Avon Gorge to reach the port of Bristol. From this port they set out to find America.

Bristol certainly keeps itself to itself. You can travel up in a bus from the Tramways Centre to the Clifton Suspension Bridge and find yourself feeling very out of it. Everybody knows everybody else even in this enormous town. 'Come and play roulette this evening, Harry.' 'Sorry, I can't, Jack – the guv'nor doesn't allow it.' 'Nice weather it's been, hasn't it?' Oh Bristol, dear Bristol, how at home you make us feel after the haggard, angry faces in London, after the crowds in the Underground. What a change is the family party in the Clifton bus. After the rush and noise, how sedately the trams screech through your streets and whirr up your almost perpendicular hills.

I was getting carried away. I meant to tell Bristolians about the lovely streets by which they are surrounded. Here is the list of some of the chief ones: Royal Colonnade. The Arcade (so much better now than the Burlington Arcade of London, which has been vulgarized). Brunswick Chapel on one side and the Doric cemetery gates and Dr Pymotre's Gothic house* further along. Portland Square, with the exquisitely proportioned tower of St Paul's church rising tier on tier, tower on tower, out of all that stateliness. King Square – tonight it was bathed in gold – with its eighteenth-century houses with fine front doors; yes, King Square, forming an ever-bright foreground for the heights of Kingsdown, where Georgian terraces command blue vistas. The Theatre Royal:† its front has been spoiled but inside it still has the quality of a playhouse where Mrs Siddons might have acted. Royal York Crescent (as fine as anything in Bath). The Paragon, Caledonia Place. The West Mall and the Mall. That little half-crescent under Clifton Suspension Bridge near where the trams to Hotwells come to an inconsequent end. The climb up Zion Hill and, further back, best of all, the streets of Clifton, Vyvyan Terrace. These are some of the places that, if they are allowed to survive, will bring crowds to Bristol in ten or twelve years – for Bristol and Bath will be the only places to retain Georgian architecture.

* Now demolished.
† Now the Bristol Old Vic.

Georgian architecture! You may be wondering what I mean by this. Well, take a look at Bristol and take a look at some of the older houses in your town or village. See if they conform to the type. Georgian houses are plain: there is no half-timber or fake half-timber about them. The windows on the ground floor are long and thin. Those on the next floor are shorter but of the same width. Those above are shorter still and almost square. The roof — if it is visible — is laid with tiles that are neatly graded: those nearest the eaves are larger and get smaller row by row till they reach the ridge. All these little tricks lend proportion — the secret of pleasing buildings. Now look at the details of Georgian houses. Notice the ironwork along the area — Portland Square, Bristol, has lovely ironwork. Notice the doors — front and drawing room or bedroom — well made, with delicate moulding and well-spaced panels. Notice the ceilings — a pretty cornice and then that absence of decoration that is decoration itself. Georgian architecture is not obtrusive. It is polite and gracious, like the nicest of our grandfathers. Bristol is full of it.

You will have noticed that I have declined to mention the few famous buildings of Bristol (and by that I mean famous to the outside world): such things as the Cabot Tower, the University Tower, St Mary Redcliffe, Wesley's Meeting House and various ye-olde things. They do not need noticing, as everybody notices them. What do need noticing are the squares and streets I have mentioned and many more whose unpretentiousness makes Bristol the best big town left in England.

The Bristol Corporation, I believe, really understands Bristol. It has established a panel of architects who assess every new design and that panel, I believe, refuses to pass vulgar villas and shops in the fake half-timber style. The engineers and architects work together in an enlightened policy to keep Bristol intact and to spare, as far as possible, the agricultural country around it. Landowners are helping them by agreeing to keep spaces on their estates open. It is the duty of Bristolians to back the Corporation up.

This evening I drove for a last time before speaking tonight round my favourite parts of Bristol with a friend. Bristol was looking at its best. Sunset behind the Avon Gorge and all that sort of thing — quiet little squares; the new Sea Mills Estate, with a surprising beauty showing off in the evening sunlight; and vistas of trees and fields and pleasant cottages that that magic estate has managed to create – and then I plunged back to Bristol. I had better not say by what road but I saw villas that were as ugly, as out of keeping, as silly, as pretentious, as be-timbered, as be-stained-glassed, as be-rockeried as any of the worst outside London. They were built by private speculators, not by the Corporation. They were as bad, even worse, as to plan and appearance as any in London. This was tragic. The beauty of Bristol lies in its individuality. It is one of the only towns in England to remain untouched by the tentacles of London. These estates were as bad as London itself. Bristol must keep away from London. No 'moving with the times', which means nothing. Keep away from London. Keep away from London.

PLYMOUTH

From the series 'Town Tours'

West of England Programme
Monday 26 April 1937
Producer: J. C. Pennethorne Hughes

. . .

Speaking as one to whom a spinnaker is the same thing as a bin-nacle, who says starboard when he means port, who can't tell the difference between a mainsail and a jib – speaking as such a one, I ought not perhaps to speak at all about a town like Plymouth. You know what an idiot you would feel if you turned up for a tennis tournament in plus fours: well, that's just how you feel if you turn up as a landlubber in Plymouth. Everything is nautical. Pink-faced naval officers drink pink gin in exclusive bars. Naval police parade the streets at night. Naval flags flutter over ominous-looking ammunition dumps. Naval gunboats race about naval waters. Almost every road looks over, at some point or other, a stretch of steel-blue water on to a horizon grey with battleships. Even the houses are grey and navy blue, out of sympathy with the general atmosphere. I would go so far as to say that the dress shops of Plymouth display more blue dresses than dresses of any other colour.

Then there is a nautical air about the details of Plymouth. Wooden floors are washed like the deck of a ship; brass and metal fittings are highly polished; if you look through the windows of the bow-fronted houses round the dockyards you will see that the barometer and the chart have replaced the usual wall decoration and the model ship has ousted the aspidistra in the window space.

The moneyed visitor stepping out of the liner onto the train, which trails over viaducts across the dreary, house-covered suburbs north of Plymouth, out into the steep green hills towards Newton Abbot, gets no idea of what Plymouth is like. The most unusual thing about Plymouth is its social life – the social strata: the position of a naval officer's wife contrasted with the wife of an officer in the merchant service; the relations between the army and the navy and the air force – all the subtle relations between the services and the town. But as this is a talk about houses and public buildings, I must leave that fascinating subject alone.

Plymouth is really a collection of towns built round various bays, pools, creeks, waters, hamoazes and whatever they are called that grace the shore of that most glorious stretch of water, Plymouth Sound. The three chief towns are Plymouth, Stonehouse and Devonport, to which we might add Stoke and Morice Town. Each town has a distinct character, even in these days of universal awfulness in commercial architecture.

Plymouth, the most easterly of the three towns, has now given its name to the rest of them. It is probably the oldest of the three. And the oldest part of it is round a harbour known as Sutton Pool. Here there is an abundance of old houses, the house of Master Hawkyns★ and various wobbly-looking and bulging timbered buildings that may well have seen Drake set out while it was 'wassail all' at the Minerva Inn and which undoubtedly watched the Pilgrim Fathers setting out in the *Mayflower* in 1620 – a fact commemorated on a piece of stone let into the roadway of the Barbican and reverenced by all blue-blooded Americans. Since those days, many an old lady has set her watercolours, many an ageing Royal Academician has squeezed blue and yellow onto his palette, many an etcher has sharpened his pen or whatever etchers do, and the old streets clustered round the port have posed for an hundred indifferent artists. Old Plymouth, though it may not be distinguished as architecture, is certainly rich in what the guidebooks call 'historic association'. And because Plymouth is still a genuine seaport, the old part still retains the atmosphere of the past without being self-conscious about it. So these lanes by the quay and the quay itself seem to be much more the genuine article than some

★ John Hawkyns (1532–95), wealthy pirate and England's first slave trader. Became mayor of Plymouth and played a key role against the Armada.

of those fishing villages in Cornwall where every other house sells Birmingham brassware, where orange curtains flutter from cottage windows and where stage sea-salts tell stage fo'c'sle yarns to gaping tourists. Old Plymouth has survived the invasions of the artists and tourists as she survived the invasions of the French from 1338 to 1403.

The next town along the shore is Stonehouse, a place that no one visits and quite the pleasantest residential part of Plymouth. Here there are neat rows of eighteenth-century houses – places like Durnford Street and Emma Place – that formed a sort of Bath or fashionable residential district for old sea captains in the evening of life. Delicate wrought-iron railings, fanlights over the doors, slate-covered walls and broad, well-proportioned streets – these distinguish Stonehouse. But its greatest distinction is the Royal William Victualling Yard down on the waterfront. This group of granite wharves, seen from the water, looks as imposing as Greenwich Hospital, London. It is undoubtedly the finest sequence of monumental buildings in the West Country. Though extremely simple, its proportion makes it majestic, so that once you are in its entrance gates, flanked by colonnades, you feel you are entering some royal palace. The Royal William, by the way, was that glorious but unimportant William IV, the sailor king. Sir John Rennie, son of the builder of Waterloo Bridge, designed this yard in 1831. He also finished the Breakwater across the Sound. He belonged to the great days when architects were not just decorators but engineers as well.

Now let's have a look at Devonport, the third and westernmost of the three towns that make up Plymouth. There are the dockyards, into which it is impossible for landlubbers like me to go. And anyhow, if I were allowed into them, they are so thick with naval secrets that I should not be allowed out alive if it were known that I was going to broadcast anything about them to the public. Much of Devonport is untidy-looking and its main shopping centre is very ugly. The only decent building in that part of the town is the Georgian Royal Hotel, which has a curved staircase – one of the wonders of the West.

The best of Devonport is some way off. It is the old civic centre and the town hall, where the Column stands that commemorates the fact that George IV allowed the town to change its name from the humble one of Plymouth Dock to the higher-sounding Devonport.

There is something very sad about this place, for as a civic centre it seems to have failed. The pavements are made of veined stone – Hardy's 'marble-streeted town' – which shines like marble after the rain but the pavements are the playground of children who ought to be provided with a decent park. The huge town hall strides over them on its handsome Doric columns but it looks as though no one has entered its portico for a hundred years. It forms a perfect termination to a street designed by John Foulston (as great in Plymouth as was John Nash in London), the man who connected the three towns by a series of terraces and crescents and fine public buildings worthy of the greatest seaport in the West of England.

Ascend the Column (after calling for the key at the police station) and you will get some idea of Foulston's scheme. Hence the best view of the towns is obtained. Straight to the east runs Union Street, planned by Foulston just over a century ago to unite Plymouth with Devonport, while Stonehouse lies to the south between them. At our end of Union Street is Devonport's magnificent but decayed (to its eternal disgrace) civic centre. At the other is that group of buildings comprising St Catherine's church, the Athenaeum (which looks like the Parthenon) and the Royal Hotel, Assembly Rooms and Theatre Royal. This group of buildings is the best thing in Plymouth and, I may say, the first time in the world's history that these three necessary buildings are combined under one roof. You will scarcely believe it, you who do not live in Plymouth, but some 'progressive' people have actually taken down this group and have ruined for ever the one remaining part of Plymouth proper that had some civic dignity.* As I speak, the Theatre Royal is white powder and broken bricks. I don't know what the building will look like that takes its place but it is bound to ruin the present group.

Beyond Union Street we can just see from this Column the ungainly towers of the Guildhall, Law Courts and municipal offices† – a cluster of turrets and an effect rather like a worn-out toothbrush with some of the hairs still standing. They are Victorian, over-elaborate,

* The buildings making up Plymouth's former civic centre in Lockyer Street were in various eclectic styles: Egyptian, Greek, Roman and Hindu.
† Mostly destroyed in the Blitz. The Guildhall, though reduced to a shell, was rebuilt and reopened in 1959.

inappropriate and in the wrong style for the town, being Gothic of a sort like London's law courts – full of points and pinnacles like a disembowelled ichthyosaurus. Compare this old civic centre of Devonport with Plymouth's Gothic ostentation, flanked by the over-restored parish church of St Andrew, and think a minute. Devonport's old centre is quiet; Plymouth's is ostentatious. One is firm and square and trim; the other is fussy and noisy and untidy. Even Plymouth's fine Library, which is in the 1910 English Renaissance style – that's to say as flat, uninspired and austere as London's new Regent Street – is a little better than the Guildhall in the way of public buildings.

I don't know whether there are any self-respecting architects with the vision of Foulston and his partner Wightwick★ still left in Plymouth. I expect so. But if there are, they must confine themselves to the docks, as they do not seem to have been given a chance outside – otherwise they would not have countenanced the destruction of the Royal Hotel.

Compared with Bristol, Plymouth is an architectural backwater. The new villas of Plymouth, especially along the Totnes Road, are among the ugliest in England. There is a special sort of villa that has spread like a rash along the whole coast of Cornwall and along both coasts of Devon. In the part of Cornwall where I used to live, it was known as 'the Plymouth style', because the men who provided what plans there were usually came from Plymouth and because the outskirts of Plymouth is full of villas of this sort. Its general effect is that of a slice of cake. If the roofs of the other houses are blue, its roof is red. If the others are red, its is blue, with a red strip like toothpaste along the top. Of course it has 'beams' painted or nailed on and nothing to do with the construction of the house. There is plenty of cheap stained glass in the windows to hide the sky. The exterior plumbing hangs about it like ribbon from a pair of pince-nez. The villa lacks all proportion and in many cases it lets in the water. In the front is an arid collection of stones called a rockery but more like a public cemetery in general effect. The front gate is in the form of a sunset carved out of wood. This villa, now unluckily known as 'the Plymouth villa', has ruined many bits of the best coast in England. It

★ Pronounced 'Wittick'.

is perhaps unfair to associate it with Plymouth, but new Plymouth is full of it.

Turn round and forget what is being done by the hydra-headed monster miscalled 'Progress' and look at the water, which they can't build villas on yet. Here you see Plymouth as Turner saw it, and as you and I can still see it from the Hoe. A garden of water and islands, backed by Mount Edgcumbe. The water flecked with vessels, the shores adorned with imposing wharves, stately terraces on the hills around us, lime-green verandahs, wide windows, quiet gardens, yellow stucco walls, the town neatly planned with clean wide streets by Foulston and Wightwick. A town to be proud of, with its slate, its bright stucco, its ilex trees, its high veronica hedges and its open iron-work verandahs. There is still plenty of the good Plymouth left – Albemarle Villas, the Proprietary Library, St Michael's Terrace, Wyndham Square, Union Street, the upper parts of Lockyer Street, the Esplanade, Mount Wise, the Custom House, St John's Church and old Devonport. Though the view from the famous Hoe is terrific, the whole of the expanse of municipal grass is littered with somewhat uninspired memorials and the usual collection of bronze wings rising from Portland stone. Wouldn't it be a good idea to see that it is cleaned up and kept safe from 'Progress'? Not even London would do itself the harm that is being done to Plymouth. Yet Plymouth has almost as much in it worth preserving as there is in London.

SWINDON

From the series 'Town Tours'

West of England Programme
Saturday 8 May 1937
Producer: J. C. Pennethorne Hughes

• • •

People who do not live in Swindon consider it a blot on the earth. It lies in an elm-shadowed valley, under the Marlborough Downs in Wiltshire, yet you can stand among the red brick villas which compose its streets and find it impossible to believe that the loveliest country in England is only a few miles away. Train travellers aren't fond of Swindon because they sometimes have to wait at Swindon Junction and there is nothing to see but goods yards and villas on every side. Motorists used to prefer to hurry through it, until the speed limit was enforced with almost unprecedented vigour through the dreary stretches of ribbon development which extend along almost every road into the town. In fact Swindon is so unpopular with the outside world that I must say something in its defence before getting down to work.

Well, first of all, there are no real slums in Swindon. And, though even a slum might be more cheerful than the red-brick monotony of most of its streets, there is no doubt that from the point of view of sanitation Swindon is much better off than some of the highly pic-turesque little towns which surround it.

Next, the people of Swindon are some of the pleasantest and politest you will ever come across. They will direct you most cour-teously through its arid avenues. They are most bright and kindly. Swindon people sing very well. They are good at getting up concerts or amateur theatricals. They aren't exactly poetic – in fact poor Alfred

Williams, a local nature writer who worked in Swindon, was none too comfortable. Even Richard Jefferies, the greatest Swindon literary figure, who lived outside Swindon Old Town, was considered a bit loopy. (But good writers always are. It's only best-sellers who are considered sane.)

The people of Swindon are also good church- and chapel-goers. In fact if you go into some of the churches in the New Town – those controlled by the famous Canon Ross, or St Augustine, with its musical reputation – you will find on a Sunday that they are almost crowded out with children and men and women of all ages.

Swindon is full of good hearts and ugly houses – and it's the ugly houses I am going to talk about.

Less than a hundred years ago, there was a small market town which stood on a hill under the downs and looked for miles over the Vale of the White Horse. It was a typical small English town. There was the big house and park with a church in it, a small market square, a comfortable-looking coaching inn, some big merchants' houses in the main street with carved doors and panelled rooms and a row of neat new houses commanding a view over the valley. This was Old Swindon, set in country which Richard Jefferies has described in the best nature books we have in the language. People can still remember the old days when men came in to market wearing ribbons in their caps – one colour meant that they were employed, another that they wanted employment.

Then the great railway line from London to Bristol was made and a nice open site was wanted for a railway works between Bristol and London. A position in the valley just over a mile away from Swindon was chosen. The railway company put their works on the further side of the line and on the side nearest Swindon they built one of the first garden cities in the world. They built several streets of cottages, each with a front garden. They put up a mechanics' institute. They bought an open space for sports. They built a church called St Marks and they called the whole thing Swindon New Town. This was the first and last bit of town planning in Swindon for years. It is still the best, though the houses may be somewhat out of date.

So far so good. But then the speculators got busy. Other factories clustered round the works. The railways boomed. People built and built. The hill slope going up from the New Town to the Old was soon covered with houses. There are many people in Swindon who can remember fields between the two towns. Now you have to go for miles through houses before you can discover, still more or less as it was, that early garden city, looking rather grimy and unhappy.

Up on the hill, also lost in houses, is Swindon Old Town. The big house and park remain but the house is empty, the park and gardens derelict. They ought, of course, to be bought by the council and turned into a public park and a museum or something more cheerful. There is nothing in Swindon you can call a public park, nothing worth looking at: only a few arid recreation grounds, fringed by a few shrubs and pent in with iron railings. Right through the centre of the town winds a dried-up canal. You would have thought this would have been planted with beds and turned into a pleasant walk. Instead, it is an untidy ditch in which grass tries to grow up between tins and pieces of paper.

The streets of pre-war Swindon are depressing in the extreme. Hardly any trees. Just rows of two-storeyed semi-detached houses, packed close together – bow window, front door, bow window, front door – for miles. Every house is two storeys high. Even the main shopping street, Regent Street, contains only about one building above this uniform two storeys. This would not matter if the houses were decent to look at. But they are not and some of the roads are often too narrow to give enough light to the ground floors. Instead of trusting to good workmanship and a plain exterior and broad streets, the speculators have thought of their money before other people's health and happiness; they have crowded the houses onto the sites and they have spent money on outward show instead of internal good arrangement. They have thought of themselves before the town as a whole – as speculative builders do.

And what I have said of pre-war Swindon applies even more forcibly to the Swindon built since the war. In the old days it was the smart thing for a man who had done well on the railway or in some other factory to move out of the New Town to the more genteel but less friendly Old Town. Now people move out of Swindon and live in houses along the roads leading to the neighbouring villages.

And what houses! All the approaches to Swindon are ranged with desirable residences – 'each one different' but each one different only in some outward showiness, so that the effect is irritatingly monotonous. Stained-glass windows, gables, standard front doors bought cheap by the dozen; sham beams in front, but the bare house behind. The idea of an ordered plan does not seem ever to have been considered by the authorities. Houses for people who cannot afford a car are situated far from a bus route. Houses exist near factories – an unforgivable arrangement in a comparatively new town. There are rows of recent cheap speculative houses situated in the pleasant purlieus of the gasworks!

The approaches to the new Swindon are still the winding lanes they were a few years ago. Now that the borough has enlarged itself, the lanes have become lined with red-brick and rough-cast Tudor-style houses instead of trees. The houses are no more Tudor than I am William Shakespeare. The road from Oxford, which is exceedingly narrow in places, is lined with some of the flimsiest-looking and most be-gabled and be-stained-glassed villas I have ever seen. To save road expenses, they are built along this approach to the town. You can see the country between the semi-detacheds – only a field away. Because they are spread out in this ribbon form, there is a speed limit all the way from Stratton two miles east of Swindon. There is just as much of this ribbon development north towards Highworth and Cricklade and Rodbourne, and perhaps the ugliest houses of all go all the way to Coate, the place where Richard Jefferies lived. Here there is an attempt at a public park, two miles from the Old Town and three from most of the New Town. Of course these long strips of main road have their bus services, but a bus can hardly be an economical proposition when it has to run down a long street with nothing but houses on either side and hardly any debouching roads.

Some attempt has been made, only very lately, to make planned estates. But, alas, there are very few council houses – and council estates are usually well laid out. Swindon is mostly the work of speculators, and they are not famous for considering beauty or town planning. There may be good new speculative houses in Swindon; I know there are bad ones.

Swindon should have been planned in small estates among green spaces and far from the factories, but linked with them and the shopping centre by roads with cheap transport facilities. The through roads have been straightened and not built upon. There are still empty spaces, uneven lumps of grass, remains of fields, right in the middle of the town. These should be turned into parks and gardens. No more houses in the middle of Swindon.

As it is, Swindon still gnaws its way along country lanes, eating up villages. Why, I saw a row of new villas yesterday on the green at Highworth, one of the loveliest little towns in England – a town such as Old Swindon was eighty years ago.

The town plan has come too late to Swindon, as it has come too late to most towns. Now the town flounders about like a helpless octopus, spreading its horrid tentacles into quiet untroubled places, waiting no doubt till one long and loathsome tentacle shall twine with that of the vile octopus London – and perhaps Bristol will stretch out a tentacle to meet it from the west. Swindon is a warning to all England to keep a watch on the speculative builder.

BOURNEMOUTH

From the Series 'Town Tours'

West of England Programme
Friday 28 May 1937
Producer: J. C. Pennethorne Hughes

• • •

Pines, rhododendrons, gorse, small oaks, tea places – a thirteenth-century cottage fifty yards ahead – hoardings as frequent as trees, then fewer pines and small oaks, less gorse and less rhododendron, more hoardings and more tea places – enough tea brewed in a week to fill Poole Harbour: that is the impression I get when I motor to Bournemouth. Bournemouth begins almost where London ends. Down every main road the bungalows and villas spread. Ha! you think, here I am in the heart of the New Forest. How terrifying! Are you in the heart of the New Forest? You may be. But look through those oaks. Isn't that a modern sham-Tudor villa? Isn't that a retired civil servant mowing his lawn beneath yonder spreading oak? It is. The main roads to Bournemouth are houses most of the way.

Now let's skip the Bournemouth suburbs and make straight for the sea coast, for Bournemouth itself.

Bournemouth holds a distorting mirror to English taste. In the 1880s, when houses in the rest of England were built with turrets and white wood balconies and stained-glass windows, Bournemouth houses had more turrets, more balconies and more stained-glass windows than any other town. Later, in the earlier part of this century, when people liked 'quaint' houses with sloping buttresses, white rough-cast walls, irregular roofs, pierced hearts in the front door and unstained oak furniture, the houses of Bournemouth were given roofs that almost touched the ground, walls with buttresses as big as a house, pierced hearts the size of a mammoth's kidney. Now, when people don't know what they like, Bournemouth flats seem to be in higher blocks than any other flats. Bournemouth sham-modern buildings have more cubes and corner windows and zigzag lines than any other sham modern. (I saw some modernistical, cubistic, imitation-functional villas in Southbourne with fawn-coloured walls and purple woodwork.) Bournemouth sham Tudor is more sham and less Tudor than any sham Tudor.

And despite all this, much of Bournemouth is, in its way, beautiful. And for this beauty we must thank the Victorians. They planned the place, decided how many houses there were to be to an acre, planted the trees and the rhododendrons, laid out the great parks in the centre of the town and preserved the pine-shaded ravines called 'chines'. They visualized Bournemouth as a series of villages lost among pines and rhododendrons and golf courses. Their dream is still partly true. Now Bournemouth is looking its best. I can imagine a worse fate for myself – should I ever reach the evening of life – than being wheeled about the chines at this time of year when the sun shines through the pines onto the purple rhododendrons; than driving in a Victoria at three miles an hour along the undercliff, where cascades of mesembryanthemum seem almost to pour into the beach huts; than sniffing the ozone and the resin; than praying my last prayers in one of those dark Victorian churches; than hearing as I pass away the murmur of the pines and the English Channel. How poetical!

Bournemouth is still a place for the aged and for relations of the aged who are expecting a legacy. Then there are the servants and the shops and the entertainment centres which get their money from the aged and what the aged allow their relations. Then there are the people who get their money from the shops and the entertainment centres. Thus there are the people who get their money from the people who get their money from the people who get their money from the aged. And there are the holiday visitors. No industries and no slums but what a mass of social distinctions! And every grade has its district. The really rich retired live in the grand houses in Branksome Park and in places like Knyveton Road. The grander you are, the nearer you get to the sea. Then huge turreted, red and often extremely ugly houses in loving settings, broad winding roads bordered with shrubs and trees for yards back on either side. Now, many of the conservatories are deserted save for a few geraniums and the turrets look a bit the worse for wear. The big houses are being turned into flats. If you want to see what really rich, royally patronized Bournemouth was like, see the Russell-Cotes Art Gallery – once the private house of Sir Morton Russell-Cotes, who was to Bournemouth what Smedley was to Matlock – a great home factor and a great house-keeper. Gorgeous with stained glass, filled with staircases, the walls painted or hung with pictures by many a capable but now forgotten Victorian artist. A riot of black and red and gold, of knick-knacks, of armour, of huge canvasses, of elaborate furniture, of panels, of pottery, of some good early English watercolours. The Russell-Cotes Art Gallery and Museum is the spirit of the old Bournemouth.

Behind the rich streets come lesser ones, for less rich but still leisured people, a little nearer the main road that runs between Christchurch and Poole at either extremity of the town. The houses are nearer together. The roads are not quite so wide and winding – take Willington Road as typical, today dropping with pink may and laburnum. The pines are not so frequent.

Then come the back streets where the workers live, on the other side of that main road I mentioned, which sizzles with trolley cars and roars with motors and is no different from any modern ugly suburb of any big town. The workers' houses are closer together still – though they all have gardens. They are just villas – rows and rows, most of them straight, not in the winding, tree-shaded manner of the smart districts. Pokesdown is the worker's part of Boscombe, Hinton of Bournemouth, Parkstone of Branksome Park and Canford Cliffs. (These last three, by the way, are in Poole, not Bournemouth, but there is nothing now to distinguish Poole from Bournemouth in appearance – it's only a matter of municipal government.)

How did this five-mile chain of villas between Poole and Christchurch come about? A hundred years ago Bournemouth and its appurtenances did not exist. Poole, a town built on Newfoundland trade, clustered round its magnificent harbour, sheltered by the great hills of Purbeck, rolling down to heath and sand. Poole is still eighteenth century. Look at those fine old houses round St James's church, or stand on the quay by Carter's pottery and walk around by the Custom House, the old Town Hall — see the plaster ceilings of the old Municipal buildings. Poole Quay was a rich, compact little fishing town. It still retains its seafaring character. Bournemouth might be a hundred miles away. I admire the restraint of commercial enterprise which has still kept the old part of Poole a town on its own — a museum piece well worth keeping. Hold back, multiple stores; hold back, speculators — remember not to ruin the look of the England out of which you make your money.

Christchurch, too, was a fishing place. The sandy common between them and Poole never bothered the Christchurch fishermen. There are fewer fine houses in old Christchurch but then Poole has not that grand priory which seems to ride like a great grey battleship over the marshes, when you see it from Wick or Tuckton. (The merchants who lived in the panelled rooms of Poole thought nothing of the sandy common which they had to cross if ever they wanted to go to Christchurch. They thought of the sea as something to trade on, not to paddle in.)

The idea of developing the Bourne valley and its sandy heath occurred to the people who enclosed the common land as early as 1802. Building started in 1835 but did not really get going until the 1850s. The popularity of Bournemouth came with the popularity of pines and Scottish scenery. Two hundred years ago, Scotland and moors and heaths were considered rude and ugly. Then Sir Walter Scott started the craze for them; Landseer painted them later. Queen Victoria went to Balmoral. Prince Albert loved pine trees. Loyal Victorians, backed by literature and art as well as royalty, started to love them too. They saw in Bournemouth a place with all the romantic pine-clad, heath-covered verdure of Scotland but without so much of Scotland's cold and rain. No wonder they filled it with houses. But they did it carefully.

What of the new Bournemouth? This has been done not so carefully. And with Bournemouth I include Poole, Christchurch, Boscombe and all the rest. Stand on Bournemouth Pier and look landwards. Towards Alum Chine to the west, the houses have conformed to the skyline and fit well into the landscape. To the east, they have made a skyline of their own — and a very ugly one too. The Pavilion seems to have no back and no front. It is an awkward shape.

The Baths seem to be all front; the roof line is cumbrous. But they are positively lovely compared with the collection of sham modern buildings which rise behind them – lines going in all directions, each trying to be more dashing and up to date than the others. As for that pink cliff of flats called Bath Hill Court, which rises behind them, that spoils the skyline from many directions.

Now Bournemouth has not only invaded the sky, it is invading with the aid of Poole the beautiful New Forest and Dorset country in which it is set. Many Bournemouth estates are well laid out. I have seen some where the old tradition of broad, winding roads bordered by shrubs and trees is still kept up. This is fine in an age which does not care for anything but money. Bournemouth must spend untold money in planting trees – good luck to it. It is the trees and the parks which will keep Bournemouth popular. Every open space in the town must be preserved.

But Bournemouth will cut its own throat if it allows its outer suburbs to go on developing as they do – treeless, uncontrolled. The speculator seems to have kept within the limited number of houses to the acre but not to have bothered about anything else. Oakdale and Sandbanks in Poole, and Southbourne beyond Boscombe, have particularly flagrant examples.

Then the new houses along the main roads, along Castle Hill Lane, towards Wimborne and Ringwood, must be kept in check. In these days of cars, holiday-makers like to see some country. Let there be some country for Bournemouth visitors to see. Most important of all, the Isle of Purbeck must be preserved as a national park. The wild shore of Studland Bay, the stretch of coast to Old Harry Rocks, is one of the finest on the south coast. Much of Poole and Bournemouth is built to look on it. Much of Poole and Bournemouth will have been built in vain if ever the isle is built upon. A smart young house agent, little knowing his poisonous words were to be broadcast, said to me, 'Yes, we hope to develop the Isle of Purbeck and Studland Bay soon. The landowners won't be able to hold out much longer.' Plan, preserve, plan – before it is too late and the speculator has ruined the whole south coast of England.

EXETER

From the series 'Town Tours'

West of England Programme
Friday 11 June 1937
Producer: J. C. Pennethorne Hughes

• • •

Exeter is double faced. There is the Exeter that strikes a visitor motoring through to the villa-bordered coasts of Devon and Cornwall. That visitor will think to himself, 'Oh, just another old-world county town. I suppose we'd better see the cathedral – there is one, I believe.' He will lose his temper in the appalling jam of traffic which there always seems to be in Exeter High Street – I hope to goodness they'll get a bypass or two finished soon – and he will think Exeter High Street is very like Guildford High Street in Surrey, a suburb of London. He will see the usual uncompromising and inappropriate fronts of multiple stores clapped onto mediaeval, Stuart and Georgian buildings. He will thread his way among buses and pert, charming little red sandstone churches – the greatest distinctions left in the undistinguished High Street – into the Cathedral Close. Then, if he is very lucky, he will find room to park his car. He will see a close not a quarter as fine as Salisbury nor a quarter the size. He will see a squat, square, stumpy grey cathedral, which he won't think as interesting at first glance as Gloucester, Salisbury or Winchester. He probably won't bother to look at the old clock in it, nor the minstrel gallery, the canopy of the bishop's throne – a piece of engineering in woodwork that makes you feel dizzy – nor the mediaeval stained glass. He will notice in the neighbourhood of the cathedral many olde gifts and olde beamed houses – so olde as to make him suspect they must be new. He will have seen all this, and he will not have got any idea at all of the real Exeter.

That is the face Exeter presents to visitors – a sort of lesser Stratford-upon-Avon but with a cathedral thrown in.

The other face, which a visitor does not see, lies away from the High Street. To understand the real Exeter, you must understand that Exeter is a conservative town. And by 'conservative' I do not mean conservative in its political sense. I mean that Exeter is a city of old causes. Oxford they call a city of lost causes; Exeter's causes are not necessarily lost, just old. She has always been the last to give in. She put up a great fight against William the Conqueror. Later she was strong Royalist; she went mad with joy when Charles Stuart came back to England. Today she is putting up a brave fight against the more repulsive elements of the twentieth century – hoardings, for instance, advertising petrol are not quite so frequent round Exeter as they are around other West Country towns. Speculative villas are not quite so ugly as they are in other parts of Devon. Petrol stations are neater than they are in Somerset. The country is allowed to creep quite near to the town without any avaricious speculator seeming to notice.

And behind her flamboyant, muddled, noisy High Street, behind her solid West Country cathedral, Exeter shelters an old-fashioned people – old-fashioned in the best sense. Don't forget that until the railways came to Exeter – less than a century ago – and even until about thirty years ago before the motor car made England hideous, Exeter was almost the capital of a kingdom. Devon squires went to Exeter, rather than to London. Very few of the country people had more than heard of London. Exeter was the most county of county towns, a really remote place. Even today, Exeter seems much further off when you motor to it than you feel it ought to be. There are several green fields between it and London. No wonder, then, Exeter is still old fashioned. No wonder she shows one face to strangers and another to those who bother to explore her side streets.

Somewhere in Exeter there is, so I used to be told as a child, a white witch. He is a man to whom farmers go whose cattle have been overlooked, a man who can cure by good white magic and ward off the evil effects of black magic. I don't know where he lives. I always like to think it is in that maze of mediaeval houses that tumble down the hill from the cathedral to the banks of the Exe. These have now mostly been removed in the name of 'slum clearance': perhaps the white witch's house still stands propped up against one of those little red sandstone churches.

Another part of Exeter that still survives almost intact is the Georgian district. Next time you go to Exeter, have a look at Bedford Circus and Southernhay; look at Dix's Field and Barnfield Crescent; walk in the miniature dell of beech- and ilex-shaded lawns called Rougemont Gardens. Nowhere in England – no, not even in Bath or Cheltenham – is such modest and satisfactory Georgian architecture to be found as round Southernhay and the crescents near it. Mellow brick walls; square-paned windows with white glazing bars; delicate ironwork of West Country design; sweeping vistas; cool pavements sheltered by ilex; the chiming of the quarter from the cathedral over the chimney pots; wisteria and clematis and vine clinging to mellow walls; old clergymen and upright solicitors walking sedately through the official parts; old ladies with parasols and pug-dogs walking in the residential quarter. Beside this calm, well-ordered place, our century of throbbing engines, lying advertisements and everlasting dance music seems a matter of no importance, something gone in the flash of a racing motorist.

Move a little further out, to Mount Radford and Victoria Park Road or to Pennsylvania Crescent or to those spacious streets above St David's station, and you will see another world – equally calm, equally remote. Here live the retired people of Exeter in places as quiet as the quietest Devon village. The houses are covered with cheerful stucco. They are plain and set back in large gardens full of all the shrubs and flowers that grow so easily in the mild Exeter climate. I was walking round some of these streets in the late afternoon last week. The sun lit up the stucco and I saw them as the unknown genius who designed them must have seen them. I suddenly realized what a genius the man who designed these stucco estates must have been. There was no fussy detail as on Exeter Guildhall (a relic of a glorious but more barbaric time), as on Exeter's new houses (relics of a less glorious and most barbarous time). Instead there was strength, the solidity conveyed by the long shadows on the angles of the house, a cool, heat-resisting effect conveyed by the broad eaves. What detail there was lay in the delicate wrought-iron verandahs and balconies, thrown up in all their beauty by the severe lines of the houses; then the colours – cream, white, pale pinks, ochre and even Pompeian red, yet all blending well together. For a moment, with the blue afternoon sky, the flowering creepers, the yews, the long walls, the warmth, I felt I was in Italy, until a gate squeaked on its hinge and an old man in a neat black suit and a straw hat stepped out to the letterbox – to post his weekly bulletin, no doubt, to some loved grandchild. Yes, it's enough to make anyone sentimental, the Regency and early Victorian part of Exeter. It represents English building at its best. The houses are more delicate and scholarly even than those round the Regent's Park, London, more original than those of Cheltenham, gayer than those of Bath: nowhere have I seen such lovely houses. Visitors never go to see these parts of Exeter. There is only one book about them that I know of and only one guidebook mentions them – and that is not the official Exeter guide.

Because Exeter likes to keep what she has got, these streets and terraces and crescents remain undisturbed. True, there is an inappropriate modern building in Southernhay but the offices that have invaded most of its houses have not defaced it with lettering and plate-glass expanses. Barnfield Crescent is not improved by a modern house in the fake-Tudor style at one end of it but on the whole Exeter seems to be aware of how lovely her old houses are.

I wish I could say that her newer houses were good. I have seen worse. Indeed one speculative builder's estate, on the road to Topsham and opposite the barracks, is really excellent – a well-chosen brick and well-proportioned houses. Each house is designed to command a view. The Exeter Council estate at Burnthouse Lane is not as good. The houses are well-designed themselves but they are in an ugly purplish brick not native to the mellow red of old Devon buildings. Then there seem to be no trees in the streets and little green space. And you may be sure that if the council is not going to plant trees, certainly the speculative builders won't. And by Jove, they don't. The post-war parts of Exeter are treeless deserts of red brick. Now the great feature of Georgian and early-Victorian Exeter is the presence of trees everywhere – copper beech, beech, oak and, best of all, the ilex, whose olive leaves look grand against the mellow red brick or cheerful plaster.

There seems to have been a pinching policy about the layout of post-war Exeter. I went up one lane in a motor car, with houses each with a garage on one side. There was a high Devon hedge on the other. The lane was too narrow even for a bicycle to pass the car. One end of the lane was dead. How it is possible for a car owner in one of these houses – and very ugly they were, with pretentious Tudor beams and stained glass such as would turn the former man of Devon sick – how is it possible for him to drive out of his house whenever any other vehicle is on the road? How is it possible for a car to turn in such a narrow passage? I pity the people who live in that lane. They have to walk a long way to the nearest bus route but I should say that is safer and quicker than trying to get there by car.

Plant more trees: plant the ilex and the beech down your new roads and you will make up for much of the ugliness of post-war Exeter. Let the country creep into the town – as it does round the canal – and Exeter will still be a country town. Copy the generous planning of Southernhay and the old terraces and crescents of a hundred years ago – you can't do better for though we may know better now about labour saving, our great grandfathers knew better about everything else connected with a house.

CONCLUSION

From the series 'Town Tours'

West of England Programme
Thursday 24 June 1937
Producer: J. C. Pennethorne Hughes

• • •

I started off on these town tours, some months ago, full of hope. I come back at the end of them sadly depressed. England is disappearing and there is growing up, where the trees used to be and where the hills commanded blue vistas, another world that does not seem to be anything to do with England at all. This new world lives in ill-shaped brick horrors, for which it has had to pay through the nose. Many of these horrors, built with no regard for one another, dropped higgledy-piggledy in the loveliest places – for all the world like huge slices of cake dropped on the tops of hills by some mad celestial picnic party – these little brick horrors are poisoning England. The people who have to live in them, sometimes – and I have evidence of this – starve themselves to pay off the instalments that will eventually make them owners of their own houses. And by the time they own the house they will find themselves saddled with a potential slum that will cost them more in repairs than ever it did in instalments. I have seen recently new houses going up in Wiltshire whose foundations were made of a concrete that crumbles like stale cake. You have all seen houses built with sham-Tudor beams and red roofs in districts where red is unknown and beams were never exposed. You have seen houses built on noisy main roads, when they should be back in the quiet: this saves road expenses to the speculator but endangers the lives of the people who live in the houses and turns every main road into one long built-up area.

Those people who can afford to live in the houses prefer to have a garage to a nursery because, presumably, they like to get away from the ugliness and noise and jerry-building by which they are surrounded. Those who can't afford to live in the new houses have nowhere to go to but furnished rooms, for there are not yet enough council houses and the old cottages in villages which could easily be repaired are condemned with too much eagerness by our anxious local councils.

So I find in most of the towns I visited that the rich and semi-rich had a huge choice of houses and the poor not enough houses. In no town, except one small estate opposite the barracks on the Topsham Road, Exeter, did I find speculative builders' estates that were anything but an eyesore. The speculator rarely considers the neighbourhood in which he is putting up his houses; he never, or rarely, plants any trees. Instead of spending money on essentials – built-in furniture, seasoned woodwork, good foundations, material suitable to the neighbourhood, trees in the road, quiet sites, the arrangement of the houses so that each has a view of greenery as in the better-planned council estates – too often he spends money on superficial attractions, though no one in his senses would call them attractions but the speculator and the poor duped fellow who wants a house in a hurry: things like sham beams, showy front gates, finicking little garden rails that a six-year-old burglar could leap in a trice, stained-glass windows. Some of the worst speculation I saw in a sea-coast town of Devon. There was a row of ugly and inappropriate villas erected only lately on a rubbish tip. A wet ditch at the back of the dump formed a boundary to tiny little back gardens. The front windows had no view, as other houses were being erected opposite to them.

The frightening thing about this bit of wickedness is that the builder gets away with it. He has his large car and plays an important part on his local council, some miles off, where he regards himself as a beneficent public figure. That man should go to prison. All people who spoil decent country should go to prison or be heavily fined. If I am found drunk and disorderly on the public highway, I get had up. But if a speculator buys a bit of land in unspoiled country – just as much your heritage as his, in fact rather more – and puts up an awful-shaped villa that spoils everybody's view and ruins a whole line of

hills with its glaring roof, if a speculator makes himself a public nuis-
ance like that, he doesn't get had up. Instead, he makes a lot of money
and thinks himself very cute. Even if I drop litter on the edge of a
common I can be fined £5. But litter can be cleared away. A speculator can put up a permanent bit of litter in the form of a bungalow
on the edge of a common and not get fined £5 and told to pick it
up and take it away. No, he clears about £50 out of his country's
scenery. *

There is nothing to cure this form of felony and greed but government control. Councils have purely advisory powers in the matter
of appearance of houses. In the Cotswolds, round Burford, the local
council is vigilant and disinterested: few ugly buildings have been put
up there since the war. What there are are coloured to conform to
the traditional buildings of the landscape. I wish the same could be
said for other districts. After all, the local councils are not always
above suspicion in their dealings. England can only be saved from
the enemies inside it – the speculators in land and houses – by either
government control or an association of local and county councillors who will have to be trained for their jobs and expelled if they
are detected in any crooked dealing. At present, the system of a local
councillor giving free evenings once a month to all the affairs of his
countryside is hopeless. It was all right when people did not worship money; now there is too much to do and too much to tempt.
Local government is a full-time job and must be an honest one. One
dishonest man in a council can ruin all the good work a council
might be doing.

But it's no good saying what might be done by other people. The
most important thing is to do something ourselves. Hoardings, for
instance. Nobody likes hoardings except the people who get money
from them. Outside Honiton and Plymouth, inside Exeter and
Plymouth, all round Bournemouth, the hoardings blare their messages to people who want to get away from the commercialism that
shouts at them all the rest of the week. Advertisements are all right
in papers but there is no excuse for using trees and cottages and
houses for them. I notice questions are being asked in Parliament

* A typical newly built semi-detached house in London cost £500 in the late 1930s.

about them. I hope something will happen. There are three acts that local councils may use, making it possible to remove hoardings that ruin the landscape. Many local councils are too inefficient to bring these laws into force, or too frightened; then higher authorities must act. Meanwhile I personally simply refuse to buy the petrol or whatever it is that the hoardings advertise.

Next there are trees. Bournemouth plants many trees each year. And I find I was unfair to Swindon in the matter of parks and gardens. Swindon – for all its ugliness – spends £3,000 a year on its handsome town gardens, the only park in the town, and I forgot to mention it in describing every green place in Swindon as recreation ground. But I attacked Swindon not because it was Swindon but because it was the supreme example in the West Country of what happens if too much is left to the speculative builder. As it is, Swindon may make itself pleasanter, as may the outskirts of every other town in England run up in a hurry after the war. This is done by planting trees. Now suppose everybody who is listening and who has a garden decided to plant a tree in it. That would help immensely. There is a pamphlet costing 6d. published by the Men of the Trees that tells you what trees grow where and how high they grow, how to plant them and what to do after you have planted them. Some trees do very well even in the sootiest towns. Among them are the rowan or mountain ash, which brings good luck to whomever plants it, and the Persian plum, which is copper coloured, and the good old white may, beneath which plants thrive even better than they do in open beds. If you have a lawn, why not plant a walnut or a mulberry in it? Then at the seaside all forms of elm – the most beautiful of English trees – the ash, the arbutus, the hawthorn, laburnum, various poplars, the London plane and sycamore all do well. There is no need to plant conifers. In nowhere but Bournemouth, among the towns I have toured, do fir trees look appropriate.

And now suppose you are going to build your house. Employ a qualified architect of the Royal Institute of British Architects; it costs less in the end. Use local material or material coloured in a suitable colour to the neighbourhood. Don't try to be 'different' from everyone else in the road (unless it's a speculator's road): it makes the whole road uglier. Don't have a low and useless garden wall; plant a hedge and use wire to keep out animals. Leaves and trees and bushes have made England beautiful in the past; there is no reason why the sootiest town should not burst into greenery. There is no reason why new houses should be ugly. They can actually improve the landscape – provided they are set on the slopes of hills, not on the tops of them.

If you all plant trees, if you all build plain houses – well proportioned like the old Georgian and early-Victorian houses of Exeter and Bristol, like the houses in the marketplace of Old Swindon, like the wide gracious streets of Stonehouse by Plymouth, like the cottages and farmhouses that still survive among the elms of England tonight – if you build plainly and fight against flashy rubbish that the speculator foists upon you, you will help to leave England fit for your children to live in. It's a hard fight but, my goodness, it's worth fighting.

UP TO LONDON

West of England Programme
Monday 2 January 1939
Producer: J. C. Pennethorne Hughes

• • •

I would like to think I'm talking tonight to people who still have illusions about London. I remember as a child those stories in *Doidge's Annual*, still published in Plymouth, about the fine city whose pavements were paved with gold and about the couple who came up from Devon and got no further than Paddington, thinking the whole of London was covered by a glass roof. I would like to think I'm talking, particularly, to someone in a remote house, who hasn't been to London for fifteen years.

Let us have a good mope together. Do you remember how it was possible early in the morning to smell the country right into the middle of London? I suppose the scent came from those market gardens in the rich agricultural land round Slough, now covered with factories, and from the carts coming in before dawn to Covent Garden Market. You can only smell petrol now and most of the Covent Garden produce comes in by lorry.

Do you remember those eating houses with humorous waiters, and horseboxes to sit in, and gaslight, and the smell of hot potatoes? Old City gents with white whiskers and red faces and enormous appetites devoured Manchester Hotpot until their watch-chains rattled against the edge of the table. Most of the eating houses are gone now. Smart new restaurants with their smart new waitresses and their glittering marble walls and dance music have taken their place. I used to go and have oysters at a restaurant in High Holborn. It was an old-fashioned

87

place where you sat at a high stool and the white-coated oyster-openers and fish-waiters passed the time of day with you between intervals of shouting their orders. 'Three stewed eels. Quick, gentleman in a hurry! – The Arsenal not doing much now, sir. – One dozen best seconds,' and so on. I went there lately and the gaiety had gone. In a fit of mistaken enterprise, someone had 'done it up' in a pseudo-modern style. The old-looking glasses and advertisements were taken down. The walls were panelled with Empire wood in a sort of neo-Tudor manner, like our uninviting new public houses. It has now closed down altogether.

Perhaps you remember how humorous the bus conductors used to be. I think of the old *Punch* joke that had a picture of a lady on top of a horse bus leaning across from the front seat to the driver on his box. 'Do you stop at the Cecil?' 'Do I stop at the Cecil, on twenty-eight bob a week?' The bus conductors haven't time now to make jokes. Buses are bigger than they were, driving is a torture and traffic blocks strain everybody's temper to breaking point.

And then perhaps you remember that rather pleasant smell of wet earth and graveyards that used to hang about the City & South London tube railway when it had those little orange engines and the cane seats and rotten lighting in the carriages. All modernized now, and the smell modernized too. One thing remains the same on this Underground: women take twice as long as men to buy their tickets. A man will have his money ready for the fare when he reaches the booking office. A woman, even if she's been waiting in a queue for some time, never has her money ready. She says to the clerk, 'Piccadilly Circus. How much?' 'Threepence.' She takes out her bag, feels for a purse, opens it fussily and then asks, 'Do I have to change?' If you're in a hurry – and everyone in London is in a hurry, worse luck – choose the queue with the fewest women in it. (I know how unpopular saying this will make me but I don't mind.)

I notice, too, talking of hurry on the Underground, that people up from the country on the moving stairways at Paddington never stand on the right as they are asked to but block up the passageway for others by standing two abreast. Sensible people, I suppose they are, because they're not slaves to time, as Londoners seem to be. Look at the time-slaves on the Underground! Yellow and white faces of Londoners, drawn, worried, with mouths turned down at the corners and haunted expressions. No wonder they're worried! They have, presumably, to travel in a crowded train to some remote suburb. The roofs of their little semi-detached houses leak; they're starving themselves to pay the weekly instalments on their jerry-built embryo slums. It takes as long to travel to most of the outer suburbs as it does for us to take an express to Swindon or Andover. Have pity on the Londoners: they have no time now for jokes and smiles. They must hurry from their houses to the office, fight for a place on the train, fight their way home again, tired, in the evening, and the little garden they took such pride in is to be turned into an ARP trench – all the standard roses to be rooted up.

Some of you may remember, when you used to go to London, the old club-men you used to see walking down Piccadilly and Bond Street. These members were the relics of the gay days before the war when it was not gentlemanly to work. They were dressed in a dapper style. They never shaved themselves: a barber called to do it for them. They got their hats at this shop, their shoes at that, their shirts at another, their ties at another and their handkerchiefs at a fifth. They spent hours looking at themselves, back view, at the tailors. They knew who you ought to know and who was 'not quite'. Look up at the club windows now when you walk down St James's Street or Pell Mell (it's never pronounced 'Pall Mall' by those who know) and you'll not see them looking possessively out into the street. The club-men are dying out. The clubs are having a hard time. Many of them have abolished their forty-guinea entrance fees. And the younger club-men get their things at the multiple stores. The old days of specially made shoes, shirts, etc. are, it seems to me, nearly over. Shade of Major Pendennis, forgive me for what I say.

And those small private 'otels (never called 'hotels' by those who know) where the brothers of the club-men used to stay when they came up from the country – where are they? Very few of them are left. The hotels are big now and the smaller ones have either been demolished or taken over by combines. As for bachelor chambers off Piccadilly, they're almost extinct. In Albemarle Street there's only one old bachelor left.

And then how the look of London has changed – in almost every case for the worse. Why is it that all the builders in London seem to think people want to live in flats? Lots of the blocks are half empty and have to resort to the old dodge of putting curtains in the windows and turning on the lights at night, to give an appearance of success. Only a small section of the community wants to live in a flat. Yet Berkeley Square is turning at this moment into a sort of well, sandwiched in between monster blocks of windows scraping as much of the sky as the bye-laws will allow. The converse is happening in the Paddington district. You may have noticed those wide streets of yellow stucco with tall, well-proportioned houses and big squares. They're being demolished and horrible little villas with red-hipped roofs are being jumbled about among them, breaking up all the symmetry and beauty of the old streets.

The London County Council is very proud of its slum-clearance schemes. You can see them all over the place now. The fine, wide two-storeyed streets of Clerkenwell, Islington, East London and South London are coming down as fast as I'm talking to you tonight. Of course, a lot of these houses ought to have come down. They're often riddled with vermin and there are plenty of streets still in London where it's safer to sleep out on the pavement on a warm night so as to avoid getting bitten by bugs. But look what is going up in their place. Flats, of the wrong height (six or seven storeys high, which is wasteful of light and space) and of the wrong-coloured bricks (a hateful red). The people who used to live in a street are forced to live in a block of flats. Now who, with a family of children, wants to live anywhere but on the ground floor? And do old-age pensioners want to climb six storeys to a flat? – for it's uneconomic to give lifts to the slum-clearance flats. Living in a London slum street isn't so bad as it sounds (I've done it myself) – I mean the actual contact with one's neighbours. The street is a sort of village in itself and the road and the pavements are a playground. People stand at their doors and talk to whomever they choose. In a flat, if you stand at your door, you've got to talk to your neighbour opposite, whether you like him or not. And the arid, sunless recreation grounds of asphalt round a flat-block are hardly a compensation for the street playground and certainly not to those who had a little garden or backyard in the past. Nor are community halls and self-conscious social clubs, for all their good intentions, a compensation for someone who's lost his house and lives in a flat. Londoners, like all English people, prefer to live in a house. London was once all houses! That was its charm and its beauty. I think the change towards gloominess which I can't help noticing in London people is largely due to the change in their surroundings, the state interference with their dwelling houses. There's a lot to be said on both sides. Let's pass on.

You must have seen, if you've been there at all, those country houses that had somehow got left behind in the middle of London. They used to be behind high walls and no one went in or out of them unless some rich person hired the ballroom one night for a charity dance. The houses have gone but not the charity dinners. Dorchester House, Devonshire House, Kingston House, Chesterfield House, Norfolk House, Lansdowne House. And on their sites great sky-scrapers have risen up. Waterloo Bridge was the loveliest in London but it came down; and now, when the new bridge is finished, it will be a huge broad thoroughfare leading from nowhere to nowhere.

Old Regent Street was a broad, sunny stretch of lovely stucco buildings, well mannered and well proportioned. The new Regent Street is a narrow chasm, blue with petrol fumes and throbbing with traffic blocks, between great grey cliffs of Portland stone that yearly get blacker and blacker. Berkeley Square, St James's Square and Leicester Square are all changing and becoming little green wells among blocks of flats and cinemas. One of Wren's city churches is coming down; eight newer churches (some of them no less beautiful) have been taken down in the west of London.

I said at the beginning of this talk tonight that I would like to think I was talking to someone who still had illusions about London. Take my advice, dear listener, if you are still listening, and keep your illusions and don't come up to London. You won't be able to get about for traffic blocks anyhow and you'll miss the old London you knew except in some of the suburbs that are hard for a countryman to find. And if you must come up, *hurry up*: soon there'll be none of the London left that made coming 'Up to London' an exciting adventure.

BESIDE THE SEASIDE

VISITORS

West of England Programme
Friday 22 April 1938
Producer: J. C. Pennethorne Hughes

• • •

'Come away, Henry, from those common little children. They're only visitors.'

'Don't have anything to do with those people, Bertie – they think they own the place.'

Who of us does not know that eternal struggle between residents and visitors which goes on from year to year round our wave-washed shores? I have arranged the first two of these talks like a boxing match. Round one, which I propose to describe now, is going to be a victory for the visitors. I'm going to show you that the poor visitors have a good deal to complain of.

While you were all thinking how cold it was this Easter, I was mooning about from watering place to watering place, being a visitor.

The first thing that the visitor complains of is high prices. High rents, for instance. I know of a modern house on the west coast of England. It contains six bedrooms (one of which is little better than a cupboard), a garage for two cars, a tiny garden, a dining room and a drawing room, two bathrooms and the usual offices. The owner lets it furnished, having first substituted linen sheets on the bed for cotton ones and removed all the better silver and ornaments, having hidden away the rugs in locked cupboards and generally cleared the place out of all but essential furniture. How much does he get a week during July, August and September for this bijou paradise? He gets thirty

95

guineas a week. It's true a gardener comes twice a week and the visitors are allowed the produce of the garden. But by August the garden doesn't contain much produce: what it did contain has generally been pinched already. Of course, the answer to this is: if someone is fool enough to pay thirty guineas a week for four walls, a roof and running water, the owner of the house shouldn't be fool enough to refuse the money.

Let me give you one instance far worse than this, though the money involved isn't so much. Here is the advertisement, such as you'd see in any local papers:

> MODERN WELL-BUILT BUNGALOW: at ——, within a few minutes of sea and shops. 4 bedrooms; recep; usual offices; garage; large garden; TO LET FURNISHED: 63 shillings a week.

I will examine this phrase by phrase, for I have visited just such a bungalow – and there are hundreds of them.

'Modern well-built bungalow'. 'Modern' means post-war. 'Well-built' means that there is an ineffective dampcourse and Tudor gables, and the partition walls inside are of some far from soundproof material. 'Modern' and 'well-built' don't necessarily go together.

'At ——'. '——' is a growing seaside town. Like most seaside towns, it grows inwards like a toenail. The local council has taken a great deal of trouble to plant calceolaria and hydrangeas in circular beds along the front and to string the pier with electric lights but the council hasn't taken much trouble with the part of the town that doesn't show and isn't mentioned in the town clerk's brochure, which describes —— as 'the most delectable of watering places' and leaves out a single adverse comment. At the back of —— are acres and acres of new building estates, indistinguishable from the dreariest post-war suburb outside any industrial town. The roads aren't properly made up and there is no proper lighting.

'Within a few minutes of sea and shops'. Certainly within a few minutes if you catch the bus which runs from the end of the road every half an hour with a return fare of 4d. Otherwise half an hour's walk from the sea and shops.

'Four bedrooms'? Well, yes. Two of these bedrooms are attics with iron bedsteads, up in those Tudor gables. When the sun has been on the tiles, the temperature is unbearable and doesn't cool off till midnight. Late hours are therefore compulsory. Of the two other bedrooms, one is undoubtedly a bedroom; the other would be more convenient as a dining room.

This brings me to the next mysterious word: 'recep'. This is presumably the room where the Turkey carpet is and the clock that doesn't go. There is a table, one armchair and four hard wooden ones. If it is wet or cold, there is a good deal of quarrelling as to who shall have the one comfortable chair.

'Usual offices'. The bath is in the kitchen and has a lid over it. The kitchen is the smallest room in the house. The lavatory is outside. The water doesn't seem to get hot – perhaps the pipes are blocked; more probably the stove's gone wrong.

'Garage'. For a small car or a perambulator, but not for both.

'Large garden'. Round this lovely little bungalow, with its view of other lovely little bungalows, there is certainly an area of grass and dandelions and a few strangled standard rose bushes which might be called a large garden, for it is a bit larger than the house.

'To Let Furnished: 63 shillings a week'. Now if this bungalow were lived in all the year round, if the things in it worked, if the rooms didn't smell of damp, mice and stale biscuits, if the garden were bright with flowers, forty-two shillings would be expensive but just reasonable. But it isn't lived in. It was bought by a man in, let us say, Bristol, for £500 fifteen years ago. Since then he has let it to successive tenants during the holiday seasons at three guineas a week. No tenant has ever been there twice. The furniture consists of not enough plates, two aluminium teaspoons, four hard beds, some torn matting, a back number of a magazine left by a former tenant, a broken lawnmower and a cake of washing soap which has stuck in the waste pipe of the sink.

If you suppose that the holiday season lasts for ten weeks at the least, and at the most five months, then you will see that this absentee landlord has been getting a good return for his outlay of £500 over the last fifteen years. So sometimes the visitor has a right to grumble about prices.

Let us turn to more cheerful subjects. The joke about the seaside landlady is now as old as the joke about the plumber and his mate.

It is even more untrue. Most, though not all, seaside landladies look after one very well. Last year I went and stayed in a little bee farm in a lonely part of the Isle of Man. I had a large room to myself, excellent food, companionship. There really was a garden and the sea really was three minutes away. We lived simply, happily and well. My bill at the end of a fortnight was £2. 5s. When I had baths, I wasn't charged extra; when I wanted to take sandwiches out, there was no trouble in getting them.

One more word on price – and this time the price of food. For some strange reason, butter and vegetables and meat are fantastically expensive in parts of the country during the holiday season. Though you stay at farms, you often have to eat New Zealand butter. You are told that all the butter made at the farm has to go to London; so does the cream and the milk. Yet, judging by the hundreds of cars that turn the narrow lanes into a terror and the thousands of people that dot the water edge and blacken the beaches, you would think London was almost empty all the same. Potatoes might be rubies, carrots culture-pearls and cauliflowers priceless chrysoprase, considering the prices one has to pay for them. In the larger seaside towns, prices are better. But in the country, one is at the mercy of the country tradesman. The butcher comes round twice a week. 'May I have some veal?' 'Veal!' – one might have asked for stewed alligator. 'We've only got beef.' And what beef: stringy, opalescent stuff, twice the price you can buy it for at home. Unless you are very rich or very clever at bargaining, I advise you to stay in lodgings with all-in terms. And be careful to look at a map of the town or country first, before you book the rooms. See exactly how far from the sea you are going to be, whether you are on a noisy main road and whether you really are in country – if you want a country holiday.

There are other things beside prices of which the visitor had better beware. The first is provision for children. He will have to look hard if he wants to find pleasant places to walk to as well as a good beach for the children. Most people cannot look after very young children *and* go for a walk or an expedition. Weston-super-Mare has foreseen this difficulty. It provides a day nursery where children can be left and cared for, for a moderate charge. By this clever device, the parents can get a bit of a holiday too. Other local councils please copy.

Then the town itself should be beautiful. The shops aren't everything. People can see shops any day of their lives. Flats aren't everything. People nowadays see more than enough of them. The front of an English seaside town, the quiet terraces and crescents with their gardens and bathing dresses hanging out to dry from bedroom windows, the pier (I am thinking particularly of Clevedon, which is a charming one) and the landscape and planting are just some of the features that give English seaside towns their special atmosphere. Foreign seaside resorts don't compare with ours. But ours lose all their beauty if they are turned into shopping centres and if the views of cliff scenery that the terraces were designed to look upon are dotted with bungalows. The lovely Georgian front of Teignmouth depends largely on the beauty of Shaldon opposite being preserved. The sweep of Weymouth Bay is helped by the outline of Portland. No one would go to Clovelly if it became 'developed'. The fronts of Brighton and Ramsgate have some of the best architecture in England. Hastings, a lovely Georgian town, has recently hit on an excellent scheme to preserve its beauty. The council has grown a quantity of trees and every householder can have a tree planted free in his garden and tended by the council.

Then again, the country round a seaside resort and within walking distance is one of the chief attractions of the place. In many towns, councils have allowed bungalows with red roofs in grey-stone districts or with black-and-white beams to dot the rolling hills and valleys. Cornwall is particularly an offender. The Cornish coast is becoming a huge suburb. This must be checked. Building must be confined to certain areas and country must be left undeveloped.

Pity the poor visitor. He comes to the seaside for a breath of fresh air and for walks in the country. He doesn't want to see a reproduction of his own town transplanted to the seaside. He often pays through the nose for the pleasure. Surely you are going to give him trees, fields, quiet lanes, farms, tracts of moor and downland. Surely you are going to give him somewhere to park his car; somewhere to escape from the noise of the internal-combustion engine, the smell of petrol and the sight of endless bricks and mortar. If you don't hurry up and legislate, you will be too late. Your town will be just like his own home and he will find it pleasanter and cheaper to remain where he is. And no amount of propaganda from the official information bureau is going to dissuade him from the evidence of his own eyes.

That is the end of round one. One up to the visitors.

RESIDENTS

West of England Programme
Wednesday 27 April 1938
Producer: J. C. Pennethorne Hughes

• • •

Last year the holiday season in most West Country resorts lasted for six weeks. In six weeks, ice-cream merchants had to sell enough ice cream, landladies had to take in enough guests, picture-postcard shops had to sell enough postcards, rock shops had to sell enough rock, and so on, for each of those people to make enough money to tide them over until the season this year. Well, a good many of them didn't. Hundreds of small traders were ruined. This year you will see empty shops in half-deserted arcades, shuttered kiosks and curtainless boarding houses with a 'For Sale' board outside them – all because the season last year was only six weeks long. Can you blame the resident trader for putting a bit on his prices when the visitors arrive?

The rates in many seaside towns are ten shillings in the pound – in some towns more than twelve shillings. Imagine yourself saddled with a large house in which you hope to let rooms. The larger and better appointed the house, the higher the rates. Then suppose that you have only a six-week season in which to make your money. You cannot charge very high prices because price-cutting in other hotels and boarding houses will take away your custom. What can you do? Starve or go bankrupt? Sack the staff? Sell the furniture?

I've been taking in local papers from the seaside towns for the last month or so. In almost all of them are letters of complaint by residents about the highness of the rates. Distracted mayors and helpless councillors try to disclaim responsibility. Nor are they always responsible.

Land has to be acquired for a car park; a new pavilion has to be built; the Winter Gardens, which everyone thought was going to be such a success, has turned out a failure; the theatre on the pier will have to be repaired; the orchestra doesn't pay (orchestras very rarely do pay directly, nor for that matter do flowerbeds or trees, but no seaside town should be without them); the residents won't patronize the entertainment places in the winter. Listen to Councillor Green of Weston-super-Mare: 'If Westonians will only support the events at the Winter Gardens pavilion during the winter season, as well as other municipal entertainments, not only will they get good value for their threepences and sixpences but they will be helping materially to reduce the colossal losses and thereby also help to reduce the rate': that is, pay your rates by going to municipal entertainments. Well, that's one way of doing it – if you have the money to pay them at all.

All this points to one thing: the residents of a seaside town pay for a large part of the entertainment of the visitors who come to it. And the residents aren't always well treated. Everything is done for the visitors. The front looks very well but what about the back? I know of streets in Exmouth that are as ugly, airless and rack-rented as a London slum. I know of a seaside town where a magnificent row of Georgian houses is being deliberately left out of repair because the landlord, who is on the local council, wants to have it condemned so that a firm in which he is deeply but anonymously interested may build a municipal edifice on its site. The amenities of the town will be ruined but the landlord will get a nice bit of compensation for his property from the council and a good profit for building the new edifice. He will himself see that the council accepts the tender of the firm in which he is interested. Oh, it's worth being on the local council if you know the ropes. Sting the residents and get rich yourself. (I shall forget myself and give away this and several other similar scandals of our seaside towns if I don't think of something else.)

Since we're on rather a disgusting subject, let's turn to another: drains. I won't say that residents only are in peril of diphtheria on our coasts: the visitors will come in for it too. There has, as you may know, been a great deal of building since the war: higgledy-piggledy, hang the amenities, muck up the country, spread out the towns, pull down the old-fashioned in the name of slum clearance, run up a railway carriage, license an army hut, pass any plans. Yes, a good deal of building goes on. Some people call it 'development'; a better word is 'growth'. Water schemes have become all the rage. But though there are lots more houses and lots more water, there aren't lots more drains. Ratepayers don't see their money's worth in drains. Since everything is money, a new pavilion or a new promenade looks better. It gets the councillors re-elected. It gets illustrated in the papers. No one photographs a drain. So drains pass by the board. When the visitors come in their thousands and drains are only just adequate for the residents, there's going to be an outbreak of diphtheria – or worse.

So you see, the resident pays for the pleasure of the visitor and runs the risk of diphtheria as a reward for his sacrifice. Is the visitor worth it? I know it's usual to laugh at colonels but Colonel Cabbage, a leaf of whose diary I'm going to quote now, would like to shoot every visitor as he once shot big game and I must say I don't blame him. Colonel Cabbage is a hotchpotch of various complaints I've received about visitors from seaside residents. The Colonel lives in a small house on the coast. He has a largish garden, which he runs with the help of one man, Spiggot. He owns a couple of fields at the back of his house, which are let to a farmer.

17 August: A little rain last night, so I went into the lower field to look at the rain gauge. Found a couple of bell tents there and a sickly socialist-lookin' fellow shavin' his pimply face, actually usin' the water in the gauge to shave with. 'Who the devil gave you leave to billet yourself here, sir?' I said. 'No one,' he replied; 'the people have a right to their own country.' 'And the farmer has a right to his own field, and so has the owner.' 'I'm not doin' any harm,' he said; 'can you oblige me with some hot water from the house?' This incident ruined my digestion for breakfast.

Took the car out to get stores from Paddlebridge. Found a fellow had left his blasted saloon car bang across the front gate. Couldn't get out. Windows and doors of the car shut and locked, so couldn't budge the thing. Half an hour before I found him. Told him what I thought. Ended by giving him sixpence to put his car in the public parking place.

Came back and found a couple of women rooting out the mesem-bryanthemums in the drive. 'D'you think you own the place?' they said. 'I know I do.' That was one up to me, I fancy.

I'll really have to get rid of Spiggot. He thinks that just because he works half the week for me, he needn't come at all. When I was away, I know he did nothing in the garden and sold the asparagus and kept the money for himself. Now he's taken to pinchin' the plants and sellin' them to other people he works for. Awful how disheartened these natives have become.

Went for a stroll down to the beach. Found a fellow had got his car stuck in the sand. Tide came up and the cushions floated through the sunshine roof. Serves him right. There's a notice to say cars aren't allowed on the beach.

The people who live in those shacks at the back will keep breakin' down the hedges and making a right of way across my fields. I'll have the upper field ploughed up next year – not that that will make any difference. These dashed visitors thinking nothin' of walkin' through a field of standin' corn.

Just settlin' down for a sleep this afternoon when a confounded wireless set somewhere or other started blarin' out one of those wretched croonin' songs. Went up the drive to investigate. Found another car stuck across the gate. A family in it readin' papers and with one of those confounded car wireless sets goin' full blast. Told 'em to move on.

Came back to find a party settlin' down to picnic tea behind the shrubbery the other side of the tennis court. 'We didn't think you could see us here.' I told them to clear out and pick up the paper. They had the impertinence to ask for hot water as they were leavin'.

Commander Cannibal dropped in after tea. Tells me that the local council is goin' to build an airport. Part of it may be on my fields. Also says the fields along the foreshore have been sold to a Plymouth specu-lator who is goin' to put up 300 bungalows there.

Can't sleep tonight. There's some blasted fellers ridin' motor bikes up and down the lane. Cannibal's children just come back from a dance. Can't they make less noise about it?

Think I'll have to sell the place. A pity, since I've committed half my pension to pay for improvements in the garden. My stars, there's one of those trailer caravans drivin' into the lower field. Wait till I slip a coat over my pyjamas.

Poor Colonel Cabbage. He seems to have had a bad day. Yet, in a more or less degree, these are the indignities with which seaside residents have to put up. And if Colonel Cabbage is afflicted, what of the Spiggots of the sea coast? What of the men of Devon, the Cornish, the Zummerset, the Dorset men, whose fathers made the villages and fields we so much admire and who built the picturesque harbours and fishing smacks that are so etched, sketched and photographed? Colonel Cabbage can escape inland. Not so the natives of the soil. They cannot afford to. Or if they can, they don't want to.

Many of them are completely demoralized. Land workers have become rough gardeners (not all of them honest); farmers have turned their farms into guest houses and retired from farming; small landowners have turned into the worse sort of speculative builder; fishermen have become stage fishermen, who lounge on the quay to tell apocryphal tales of King Arthur and John Wesley at a half a crown apiece or to take out London businessmen and make them seasick at ten bob an hour. The avariciousness which is the least charming thing in simple people has been exploited to the full. It's not their fault that this happened: it's the fault of the visitors who have corrupted and uprooted them. The harm is done now to the residents just as surely as the harm is done to the scenery of our coasts. I don't know what we can do about it beyond praying. But I know that, in the balance of justice, the scale is heavily weighted against the visitor. The men of our coasts are no longer sea-dogs but land-dogs, 'Laden with spoil of the South, fulfilled with the glory of achievement,' but not, I fancy, 'freshly crowned with never-dying fame'.*

* Sir Henry Newbolt, 'The Death of Admiral Blake'.

SEAVIEW

West of England Programme
Wednesday 11 May 1938*
Producer: J. C. Pennethorne Hughes

• • •

Which are you? I don't know which you are.
 Have you children still of the age that finds pleasure in exploring caves? Children who might easily tumble over steep cliffs in search of seagulls' eggs? Children who come back tired in the evening with a bucketful of jellyfish and upset them over the bedroom floor? Children who get up monstrously early and long to get down to the sea? Children who still believe in ghosts and smugglers? Children who expect to find the wreck of a Spanish galleon in the next bay and the sea-smooth skeleton of a pirate wedged in a hollow of the cliffs?

And are you susceptible to this sort of thing yourself? Do you like to lean over the edge of a dinghy on a calm day and see at the bottom of the green water the remains of walls on what was once dry land? Do you want to get away from the noise of cars and things, like me talking to you now, and telephones and aeroplanes and the other inestimable advantages of our civilization?

If so, go to the Scilly Isles. There aren't many of them that are inhabited so you can't all go, even if you can afford it. But they are all they're cracked up to be. There are haunted uninhabited islands

---

* This was the concluding talk in a series of four talks entitled 'Seaview', of which 'Visitors' and 'Residents' were the first two. The third, not included here, was a fictional account of an unhappy holiday spent at 'Port Blanket', based on various real experiences.

and islands with ruins of houses on them. There's St Mary's (the biggest island) with Hugh Town, the little capital, a place with hardly one ugly building in it; Tresco, with gardens containing palms, camelias and tropical plants at one end, bare and frightening moor at the other; Bryher, with little beaches and high enormous hedges; St Martin's, for cliff scenery; St Agnes, which is like unspoiled Cornwall; Annet, where you crush birds' eggs with every step you take on the spongy thrift; and rocks and tiny islands – all within a few minutes' sailing of one another. The Scillonians are long, lanky people. And, blessed advantage, they don't get their letters every day of the week. A warm and mild breeze blows among the high-hedged flower fields and the only sounds you hear are the waves rumbling and the creak of rowlocks and splash of the oars and the grate of a keel as the dinghy puts in at the row of fishermen's houses. Scillonians are fishermen, gardeners, carpenters, everything.

There are parts of Cornwall where you can find equal quiet and wilder, grander scenery, for the cliffs are much higher and the Atlantic rollers come tumbling in as high as a house in stormy weather – crash; a hiss up the shingle; an echo against the rocks; silence; then crash again. Then there's the happy terror and escape to a fire of driftwood when the wind howls up the chimney – the ghost of Jan Tregeagle with his hounds of hell. That's the advantage of Cornwall: it's as thrilling in rough winter as it's beautiful in fair. You don't huddle into a shelter on the promenade: you meet the wind and let the rain whip against your face, and like it.

I shan't tell you where all the lovely places are: I want them to myself. But I'll tell you where to look: between Falmouth and St Ives, between Pentire and Tintagel, and right up in the north beyond Bude where Cornwall thins out into Devon and Hartland stretches on into the Atlantic.

Which are you? I don't know which you are.

Are you getting on in life and anxious for a little sea air but not too much? Do you like what the guidebooks call a 'salubrious climate' and a 'respectable residential neighbourhood'? Do you like to hear a little good music on wet days? Do you like to sit on a municipal seat and listen to the breeze in municipal trees and smell the frequent municipal flowers? Then you want somewhere where the children, married now or working, can come down to see you and get a little fun too – tennis clubs of an exclusive, respectable kind; baths with high diving boards for the daring; golf links adjacent; cinemas; and something classy at the Theatre Royal?

Then go to Bournemouth and more particularly to the exclusive Branksome. Here the pine trees and rhododendrons and heather are allowed to grow beside twisting roads – steep climbs for him who pushes a bath chair – and houses hide respectably among the foliage of their spacious gardens. There are more than three million pines in the sandy soil of Bournemouth. The municipal council is sensible about planting them. Whether it is the terebinthinate sap or the mixture of ozone and resin, I don't know, but Bournemouth is said to be just the place for the lungs and bronchial tubes.

Or there's Budleigh Salterton with its tennis and its grown-up tennis players, all muscle and freckles and tan. Or there are the delightful Regency towns of Sidmouth, Teignmouth and Dawlish – what is left of that great gracious age in them. I know few pleasanter sights than the view of Shaldon from the front at Teignmouth. Keats wrote about Teignmouth:

> Here all the summer could I stay,
> For there's Bishop's Teign
> And King's Teign
> And Coomb at the clear Teign head –
> Where close by the stream
> You may have your cream
> All spread upon barley bread.
>
> [from 'For there's Bishop's Teign']

And here, while I'm on the subject of views, is a piece of advice. When you're choosing where to stay, don't mind how ugly it is itself so long as what it looks on is beautiful. If it's pre-war ugly, it's pretty certain to be well built at any rate, which is more than can be said for the 'desirable' bungalows and villas that have made so much of the West Country nauseous. More than often, advertisements show a view *of* the house but not the view *from* the house, which is what you see – so be careful.

And yet another place for those who like a respectable, equable atmosphere: tropic Torquay, so magical at night when street lamps dot the hills and strings of lights are seen among the palms and over the pavilion.

Which are you? I don't know which you are.

Perhaps you're the man who likes a bit of everything: a good cinema in the evening, a promenade, a bus service, good scenery, good bathing, good music, good country in the near neighbourhood for walks. A modicum of everything and not too much of anything. A pier not too long; country not too wild and dangerous; cinemas not too big; the promenade not too crowded. If that's the sort you are then there's Weymouth, that noblest sweep of bay in all the South-West, where the charming red-brick Georgian houses that have been allowed to remain by short-sighted local councils curve round still, very much as they do in the Turner picture. And fine country is near to Weymouth: Portland Island, grey, forbidding, almost treeless, with long, fair-haired Portlanders who marry among themselves and regard people as near as Wyke Regis as foreigners. Have a look at the old church at Easton-upon-the-Hill, with its miraculous carved classical steeple in Portland stone. And to the west is Abbotsbury – a grey limestone village, rolling downs behind, the swannery before, protected from the sea by that extraordinary Chesil Beach. The beach is a long mound of rounded pebbles, huge at Portland and stretching in diminishing size of cobblestones in a great curve all the way to Lyme Regis. Or there's Lyme Regis, a town where still you feel you might meet Jane Austen after getting her books from the circulating library. Or Beer, with Branscombe's unspoiled church near it and that terrific stretch of coastline where the red of Devon turns into chalk and limestone.

And in North Devon is Ilfracombe, steep cliffs, jagged and rocky, with green patches of grass here and there. Or dizzy heights by Lynton and Lynmouth, those two superbly situated places, lost in folding hills and wooded valleys where the country stretches back with little fields – that's a funny thing: the further west you get, the smaller the fields seem to become – to the smooth heights of Exmoor. There's also Clevedon in Somerset, a quite respectable place, an unspoiled Victorian town.

Which are you? I don't know which you are.

Do you like twisting streets and genuine fishermen, as opposed to the fake fishermen of artist-ridden, tourist-haunted ports where every other cottage is a tea place and the ones in between sell fake antiques? Do you like grey alleys with high walls, tufted with stonecrop, and slate roofs, feather-grey, down a steep hillside (impracticable for motors)? Do you like a stream running down between the slatey houses, gaunt square Methodist chapels and the brilliant brick and slate of the seamen's institute? Then take a look at Padstow – they were trying to spoil the quay when last I was there – or at Port Isaac, both in Cornwall. Or try Kingsbridge and Dartmouth in Devon, and even Brixham, if it's still not too self-conscious.

Which are you? I don't know which you are.

Probably you are of the biggest lot of all – those who want cinemas, dance halls, theatres, fun, noise, splendour, sand stretching for miles, bathing machines, mixed bathing, lights, winkles, rock as opposed to rocks, souvenirs, postcards, funfairs. Probably you've seen enough of the country all the rest of the year and want a contrast now. More probably you like the town – country frightens you – and you want more of it, and some sea and bathing chucked in as well. Kind sea that washes away all our waste paper and uneaten, sandy sandwiches; kind sea that looks so very kind when there isn't a stiff breeze blowing against the tide; kind sea, what else have you drawn to your shores for those of us who want to spend our year's savings like your own lavish waters? Well, there's Porthcawl, Paignton, Newquay, Weston-super-Mare. They have all the delights for the majority. They are inland town life, settled down beside the sea.

Which are you? I don't know which you are.

But don't blame me if it rains after all this fine weather. Don't blame me if I haven't mentioned everywhere: there isn't time in my thirteen minutes. Don't blame me if you find yourself stuck in a hideous little place, neither town nor country. I only hope I've given you some idea of the tremendous choice there is in green Somerset, white-chalky Dorset, in the red little hills of South Devon, bare yellow clay of North Devon, grey slate and granite and steep flower-spread cliffs of Cornwall.

And now a few fleas in the ears of local residents. Don't make such a fuss about bathing dresses and mixed bathing: the human body, even at its fattest or skinniest, isn't half so ugly as the simply hideous bungalows you allow to ruin the country that was once the attraction of the place you govern. Don't spend all your money on promenades, pavilions and fairy lights along the front. Remember the back. Remember the speculative builders' estates that will soon be slums stretching away, miles from the sea, but still called 'the Borough of ——', which will get you a bad name and which deface England more and more every minute. Don't rob your visitors or they won't come back again. Don't give them bad food. Don't build bad houses out of keeping. Don't forget to have enough drains and sewage. Don't think you're being progressive when you take down the old buildings that could perfectly well be repaired: you're cutting off your own noses to make your face jolly ugly. Don't – but if I go on like this I shall never stop. Goodbye. Enjoy yourselves.

WARTIME REFLECTIONS

SIR HENRY NEWBOLT

Home Service
Thursday 4 January 1940
Producer: J. C. Pennethorne Hughes

• • •

I should think that everyone listening today knows at least one line
of the poetry of Newbolt. Even those who dismiss poets as long-
haired men who do not wash behind their ears – and how true this
description often is of poets, despite rumours to the contrary – even
those who regard all poetry as unhealthy or boring can quote a bit of
Newbolt. I will just give a few familiar phrases or lines of Newbolt,
in order to prove to you, whatever you think about poetry, that you
know his work.

> Drake he's in his hammock an' a thousand miles away
> (Captein, art tha sleepin' there below?)
>
> Admirals all, for England's sake,
> Honour be yours, and fame!
>
> The Dons on the dais serene
>
> A bumping pitch and a blinding light,
> An hour to play and the last man in
>
> Play up! play up! and play the game!

Sophisticated people will call it blood-and-thunder stuff. Others love
it. A distinguished military gentleman once told me that verse only
turned into poetry for him when it sent a shiver down his spine.
Newbolt nearly gives him St Vitus's dance.

> To honour, while you strike him down,
> The foe that comes with fearless eyes . . .

Blood-and-thunder stuff it may be but you cannot forget it. It is what Newbolt unfortunately was chiefly known for, just as Rachmaninov is known chiefly for his *Prelude*. Yet almost until his death in 1938, Henry Newbolt was writing better and better poetry and the blood-and-thunder poems appeared first in the 1890s.

People like to know what a poet looked like and where he lived and what he did. Maybe you think of Newbolt, having heard his better-known poetry, as a fire-eating colonel on half-pay in Cheltenham, or a large beer-drinking fellow who slaps you on the back, or a sea captain living in Plymouth Hoe. He was none of these things.

I like to think of Newbolt as I saw him about six years ago. Picture to yourselves a sunny summer day in a chalky Wiltshire valley within sight of Salisbury spire, a little brick and stone and chalk village, a Victorian church and a mellow stone manor house, mostly of Queen Anne date, with a wide garden full of grass walks and the great trees of Wilton in one direction and quiet downs in another, giving shelter. Here by the open door stood Sir Henry Newbolt. He was very tall and handsome, with sharp, lean features, a pale face, piercing blue eyes and silver hair. When he spoke, his voice was gentle and mellow. He had the sort of commanding presence that makes you careful not to talk rot to him or tell a lie.

Inside, the house was white and I remember that long attic study across the top of the house, with white walls and white beams, and rows and rows of books – rare editions, leather-bound poets of the eighteenth century, printed yellow-paper volumes of modern poets, rows of Greek and Latin classics – and from the windows all along the south of the room a view of the green swell of distant downland. If ever a house had an atmosphere of English peace, it was this old manor of Netherhampton, Salisbury.

Newbolt was born in 1862, the son of an evangelical vicar in Staffordshire. His father died when he was four and soon after the family left the Midlands for the West Country about which Newbolt wrote his poetry, so that he has rightly come to be thought of as a West Country poet. Indeed, his mother settled in Clifton in order to send her sons to the public school there. Almost as soon as he started writing for the public, Newbolt was a success. It is pleasant to read in his autobiography, *My World as in My Time*, of the success of his first volume of poems, *Admirals All*:

> As I passed down the Strand on my homeward way from Lincoln's Inn [he was a young barrister at the time, as many young men were when they came down from Oxford], I stood for a moment or two at the wide entrance, half-doorway, half-bookshop, of the Dennys' shop at the west end of Holywell Street – the Booksellers' Row for which the present generation will look in vain. One of the Dennys said the usual 'Good evening' to me and added: 'Have you come for your book, sir? You are just in time, we've hardly a copy left tonight.' 'How many had you this morning,' I asked lightly. 'I don't know, but we shall have five hundred tomorrow if we can get them.'

Admirals All sold four editions in a fortnight: not bad for poetry, as poets will know – especially for poetry that is worth reading. Twenty-one editions were sold in the year.

From then on, Newbolt was a made man and gave up the Bar for literature. He had already lived happily and successfully at Clifton and at Oxford he continued happy and successful. He married the woman he wanted to marry; he retained his old friends and was always making new ones. A happy life for such as him in pre-First War days. A happy life. Country-house parties, vintage wines, good conversation, driving in rolling carriages through ordered parks to country railway stations, cigars and foot-warmers, literary circles. In those days Stephen Phillips, William Watson, Housman and Hardy were the poets people talked about. Particularly they talked of our late Poet Laureate Robert Bridges. At one time the Newbolts lived at Yattendon, a little Berkshire village, in the next house to the Bridges. There was a door between the gardens known as 'the hole in the wall'. Through this one morning came Newbolt. Bridges was lying on the steps of his house, basking in the sun, wearing an old felt hat, a shabby coat and grey nankeen trousers. His dog was beside him. Nervously Newbolt showed him 'Drake's Drum', which had just come out in the *St James's Gazette*. There was a silence. Then Bridges said, as if to himself, 'Awfully swell, awfully swell.' And after another silence, in which he re-read it, 'You'll never write anything better than that. I wish I had ever written anything half so good.'

More friends, more talk, more poems, still a great success, country-house parties, gaslight, electric light, art, music, the first motor car, some years editing the *Monthly Review*. More petrol in use, more motors, a slight champagne hysteria in the world – then crash, the Great War of 1914 and all the old values gone. Newbolt lost his only son* and he found himself in a new world. After the last war, poems about Empire, blood-and-thunder and death were at a discount. People had had enough of them. Poems that scanned were looked down upon by some and poems that, not content with scanning, went rollicking along, delighting in their own metre – as some of Newbolt's do – were thought quite awful. For many years Newbolt had been experimenting in new metres but only his early poems were remembered. He was never allowed to forget them. 'Play up! play up! and play the game!' It was hard on a sensitive man, who knew more about what these young people were doing than any of his contemporaries, to be treated as a colonel with a gift for patriotic verse. But he played up undismayed and his criticism and understanding of T. S. Eliot, Peter Quennell, Ezra Pound and other important poets of the 1920s is still the best.

To understand Newbolt, you must understand his generation. He came from a comparatively leisured class; he had the education which is now, on the whole rightly, laughed at as 'the old school tie'. He lived among people who were expected to blow their brains out if they cheated at cards; who were believing Christians of a sincere and rather liberal sort; who, above everything, kept their word and fulfilled their obligations. Some still survive of this old generation: they live in Bath and Cheltenham and in certain country houses. They sit dazed among these new values of broken oaths, business deals, 'progressive' local councils and the destruction of beautiful buildings and country that is fortunately coming to an end in this war. They are still honourable personally and intensely loyal to their friends; above all they are loyal to their country. They are not internationalists. You may call them narrow, conservative, stiff-backed – but you must admire their goodness. Newbolt was their chosen poet. He outgrew them. But they are

---

* Not true – fortunately for Newbolt, unfortunately for Betjeman. See the Introduction, pp. 16–17.

still loyal. And he never went back on his word. In the last volume of his poems, Major Ralph Furse describes his attitude. 'He was criticizing some practice he disapproved of in men of letters.' I have no doubt it was some slightly shady practice. 'One of the company, reddening, acknowledged that he had been guilty of this enormity and began to defend himself. Newbolt cut him short by saying, "I'm very sorry to hear it. Let's talk of something else"; and did so. That was often his way – quiet, brief and rather formal.'

Newbolt was no bohemian, though he was tolerant of the bohemians. He looked at unconventional people from the light of his own austere stronghold, but he gazed kindly. W. B. Yeats, for instance, who always looked like what poets are supposed to look like, once stayed with Bridges at Yattendon and Newbolt joined the two in a game of 'small cricket' on the steps of the manor. Yeats had been talking wonderfully but at cricket he was less successful. This is how Newbolt describes the game:

His costume was inappropriate – he wore throughout his visit a long frock coat with gracefully flowing skirts, and round his neck an enormous tie of purple silk, tied in a bow and floating down to his waist uncontrolled by waistcoat or pin. The effect was to make it difficult to catch a ball and impossible to hit one. Bridges, when I left at seven o'clock, made a kind of apology for his guest's cricket and added: 'But he's a great poet; a better poet than I am.' I was silent; so he went on.

In case you should think that this austere, honourable and patriotic man I have described was self-confident or unfeeling, let me deny it at once. He came of a class that concealed its tenderest emotions from the public. I wish there were more like him now. To a critic who doubted his sincerity he once wrote these lines describing himself:

> . . . A nature too complete,
> Eager and doubtful, no man's soldier sworn
> And no man's chosen captain; born to fail,
> A name without an echo; yet he too
> Within the cloister of his narrow days
> Fulfilled the ancestral rites, and kept alive
> The eternal fire; it may be, not in vain . . .
>
> [from 'The Non-Combatant']

Newbolt's trouble after his first blazing success was his lack of confidence. He knew so much and felt so much that he scarcely dared set pen to paper. He has written, despite his fame, surprisingly little poetry. He gave much of his time to public work in his village and country instead.

I will end by turning to his poetry; there is not time to tell you of his prose. Very few poets in any language have been able to write whole poems which you cannot help remembering; lines, maybe, but not whole poems. William Cowper did it on the loss of the *Royal George*: 'Toll for the brave . . .' You can read through that poem three times and remember the whole thing. Newbolt did it, too, in 'Drake's Drum' and other patriotic poems.

I think he described this gift very well in a lecture to Bristol University nine years ago. 'Among others, what matters is delicacy of feeling, elasticity of thought, simplicity of diction and the power to make the sound of the meaning pulsate in the blood and echo in the memory of the reader.'

I see at once one of those old oil-painted sea pieces of sailing vessels crowding home in these two lines:

Sweeping by shores whose names are the names of the victories of
   England,
Across the Bay the squadron homeward came.
> [from 'The Death of Admiral Blake']

I can think of no simpler nor more effective way of writing patriotic poetry that is not truculent or boastful or oratorical than thus:

Over the manhole, up in the iron-clad tower,
Pilot and Captain met as they turned to fly;
The hundredth part of a moment seemed an hour,
For one could pass to be saved, and one must die.

They stood like men in a dream: Craven spoke,
Spoke as he lived and fought, with a Captain's pride,
'After you, Pilot.' The pilot woke,
Down the ladder he went, and Craven died.
> [from 'Craven (Mobile Bay, 1864)']

And, for a softer scene, here is an example of sound and meaning meeting in a description of a girl dancing:

All through the night from dusk to daytime
   Under her feet the hours were swift,
Under her feet the hours of playtime
   Rose and fell with a rhythmic lift:
   Music set her adrift, adrift,
   Music eddying towards the day
Swept her along as brooks in Maytime
   Carry the freshly falling may.

[from 'Imogen']

And, in a less obvious manner, in this description of a bird's nest in a white citrus bush:

Come nearer, and speak low; watch while I put aside
This thickly, flow'ring spray, and stoop till you can see
There in the shadowy centre, a tiny nest
And on it, facing us, a bright-eyed bird sitting.

[from 'The Linnet's Nest']

Newbolt has suffered among literary people because he has never been hard to understand. But he is honoured because he lacks truculence and there is no doubt that he was profound. One poem of his, 'Moonset', seems to me to combine all his qualities. Imagine a chill, bright morning, before dawn at this time of the year, and yourself driving through the park of an English house in an Edwardian coach, catching the early train.

Past seven o'clock: time to be gone;
Twelfth-night's over and dawn shivering up:
A hasty cut of the loaf, a steaming cup,
Down to the door, and there is Coachman John.

Ruddy of cheek is John and bright of eye;
But John it appears has none of your grins and winks;
Civil enough, but short: perhaps he thinks;
Words come once in a mile, and always dry.

Has he a mind or not? I wonder; but soon
We turn through a leafless wood, and there to the right,
Like a sun bewitched in alien realms of night,
Mellow and yellow and rounded hangs the moon.

Strangely near she seems, and terribly great;
The world is dead: why are we travelling still?
Nightmare silence grips my struggling will;
We are driving for ever and ever to find a gate.

'When you come to consider the moon,' says John at last,
And stops, to feel his footing and take his stand;
'And when there's some will say there's never a hand
That made the world!'
    A flick, and the gates are passed.

Out of the dim magical moonlit park,
Out to the workday road and wider skies:
There's a warm flush in the East where day's to rise,
And I'm feeling the better for Coachman John's remark.

Nor was it an unfeeling blood-and-thunder writer who composed
this – called 'The Only Son':*

O Bitter wind toward the sunset blowing
    What of the dales tonight?
In yonder grey old hall what fires are glowing,
    What ring of festal light?

'*In the great window as the day was dwindling*
    I saw an old man stand;
His head was proudly held and his eyes kindling,
    But the list shook in his hand.'

O wind of twilight, was there no word uttered,
    No sound of joy or wail?
'"*A great fight and a good death,*" he muttered;
    "*Trust him, he would not fail.*"'

What of the chamber dark where she was lying;
    For whom all life is done?
'*Within her heart she rocks a dead child, crying,*
    "*My son, my little son.*"'

---

* Betjeman wrongly referred to this as 'My Only Son' and thought it gave evidence
of the death of Newbolt's son.

BACK TO THE RAILWAY CARRIAGE

Home Service
Sunday 10 March 1940★
Producer: J. C. Pennethorne Hughes

• • •

This is an odd thing to ask you to do on a fine Sunday morning, but I want you to imagine yourself in the waiting room of a railway station on a wet evening. You know the sort of room: let me recall it – a wind whistling down the platform, a walk battling against the breeze to the door marked 'General Waiting Room', the vast interior, the black horsehair benches and chairs, the mahogany table, the grate with its winking fire, the large framed photographs of yellowing views of crowded esplanades and ivy-mantled ruins, the framed advertisement for the company's hotel at Strathmacgregor (electric light, exquisite cuisine, lift to all floors, within five minutes of sea and pier), the gaslight roaring, a friendly buzz of restless conversation of other people also awaiting trains.

Just such a scene as this, which may be witnessed this very evening at a hundred junctions, lost among the suburbs of industrial towns or far away in the country where branch line meets main line – just such a scene as this was witnessed sixty, seventy, eighty years ago. I shall have the railways complaining that I'm calling them Victorian. Let them complain. They *are* Victorian: that is their beauty. But they aren't only Victorian: they're Edwardian and modern as well. Now they are here, I hope they'll never be taken away and I, for one, am grateful for the opportunity these times have given me of using them

★ This talk was given (four months late) to mark the centenary of *Bradshaw's Railway Guide* in November 1939.

again, more than I did in the old petrol-clouded civilization of before the war.

Think yourself back into that waiting room and learn with me the first lesson the railway teaches us: to pay a proper respect to the past. Railways were built to last. None of your discarding last year's model and buying this one's. That horsehair seat has supported the Victorian bustle, the frock coat of the merchant going citywards first class, your father in his best sailor suit when he was being taken to the seaside — and now it is supporting you and it's far from worn out. That platform has seen the last farewells of sons and parents, has watched the City man returning home to break the news to his wife that he's bankrupt, has watched his neighbour come in a new suit one morning and with a first-class, instead of a third-class, ticket.

Turn from human history to the history of stone and steam and iron. The railway station in the old days was a monument to science. Euston, whose fine Doric portico — one of London's noblest buildings — was the new gateway to the North; King's Cross, whose simple outlines are a foretaste of all that is good in modern architecture; Temple Meads, Bristol, in the Tudor style: far from gimcrack but cut out of local stone; Newcastle Central station, a lovely classical building worthy of ancient Rome; and many a lesser station. I know little stations among the Shropshire hills built in a solid but picturesque Gothic style to tone in with the romantic scenery. I know of huge suburban stations that are dusty from disuse and full of top-hatted ghosts in the corners of echoing gaslit booking halls. Best of all I know that station in Cornwall I loved as a boy — the oil lights, the smell of seaweed floating up the estuary, the rain-washed platform and the sparkling Cornish granite and the hedges along the valleys around, soon to be heavy with blackberries. I think of Edward Thomas's lovely poem 'Adlestrop', on a country station in the Cotswolds:

> Yes. I remember Adlestrop —
> The name, because one afternoon
> Of heat the express-train drew up there
> Unwontedly. It was late June.
>
> The steam hissed. Someone cleared his throat.
> No one left and no one came

On the bare platform. What I saw
Was Adlestrop – only the name.

That verse recalls one of the deeper pleasures of a country railway station – its silence, broken only by the crunching of a porter's feet on the gravel, the soft country accent of the stationmaster and the crash bang of a milk can somewhere at the back of the platform. The train, once in the centre of a noisy town, has drifted into the deep heart of the English country, with country noises brushing the surfaces of a deeper silence. Edward Thomas expressed this in the last stanza of his poem on Adlestrop station –

And for that minute a blackbird sang
Close by, and round him, mistier,
Farther and farther, all the birds
Of Oxfordshire and Gloucestershire.

For if you want to see and feel the country, travel by train. Roads are determined by boundaries of estates and by villages and other roads; they are shut in by hedges, peppered with new villas, garish with tin signs, noisy with roadhouses. A town spreads out along its roads for miles, leaving the country in the fields at the back that you don't see. From Reading to London it's town almost all the way, by road. Yet by rail the country creeps surprisingly near to London. This is because railways are built regardless of natural boundaries and from the height of an embankment we can see the country undisturbed, as one who walks along an open footpath through a field. Roads bury themselves in the landscape. The railways carve out a landscape of their own. Ninety years ago some of the best artists were proud to draw the scenery of railways: their stations, viaducts, banks and cuttings and locomotives. The large railway arch over the road at Chippenham was one of the wonders of the West. (Now it's covered with advertisements, so that you can't see it.) Railways were built to look from and to look at. They still provide those pleasures for the eye.

Personally I don't like new, smart jazz expresses with cocktail bars and heat which to me is stifling. I like an old, bumpy carriage with a single gaslight in the ceiling, that peculiar design only known to railways on the upholstery, views of Tenby, Giant's Causeway,

Morecambe Bay, Bala Lake and so on under the rack marked 'For Light Articles Only'. I like to see a loop of upholstered leather in the corner seats of first-class carriages into which you are meant to put your arm should the train travel fast. I've never seen one of these loops used by a passenger but I'm told that they're a survival of old coaching days. As you know, the earliest covered passenger compartments were little more than post-chaises clamped together and fastened down on to a four-wheeled tramway wagon. Sometimes, inside old landau taxis that ply from country stations to the rectory, these loops survive. They are the sole relic, in motors, of Georgian days. I like a locomotive with a brass dome and the arms of the railway company in all its splendid Victorian heraldry on the tender. I think the railway companies are making a great mistake in trying to imitate the streamlining of motor cars, the gashes and cubes of pseudo-modern fabrics in the upholstery and other futile devices to appear up to date. Railways are essential and this new surface decoration is, it seems to me, quite unnecessary. They've a fine tradition of solid Victorian beauty that they're trying to destroy. One company is spoiling the look of its engines with a new and hideous monogram in distorted lettering designed to save space. This seems to me to be spoiling the engine for a ha'p'orth of paint. But of course I know that I may be in a minority about this: no doubt thousands of people love it.

You need never be bored in a train. You can always read a book and an even more interesting book to read than that on your knee is the faces and habits of your fellow passengers. I know the types so well. The fussy type: the old person who wraps a travelling rug round his knees and gets up to lean out of the window at every station and ask if this is the right train for Evercreech, receiving the answer 'Yes' every time. He continues to look out, as though his anxious face will cause the guard to blow his whistle sooner. The vacant fool who taps with his toes on the floor and whistles to hide his embarrassment when the train comes to an unexpected halt between stations. The talkative person who tries to get into conversation – the war has brought on a big increase in this type – on general topics. I very much enjoy listening to the battle of wits in which people try to avoid being caught into the talk:

'Colder today, isn't it'

'Yes.'

'But the days'll be getting longer soon.'

Silence.

'Anyone here know whether this is right for Bristol?'

'Oh yes.'

'Ah, I suppose we stop at Didcot, Swindon and Bath?'

Mr Knowall struggles between a desire to go on with his book and a desire to correct the speaker. His desire to correct wins.

'You've left out Chippenham. We stop at Chippenham and, I think, at two other stations.'

Me: 'Yes, at Challow and Uffington.'

'Ah, thank you.' (*To Mr Knowall*) 'Pretty place, Chippenham.'

'Yes.'

They're off.

But the greatest gift the railways give to us is the proper treatment of time. Of course there are expresses that will hurtle you from place to place in no time. But the others – no longer that mania for getting from one town to another volleying along a tarmac road at sixty miles an hour, but a leisurely journey, seeing the country, getting to the place much sooner and much more comfortably in the long run and with the pleasant discipline of having to catch a train at a stated time. And if the train is a bit late, what matter? There are one's fellow passengers to study, the unfamiliar view of a place one knows well from the road seen at an odd angle from the railway, the photographs below the rack to see, the railway noises to listen to. And for me there's the pleasure of a railway timetable. It's one of the ironies of this war that the centenary of *Bradshaw*, which occurred last November, should have been obscured by the war. The original Bradshaw was a Quaker and a great worker for peace. How I enjoy his pages, particularly those at the end that deal with the Great Southern Railway in Eire. 'Stops to take up at Inny Junction Halt on Thursdays and Saturdays.' Inny Junction Halt is hidden away among the footnotes of *Bradshaw*. What romance there is in the name! For Inny Junction is a station lost in an Irish bog in the middle of Westmeath. There's no road to it, nothing but miles of meadowsweet and bog myrtle and here and there the green patch and white speck of a distant Irish smallholding and the silence is only livened by rumblings of distant turf carts and the hiss of a waiting Great Southern engine on Thursdays and Saturdays.

Trains were made for meditation.

> . . . Meditation here
> May think down hours to moments, here the heart
> May learn a useful lesson from the head,
> And learning wiser grow without his books
>
> [from *The Task*, Book VI]

to quote Cowper, who was writing about something else. And I advise slow trains on branch lines, half-empty trains that go through meadows in the evening and stop at each once oil-lit halt. Time and war slip away and you are lost in the heart of England.

When I was a boy, the old North London railway stopped running on Sundays during church time. It's about to strike eleven o'clock on a Sunday morning and I must be stopping, too.

SOME COMMENTS IN WARTIME

Home Service
Thursday 4 July 1940
Producer: J. C. Pennethorne Hughes

• • •

The title of this talk might lead you to think that I was going to make some sort of political comment. But I'm afraid you will be disappointed. I don't know anything about politics. Instead I am going to talk about some of the pleasant things I have discovered as a result of this war and observations about things, scenery and people in these islands. For instance, I have become grateful for small things that I had not time to notice in that hurried turmoil we called civilization before the war.*

For instance, the country – which people who don't live in it call 'the countryside'. It used to be the thing to say, 'Oh, the country's all right in the summer but I should go mad if I had to live in it all the year round.' By now, many thousands of town people will have spent a winter in the country for the first time. They will have seen that the country in winter is as full of life as in the summer. They will have noticed how willows burn red in the meadows before they bud

---

* Betjeman had intended to start his talk by saying, 'I must confess that I have never been more awake than I have been in the last few months. I am not referring to any disturbances from air raids. I mean that my wits have been sharpened. I notice a lot more about scenery, things and people. In fact I regard this as one of the blessings of war, the awakening of my wits. I have become grateful . . .' This form of introduction seems to have fallen foul of the censor and changes were asked for that accentuated Betjeman's role as a lightweight and made him deny that he had any competence as a political observer.

and how oaks turn gold with early leaf. They will have known the pleasure of feeling rain on the face and retreating to a warm cottage and the comfortable feeling of listening to the storm outside.

The country has ceased to be a great park to which townspeople could come in their motor coaches and drop paper about the lanes. Country people have ceased to be 'rustics' and 'yokels': they have become flesh and blood, foster-parents of the towns. To many children who have been evacuated to country districts now for some months, the country is a great farm instead of a great park and I don't think any child who has migrated from the town to the country will ever again despise country life. I know of many who would like to be farmers when they grow up. Evacuation may have brought about what is so badly needed: the return to the land.

The country seems to have gone back to the peace of the last century. It's a relief to see the hideous tin signs of place names removed from the walls of cottages, to hear the comfortable plod of horses and rumble of iron-rimmed cartwheels instead of the endless gear-changing of motors. I have never disliked the noise of aeroplanes – not even of enemy ones – because at least they do not change gear in the air; and except for a few types of machine, the roar is rather heartening. One sound alone we will miss in the country: the church bells. The mellow *lin-lan-lone*★ across the hay. And here I would like to put in a word of advice. If any country air-raid warden thinks he is going to be able to ring the church bells as a warning of a raid, let him be sure he knows how to handle a bell. I picture to myself an excited warden running up the belfry stairs, giving a colossal pull at a bell rope and finding himself either hauled up to the belfry roof and crashing down unconscious on the floor with his skull cracked open, or else I see him with the skin ripped off his hands as the bell slides through it, or else I see him hanged by the neck as the rope end coils itself around him. Bell-ringing is an art and I wonder how many country wardens have learned it. (As this is not a talk on bell-ringing and I have not the time to tell you how to ring a church bell, I beg all wardens who contemplate ringing to consult a ringer immediately.)

★ 'Lin-lan-lone' is Tennyson's characterization of the sound of distant bells in his poem 'Far-Far-Away'. Betjeman quotes it again in his own poem 'The Dear Old Village'.

The time came for me to leave my family in the country and take up work in a big town. And the town, instead of being the roaring hell of the past that I dreaded visiting, had submitted itself to a decent discipline with comparatively few motors on the roads. Now the buildings stand out and I have time to see them: decent Georgian terraces built of brick, with windows neatly graded in height; fanciful and often beautiful Victorian churches with their tall spires and towers; towering office blocks in all sorts of fancy styles, made more fanciful still by strips of paper pasted across the windows; luxuriant plane trees hanging over squares; that healthy smell of tar melting in the sun, instead of the blue petrol vapours of the past.

Best of all is the evening's pleasure of bicycling in the suburbs. Before the war I used sometimes to give talks on architecture and town planning. I remember referring to Swindon as a great octopus or starfish or something stretching out its tentacles of jerry-built houses into the quiet country (Swindon forgives me). But now I am so forgiving. I *like* suburbs; nothing is ugly. Bicycling in the suburbs of a great city, I see a strange beauty in those quiet deserted evenings with the few remaining children showing off in the evening sunlight, laburnums and lilac weeping over the front gate, father smoking his pipe and rolling the lawn, mother knitting at the open window, the little arcade of local shops, the great outline of the cinema, the new bricks pinker than ever in the sunset, the sham-Tudor beams, the standard roses, the stained glass in the front doors, the pram in the hall, the drainpipes running zigzag down to the side door. Now that the hedges are growing up and the trees are giving a greenness to it all, I see a beauty in it. I mean, there they are, those houses: they are part of England; I've got to put up with them. Then I will try to see the best in everything – even in the half-baked Tudor dreams of the man who designed that deserted roadhouse. And in the moonlight, when the colours disappear, not the maddest, flashiest modern factory looks anything but beautiful.

I have bicycled by stucco terraces of George IV's time and seen the great Corinthian columns and uneven chimney pots bathed in silver moonlight and I've almost fallen off my bicycle with genuine emotion. I thank heaven for the blackout, for without it I would never have known how beautiful a city can look in the moonlight.

I know of a soldier who was left on a rather deserted beach in South Africa during the Boer War and there he started to collect the sea-water snail shells he found in the sand. He classified these shells and started to take an interest in the subject. Soon he was collecting snail shells all over the place – and now he is a great malacologist and has a room in the Natural History Museum and has written standard books on the subject. Malacology, I should say, is the study of snail shells. I wonder how many people will find themselves specialists as a result of this war, in subjects that the war has drawn to their attention: freshwater fishes, astronomy, cow parsley, planning, geology, building materials, patent manures, marsh plants, refuse, trees, cloud formations, winds, tides, seaweed, rhododendrons – all subjects that we never bothered about when we had not the time but that have now, one or other of them, forced themselves on our attention. War has a splendid effect in making you aware of your surroundings and the best way to get to like them is to find out all about them: why villages are where they are; why the roads wind; why certain fields are of such peculiar shapes; how old the church is. It does not, by the way, take more than a week or two to tell the date of a building from its appearance. You can soon learn to compare it with others whose date you know and see how it differs.

Yes, the war has wakened my wits a bit and shown me the beauty of England in all sorts of places where I did not expect to find it.

It has done something else. It has made me see that what really matters is people, not their possessions. As a result of billeting and various war occupations, I have had to meet all sorts of strangers and as a result I like to think I have made a new lot of friends. Neighbours whom I hardly knew in the past I now consider friends. War brings out the best in people: dithery old fusspots suddenly cease to fuss, the most unexpected people show great courage and pessimists become cheerful. War divides us into where we really belong. Class nonsense becomes unimportant. The cake is cut at right angles to the way it was cut before. The potential fifth columnists of this country are not only those who hold divergent political opinions from the majority but those who are still out for themselves only: people who are so afraid of losing their job that they will stop at no dirty trick to retain it; self-made men willing to sell their country in order not to lose any more of their incomes; rats who repeat and invent evil gossip about their neighbours in order to appear more loyal than they know themselves to be. They are the people who are determined that nothing matters so long as things remain as they used to be for them – the narrow man who has worked his way up, betraying his friends in the process; the man who thinks only in terms of money; the man who isn't sure of himself and hasn't the guts to see his own defects. War sorts us all out and the process is sad and painful – very sad and very painful for some of us. But also it teaches us new interests. Better still, it teaches us to consider other people and to value a man not according to his income but according to his heart.

COMING HOME, OR
ENGLAND REVISITED

Home Service
Thursday 25 February 1943
Producer: Geoffrey Grigson

• • •

First, for the benefit of those who have not done it lately – leaving home. The boat slides away from the quay. There is a moment's pain. Those lucky people waving from the shore, they can go back to change their books at the library, read the evening paper, fix the black-out curtain, put the kettle on, let the dog out or go to a crashing lecture in the Home Guard. But for you and me it is diminishing cliffs, then sea, then a landscape that is not England. We buoy ourselves up with thoughts of adventure before us; we think of soul-stirring articles about democracy, freedom of speech and thought, about how awful the Nazis are. We may even think that we are helping to build a new world. Or we may turn in and have a drink – or be seasick. But deep down in our innermost selves, or rather in my innermost self, I think we put ourselves to the inconvenience of leaving our homes not because of these advertised abstracts but because we want to see England again.

It is something really terrible, this longing for England we get when we are away. The other month I found my eyes getting wet (fortunately there was no one about) at the sight of moonlight on a willow stump covered with ivy. It reminded me of a willowy brook in the Berkshire village where we used to live before the war. And then I looked at the stars and even envied them in their icy remoteness because they were also shining on my home village. We have all been taught in my generation to avoid the sloppy and sentimental.

Exile from England★ has uncorked the bottle of sentiment for me and I could go on gushing for hours, indulging myself at your expense.

I remember the most trivial things about home. The trouble about the cow parsley, for instance. (I hope any listeners at home will forgive my bringing up again so publicly something that was over years ago. Someone had decorated the altar of the parish church with cow parsley. One side said that cow parsley was an unworthy flower for such prominent a place; the other side said that cow parsley looked very nice on the altar – much better than garden flowers – and it was always put on the altar at that time of year, anyway. I have forgotten what happened.)

Then I think of a story someone told me during the Battle of Britain, before I left England. She had to go and judge a Women's Institute competition for the best-decorated table centre in a village in Kent. Bombs and aeroplanes were falling out of the sky, guns thundered and fragments of shell whizzed about. 'I am afraid we have not *everybody* here,' said the head of the Institute. 'You see, several of our members had to be up all night – but we have quite a little show all the same.' And there they were: the raffia mats, the bowls of bulbs, the trailing ends of smilax writhing round mustard and pepper pots. God be praised for such dogged calm.

My eyes, my nose, my ears all strain for England when I am away: oil lamps on bold Gothic mouldings at evensong in a country church; tattered copies of *Hymns Ancient and Modern*; the crackle of the slow-combustion stove; the pleasantly acrid smell of flowering currant bushes on the platform of a local station; the cat in our backyard 'licking the sunshine off its paws' on a still summer day; shopping in a big town; and, for me, the gambling den that will one day bring my wife and children to starvation: the second-hand bookshops, the stalls in Farringdon Street, London, the remote haunts in Highbury and Islington.

There used to be a funny illustrated joke. It showed Englishmen in the tropics dressing for dinner. I don't think that joke funny any more. I believe these Englishmen did it because they wanted to pretend they were home again, not because they were highly conventional.

★ Between 1941–3 Betjeman was the UK's press attaché in Dublin.

Really, this self-pity must stop! I am not half so badly off as thousands of others. I don't dress for dinner. I have a job that enables me to return to England quite often. I am not some luckless prisoner or a wounded man sweating in a hospital in the East. I shall see England (*Deo volente*) every three months or so. But there are certain things about England I have noticed on my more recent visits that you in England ought to know about.

First, English people — persons who in the old days would get into the railway carriage with you on a cold day and leave the door open. They shut the door now. People in public buses and trains are much pleasanter. Heaven protect us from the railway-carriage military strategist! But if you have luggage, people will help you to lift it in — even if you are a civilian like I am. Why, the other day in the train, a party got in with a luncheon basket and insisted on sharing out their sandwiches and drink with the rest of us in the carriage. Twice in a week I was given a free cup of tea in country public houses. Everywhere I went I found people much nicer to one another than I ever remember them before the war. From only one stranger did I receive a rebuff — a formidable spinster in some uniform or other. We were passing through a village I knew, and I enquired whether Mrs So-and-so still lived there. She said 'Yes.' Then she looked at me and I saw behind her cold grey eyes an argument going on. 'This unhealthy-looking brute is trying to get military information from me.' So she suddenly added, 'No, she doesn't.' I cannot say I minded, for her attitude showed the trained, cautious behaviour of my countrymen, still on the watch for paratroops.

And if strangers are pleasanter, my friends I find kinder still. They uncorked their last bottle of wine, they shared their sugar ration with me they were delighted to see me, although they were all intensely busy. I was warm, comfortable and well fed during the whole of my visit. Indeed I would go so far as to say that a certain chain of hotels, one of whose houses I patronized, has improved since the war. The food is no longer so pretentious and you can see what you are eating. The prices are lower too.

But the two most noticeable things of all about English people since the war are these: the breakdown of class distinctions and the new standard of values. It seemed to me as though people now take you for what you are like personally, not for how you stand in the social scale. Then there seemed to me to be less materialism about, less bother with money. I noticed people reading books on philosophy and religion sitting next to me in trains. I could swear that these people, before the war, would have been reading the financial news or filling in competition crosswords. Of course, all this sudden revelation that has led me to make what may seem sweeping statements may be due to absence from England. Possibly everyone was simply delightful before the war and I didn't realize it.

I did realize, however, and I realize more strongly than ever today, how exquisitely beautiful are the villages and old towns of England. There are the obvious things: Ludlow's great sweep of old houses up the hill from the rich Shropshire valley; the flint towers of Norfolk and Suffolk, where roads wind like streams among the elms; the bulging barrows of the chalk downs, where thatched houses cluster among elm trees in hollows and white roads wind up from them to the sheepfolds; Salisbury Close with its ancient houses, stone walls, wide sweeps of grass and cloud shadows chasing over the silver-grey magnificence of the cathedral; hundreds and hundreds of place names of hundreds and hundreds of unspoiled places with stone churches, heavily ticking church clocks, modest post offices, creeper-clad wardens' cottages, rusty croquet hoops on rectory lawns, swinging inn signs, and well-stocked gardens where brick paths lead through thyme and vegetables. To think of the names is to feel better – Huish Episcopi, Whitchurch Canonicorum, Willingale Spain, Tickencote, Bourton-on-the-Hill, Iwerne Minster, Piddletrenthide, South Molton, Wotton, Norton, Evenlode, Fairford, Canons Ashby, Bag Enderby, Kingston Bagpuize. The broad sweep of England's beauty is obvious enough – the immense variety of building stone and sorts of landscape to be found in a single county. But this is so easily destroyed, not by bombs but by witless local councillors, people on the lookout for building land, electric-light companies, county councils with new road schemes, the wrong sort of 'planner'.

Planning is very much in the English air now. Let the planners be careful. It would not be worth our being away from England, those of us who live in the country, if we had to come back to find our villages transformed into single blocks of flats towering out of unfenced fields, with an interdenominational religious room at the top of each tower for services conducted by wireless (voluntary attendance). And those of us who live in old towns do not want to see everything swept away to open vistas where vistas were never intended. Hitler has opened up a few good ones. Let us leave it at that.

Of course we do not want slums to remain, nor to live in cottages in the country where there is no water and where the roof leaks. But slums can be rebuilt into habitable places – not always as flats – and cottages can be repaired. Perhaps we shall be allowed to live in the sort of England recommended by the Scott Committee,★ where country shall still be country and town shall still be town and where we will not all be thought cranks and reactionaries who wish to keep the country worth looking at.

Think of a single old brick or piece of stone in an English house or garden wall: centuries of sun and rain have mellowed it and overgrown it with lichens and moss and shaved off its sharp angles. Think of the slopes and swags of an old tiled roof seen from the top of a country bus. Think of the layout of an old town or village, the winding roads to it and Georgian merchants' houses in the middle, the L-shaped farms on the outskirts, the church tower gathering the hours round it like a hen her chicks. In a single week of our planning, centuries of texture can be brushed away. Is all to be replanned? Are we only to bask on our own flat roofs and swim in municipal pools and feel half naked at home because our outside walls are all of glass? Are all roads to be straight and all wild-rose hedges to be swept away? All trees except quick-growing conifers to be cut down? All this for the rather doubtful advantage of running hot water in everybody's bedroom and aeroplanes for all?

I do not believe we are fighting for the privilege of living in a highly developed community of ants. That is what the Nazis want. For me, at any rate, England stands for the Church of England, eccentric incumbents, oil-lit churches, Women's Institutes, modest village inns, arguments about cow parsley on the altar, the noise of

★ In 1942 the Committee on Land Utilization in Rural Areas, chaired by Sir Leslie Scott, reported on uncontrolled development and the loss of agricultural land. It proposed compulsory purchase and a system of national parks to be set up after the war to resist the spread of towns.

mowing machines on Saturday afternoons, local newspapers, local auctions, the poetry of Tennyson, Crabbe, Hardy and Matthew Arnold, local talent, local concerts, a visit to the cinema, branch-line trains, light railways, leaning on gates and looking across fields. For you it may stand for something else, equally eccentric to me as I may appear to you – something to do with Wolverhampton or dear old Swindon or wherever you happen to live. But just as important.

But I know the England I want to come home to is not very different from that in which you want to live. If it were some efficient ant heap which the glass-and-steel, flat-roof, straight-road boys want to make it, then how could we love it as we do?

When I am attacked by my country today – when people make generalizations about the British without having lived in England themselves – I no longer lose my temper. I know how useless it is to explain to them about cow parsley on the altar, villages, Women's Institutes, life in English towns. One cannot explain anything at once so kind and so complicated. If I could explain England, if it really were a planned ants' nest that we could all generalize about, I, like thousands of others, would have no home to which to return.

YESTERDAY'S FICTION

From the series 'Book Talk'

Home Service
Monday 21 August 1944
Producer: Godfrey James

• • •

Instead of telling you about the best of this week's latest books, because there are so very few being published just now, I am going to review some old favourites. I am going to review some Edwardian novelists – the sort of people who were very popular before the last war.

I choose Edwardian novelists in particular because their books are to be found more often than most. There they are, small red-bound volumes, decently printed, on good paper, in Nelson's Sevenpenny Library or cheap editions issued by other publishers. There they are, up on that shelf in the sitting room, dusted but unread for years, or in the junk shop, bought in with a sideboard and dining-room effects, or at the village fête, spread out over a table on the rectory lawn. Wherever people of the older generation live – and, I may add, discerning people of the younger – you will find the works of Edwardian novelists. Look in your own shelves: look and weep, if you gave them away to the paper salvage campaign. We shall not look upon the like again.

The names I shall mention will be ones that were famous once. Temporarily some may be eclipsed; the fame of others may have survived. The list is by no means complete – how can it be in a short talk? – and the writers are not world-shakers. I suppose the only great novelists from these islands who stand head and shoulders over us all during the last half century have been Thomas Hardy and James

Joyce. Thomas Hardy, inimitable in his writing because it was often so cumbrous and individual, like a country cart lumbering up a harvest lane; Joyce because of his pioneering manner that has been adopted with varying success, consciously and unconsciously, by most novelists since.

The names I shall mention are probably to be found on the back of a book within three miles, possibly within three yards, of everyone listening this evening who lives in these islands. I shall choose authors who have never produced a wholly bad book and often produced a very good one. And while you are going away to get a pencil to take down the new names I mention, I will indulge in a short background sketch of Edwardian novelists.

Think yourself back into a time when streets were cobbled in towns and main roads were dusty; when villages really were remote; when branch-line trains full of passengers stopped at oil-lit country stations; when clubs were tremendously exclusive; when you knew someone who knew someone who knew King Edward; when multiple stores were unknown; when elk horns were a feature of every large entrance hall and a flowered paper was a feature of every small one; when electric lights were in 'pear-shaped globes' and gas lighting was more usual; when the sun seems always to have been shining; when there were ices and stable smells, and horses and cigar smoke blended with the popping of champagne corks; when war seemed impossible and 'progress' was not sinister. The age summed up by Belloc:

> The accursed power which stands on Privilege
> (And goes with Women, and Champagne, and Bridge)
> Broke — and Democracy resumed her reign:
> (Which goes with Bridge, and Women, and Champagne).
> [from 'On a General Election']

In those days the English genius for writing — and it has always been there, whatever people may say today — was not to be found in poetry, nor autobiography, nor economics as it is now, but chiefly in the writing of the romantic novel.

In those days Anthony Hope was at his height. Most people have read his *The Prisoner of Zenda* and *Rupert of Hentzau*. He wrote these when he was a very young man studying the law after he had gone down from Oxford. Indeed the success of his Ruritanian novels made things awkward for him. His ambition had been to be a politician – Liberal. His success in literature left him with the choice – politics or literature – and he chose the latter.

His many books, besides those two that are still read, are all worth reading. Indeed I would say that another Ruritanian novel of his, *The King's Mirror*, is the most exquisite bit of writing he produced. I remember him telling me that it was the novel he liked best of those he wrote. It has not such wildly exciting adventures as those that surround Rupert and Black Michael but it translates you into a small civilized court life, glowing with chandeliers and looking glass, that you can never forget.

Nor is the other side of Anthony Hope to be forgotten: the writer of the witty society novel, all about lovely women tinkling among the teacups or setting sun in Rotten Row. *The Dolly Dialogues*, which are short stories carried along by brilliant conversation, seem to me a cross between Kipling's *Plain Tales from the Hills* and Wilde's comedies. Let me quote:

> 'You oughtn't to yield to temptation –'
> 'Well, somebody must, or the thing becomes absurd.'

or even better known:

> 'Bourgeois', I observed, 'is an epithet which the riff-raff apply to what is respectable and the aristocracy to what is decent.'

And there is this description of the sort of person who was just then rising into prominence, who went in for handwork at home:

> 'He is very fond of making things which he doesn't want, and then giving them to people who have no use for them.'

His later books took a more serious turn. They went in for describing why people did what they did or said what they said. One of the best of them is *Tristram of Blevit*. But all that Anthony Hope wrote is worth reading. I put him top of my list of Edwardian novelists for consistent high standard.

Anthony Hope wrote of the prosperous world with money of its own and peace of mind. The fact that he was a Liberal is probably more due to the fact that he was the son of the Whig tradition – the evan-gelical clergy – than to embryonic socialism. Were he alive today – and would he were, for he was the most handsome and charming of men, with his mellow voice and shrewd, dry humour – he would probably be a Liberal still: what is called 'an old-fashioned Liberal'.

George Gissing, on the other hand, was a Liberal who would today have been a socialist. He was a Mancunian of Suffolk ancestry and he was more interested in the wronged, misjudged, lower middle class and in the oppressed than in the world of Anthony Hope.

He is an uneven writer. There were two sides to him. The classic-al side, which delighted in writing of the ancient world, is less important and there is no need for me to mention his works written in that vein. The other side is the squalid side – the 'pessimistic side', as it has been called – which delighted in refined gentility, in the dis-tresses of small shopkeepers and long evenings of wasted love amid the silent, respectable suburbs of a manufacturing town. Gissing is a great writer. He made what had been ugly beautiful. He infused life, by his magic powers of description, into long, lifeless avenues of brick houses. He makes one think after one has read him and when one is walking, say for a bus, down a long, dreary town road, 'This is very Gissing.' His best book, I think, is *The Odd Women*. It is the story of a doctor's family at Clevedon, near Weston-super-Mare. There are three daughters – two ugly ones and the youngest one is less plain. They have been brought up as 'ladies' and when the doctor is suddenly killed in his gig they are left penniless and alone in the world. Oh, what a tale of misery this is! Going out as governesses, going out as companions, tiny furnished rooms in South London, not enough to eat, but always respectable. Then the youngest one mar-ries a possessive, pernickety self-righteous man. One of the plainer girls takes to drink. I shall not soon forget the description of her yielding to the temptation to have a nip of brandy in the buffet at Charing Cross Station before returning to her arid bedsitter. *The Odd Women* is a deeply agonizing book. So is *Born in Exile* and so is *The Unclassed*. *The House of Cobwebs*, a collection of Gissing's short stories, displays him at his highest level throughout.

Do not let me give you the impression that Gissing is all tears and gloom. He had a fierce humour. His short story 'A Charming

Family' in *The House of Cobwebs* is an ironic masterpiece. A good-hearted spinster lives on the rent she receives from a small villa in West London. She lets it to a charming family, who do not pay the rent. But they are so charming that they suggest she comes to stay with them in lieu of rent. What a charming idea; and she loves children. So she leaves her boarding house. Gradually she finds herself becoming maid of all work to them but they are so charming she feels she must help them. Indeed she eventually helps them with her tiny capital – oh, so charmingly, they leave her life for ever.

Gissing died in 1903 and he is mostly, I suppose, a late-Victorian novelist but it was the Edwardian age that appreciated him. The two books of his still fairly easily obtainable, *By the Ionian Sea* and *The Private Papers of Henry Ryecroft*, are not half so good as those I have mentioned. It is of interest to notice that in 1897 H. G. Wells went to Italy with Gissing, and I have no doubt that the early work of this writer was influenced by Gissing. My two favourite Wells novels – *Kipps* and *Mr Polly* – are in the nature of cheerful Gissing.

An altogether lighter and totally forgotten author is Miss S. MacNaughton. I had seen her books going for fourpence and six-pence in secondhand shops. We had them at home. I was always seeing them; I still see them. But I never thought of reading them until two dissimilar lady novelists advised me to do so – Miss Elizabeth Bowen and Miss Rose Macaulay. Miss MacNaughton specializes in good, kindly people in fairly easy circumstances and her novels have happy and probable endings. Her best book is *A Lame Dog's Diary*, the recollections of a Boer War officer who lives in a small country town. It is rather as though Captain Brown were to write his recollections of an Edwardian Cranford. Then she wrote *The Fortune of Christina McNab*, the story of a raw Scottish heiress let loose on smart London society.

I would have liked to have gone on with this list but it runs the risk of becoming a catalogue – Conan Doyle, Booth Tarkington, Leonard Merrick (always good), E. F. Benson (nearly always), N. and A. M. Williamson, Rider Haggard, Stanley Weyman (according to taste), Seton Merriman (often good), 'Q', Somerville and Ross (to me, always good), H. A. Vachell, A. E. W. Mason and many, many more.

Instead I will conclude with two novels that will always be the only novels by which their authors are known. These two novels, if not in print, are generally obtainable second-hand, despite the paper salvage campaign: *The Riddle of the Sands* by Erskine Childers and *Red Pottage* by Mary Cholmondeley. *The Riddle of the Sands* was written at the beginning of this century. It is a spy adventure story and I have never read its equal and there has probably never been written so alluring an account of the delights of the amateur yachtsman.

The scene is laid among those islands running from the Zuider Zee to Germany. But even more remarkable is the prophetic importance of the book, for Childers in *The Riddle of the Sands* foretold the war with Germany and Germany's methods with terrifying accuracy. He was himself a remarkable and high-principled man whose life would make almost as thrilling reading as his novel. If I start talking about it I involve myself in the forbidden topic of politics. But the outline of this fine man's career should be known in England. He was half Irish: he fought in the Boer War and wrote the story of the Honourable Artillery Company's part in that war. He was in the Admiralty in the last war and in the then equivalent of the Fleet Air Arm, where he behaved with great bravery. He had long been interested in Irish politics and while at one time he wanted Home Rule for Ireland, by the end of the last war he was in favour of Dominion status. Then, when he thought that the time was too late for this, he sided with the Irish Republicans under his friend Eamon de Valera and in the civil war between Republicans and Free Staters he was caught and executed by the Free Staters in 1922. An unusual career for a novelist. But Erskine Childers was a man of action and principle first.

Red Pottage by Mary Cholmondeley is not her only but by far her best novel. I believe it is autobiographical and autobiographical novels are often an author's – and in particular an authoress's – best novel. It is the story of a girl who wanted to write but was not allowed to do so by her family. It is a picture of rectory life and mental cruelty and frustration and stupidity therein among the lush, lovely and uncaring landscape of Shropshire.

I am afraid there has been no logical sequence in my selection of Edwardian novelists. I have taken them just as they appear on some neglected shelf. Lots of excellent novels are missing, just as they would be from a shelf at home. But if I have caused you to put down your latest thriller and turn to that era that liked a love story to have a plot, which did not despise the sentimental, which enjoyed splashing on the surface rather than swimming underwater (though it could do both) – if I have caused you to take a look at some of your parents' old favourites or some you enjoyed in youth yourself, this talk will have served its holiday purpose.

WARTIME TASTES IN READING
From the series 'Book Talk'

Home Service
Monday 4 September 1944
Producer: Godfrey James

• • •

There is a sure way of finding out what people are thinking about, or would be thinking about if they thought, and are at present feeling but unable to express and that is to turn to modern poets. Poets express the convictions, or lack of them, of the age. Poets always do, always have done. By turning to the modern poets, I am not holding a brief for contemporary poetry. It is struggling out of the obscurity of the past decade into a certain clarity but it is still, much of it, unmemorable and unmusical. Before the war, many modern poets were buoyed up by the belief in a new dawn that would arrive on this earth. They were always talking about manning the barricades. Some of them even manned them on behalf of Republican Spain and died there. They were the heralds of the Marxist revolution. They were putting into poetry the ideas behind those little orange-covered, far-from-poetical publications of the Left Book Club that graced the unstained oak shelves of many intellectual people. Then doubt set in. 'My sympathies are with the Left on paper and in my soul,' wrote one of them, quoted in Mr Paul's important book *The Annihilation of Man*, which I shall be noticing in more detail in a minute. 'My sympathies are with the Left on paper and in my soul. But not in my heart or my guts. On paper – yes.' And that doubt has now turned to despair with many of the younger generation of poets. Let me say at once, this is not despair about the war especially but despair about civilization, about new dawns in the immediate future, about material progress.

Neither despairers nor Christians believe in the progress myth that was all the rage in the last century – that heresy that because a thing is new it is better, that if it is bigger it must be more efficient, that everything is getting bigger and better all the time: the brave-new-world idea, when you just lie back in the sun and science does all your work for you, while you . . . goodness knows what you do – contemplate the marvellousness of scientific invention, I suppose. Well, that progress myth is dying. Just listen to this, one of the most beautiful passages of prose in the English language, written in the middle of the last century by James Anthony Froude, the historian. I often wonder whether it does not express that first tremor of fear about the machine that has now, in the modern poets, become a real terror. Here is a passage taken from Froude's *History of England from the Death of Cardinal Wolsey to the Defeat of the Spanish Armada*. It is in such beautiful prose because it was written before the present sort of history was popular; it was written when a man stamped his personality on what he wrote instead of writing a dry Civil Service minute, seeing eight sides to a question that only has two and even then taking none of them. It refers first to the New Learning and Protestantism and then to the industrial age in which Froude lived and which we have inherited:

> For indeed, a change was coming upon the world, the meaning and direction of which even still is hidden from us, a change from era to era. The paths trodden by the footsteps of ages were broken up; old things were passing away and the faith and the life of ten centuries were dissolving like a dream. Chivalry was dying; the abbey and the castle were seen together to crumble into ruins; and all the forms, desires, beliefs, the convictions of the old world were passing away, never to return. A new continent had risen up beyond the Western Sea. The floor of heaven, inlaid with stars, had sunk back into an infinite abyss of immeasurable space; the firm earth itself, unfixed from its foundations, was seen to be but a small atom in the awful vastness of the Universe. In the fabric of habit which they had so laboriously built for themselves, mankind was to remain no longer.
>
> And now it is all gone – like an unsubstantial pageant faded; and between us and the old English there lies a gulf of mystery which the prose of the historian will never adequately bridge. They cannot

come to us, and our imagination can but feebly penetrate to them. Only among the aisles of the cathedral, only as we gaze upon their silent figures sleeping on the tombs, some faint conceptions float before us of what these men were when they were alive; and perhaps in the sound of church bells, that peculiar creation of a medieval age which falls upon the ear like the echo of a vanished world.

I have collected the evidence – from the booksellers, from poets – and it looks as though today all we seek in what we read is escape from the present: escape into the past of James Anthony Froude or into the future. Either that or we are Christians. The meaning and direction is still hidden from us – but not from those, I maintain, who read Leslie Paul's *The Annihilation of Man*. This new book requires concentration but it is written in simple language and I cannot hope in the space of this talk to present its arguments. I can only sketch its plan of action, which is first to show why Britain is at war, then why Germany is at war, then to show that capitalism is not the foremost reason for this war any more than Marxism is.

Indeed, Mr Paul has convinced me, at any rate, that this is not solely a war about money nor a war about the balance of power or markets or this world's goods. It may be partly to do with these things but primarily it is a war of beliefs. His arguments lead to the conclusion that beliefs are supreme: what mankind believes governs mankind. Europe, he says rather dramatically, gets its ideas of democracy from Greece, of law from Rome and of freedom and equality from Christianity. It is in defence of these that all the Allies, and Russia included, are fighting, for fascism is a revolutionary force that believes not in democracy, law, freedom or equality. It too is a strong if half-baked belief philosophically – something to die for, fanatically in defeat. *Herrenvolk*, purity of blood, soil, the leader (that personification of the state), the group mind, the state instead of the individual, theory instead of man himself, theories instead of human beings, the annihilation of man as an individual, the setting up of the ants' nest.

At the beginning of the book, he asks, 'If the enemy is destroyed, is all safe? Is it possible that the trouble is universal, after all, and that civilization is somehow failing to satisfy even those peoples of the West who yet defend it?' And having shown the importance of beliefs in Europe today, he ends the book by saying:

If you believe that football pools, cinema, motor cars and the road-house can be desired above all other things, if your ideal is to live in the glitter and luxury of a Hollywood film set overwhelmed with a cornucopia of material goods, housed in a childless palace in which you parade in impeccable clothes, it is illogical to complain of the power of economic forces over your life. You are creating the power . . . It will subordinate man's efforts to the need to increase constantly the volume of consumers' and producers' goods: and man will be just as much a prisoner of the economic process whether his gaoler is a commissar, a banker or a party boss: the economic tyranny in the end will be just as unendurable.

Just think for a moment what the subordination of man's efforts to increasing the volume of production of goods for the Hollywood type of world means. It means longer hours of duller work; not families but crèches, so that your wife can work too; none of that gardening in the evening – there will be a machine to do it for you; no hobby beyond the filling-in of forms; no hedges, because they waste valuable land; no trees, because the roots take up too much space; no villages, because houses take up too much space and a single block of flats is more economic; no work that you may do with your hands, because machines can do it so much better; infinite labour to save labour – for what? For the grave. Friends, familiar landmarks, separate identity gone. All of us living in a streamlined, air-conditioned ants' nest.

Mr Paul sees the only revolutionary force likely to contend with fascism or its future equivalent, which he has just described, to be Christianity. Indeed, our revolution is for those rights of European man for which we are fighting now, even though some of us may not have realized that they are part of the Christian ethic – freedom and equality. (By 'equality' I don't mean all the same but equality of opportunity.)

Unfortunately, Mr Paul does not suggest how a man who does not believe in the Son of God may come to believe in Him. I fancy that few are even convinced intellectually of the mysteries of the true faith. Indeed, the intellect is a stumbling block to belief. Speaking as a non-intellectual and as a believing member of the Church of England, I can well understand the bewilderment of someone who

has lapsed from it, who is of another faith or who has never considered the importance of religious belief when they read the Church
catechism in the prayer book. It requires as big a surrender of pride
to accept those few but inspirational demands as it does to accept the
demands of any defined faith, even Nazism. It involves taking a lot
on trust from the centuries. But when we are bewildered by the present – so tiny a fraction of the whole of man's existence – we may at
any rate be conditioned to a state of willingness to believe by such a
book as Mr Paul's. The evidence of what people are reading and feeling and thinking at present seems to point to the fact that we are ready
to turn again to that faith that made the Europe for which men are
fighting now.

ECCENTRICS

ADOLPHUS COOKE ESQ. OF COOKESBOROUGH

From the series 'Eccentrics'

Regional Programme
Friday 24 September 1937
Producer: Guy Burgess

• • •

Ireland is the breeding ground of eccentrics. And the finest, grandest, most lovable eccentrics are to be found among that fast-dying race the Anglo-Irish. Transport yourselves, dear listeners, to that green island of white cottages, peat smoke, mountains, lakes, little fields, quiet lanes unspoiled by the motor car, wide skies uninvaded by the aeroplane; to those peaceful counties with their crumbling Georgian houses, the tall beech plantations around them, the mouldering garden walls, the grass-grown avenues. Think of the last century there when, amid mortgages and occasional discontent, the peers, the baronets, the squires and squireens hunted, laughed, joked and drank away their time in an expansive, hospitable manner in what is still the most hospitable country in Europe, where every inhabitant is a wit and every other inhabitant a poet.

And transport yourselves into the very middle of Ireland, to its quietest and loneliest part – the county of Westmeath. The year is 1876 and the time summer and the town is Mullingar. We are here to witness the great dispute over the will of Adolphus Cooke, to be heard in the granite assize court beside that enormous railway station, even bigger than the imposing court, and with a refreshment room that seems to be out of all proportion to the size of the station.

The court and, for all I know, the station refreshment room, is crowded with people of every sort. What has happened is this:

Adolphus Cooke, a Westmeath squire lately deceased, has left his money to the younger son of a neighbouring peer. The will is contested by the plaintiffs, partly on the ground that Adolphus Cooke was off his head and not in a position to make a will. That is the part of the trial that will concern us. Legends about Adolphus Cooke are rushing about. The two half-wits are remembered whom he called his guides, philosophers and friends. One, of military bearing, was said to have drilled the geese at Cookesborough, Mr Cooke's estate. When he met Mr Cooke, they would exchange military salutes. The other half-wit was far less military. He was more for conciliation. Mr Cooke would consult these two men when his neighbours asked him questions – to show, some said, his opinion of the intelligence of the surrounding gentry.

Then there were the rumours of poor old Mr Cooke's theories of the soul. Mad with learning he seemed, to Christian Ireland. He believed in the transmigration of the soul. Was he not supposed to have employed a man specially to look after an aged turkeycock, and was not this turkeycock said to contain the spirit of his grandfather? Then there was the strangest rumour of all, a sort of ghost story. Mr Cooke was supposed to have thought he might turn into a fox in the next life. 'Very useful,' he said in his slow, precise way, 'for I know this district well.' And shortly after his death there had been a meet of the Westmeath and a fox was killed in the kitchen of Cookesborough. 'The right place to find a Cooke,' said a local wit. But the story is more sad than witty, for Mr Cooke disapproved of fox hunting and the killing of animals of any sort.

Those were the rumours. Now for the facts. Mr Cooke's family had been settled in Westmeath after one of the English invasions of Ireland. Their house was like many other big houses of that country – a late Georgian structure, plain without and decorated within with many pieces of delicate Chippendale furniture, glistening silver, and ceilings and fireplaces adorned with exquisite plasterwork and carving. Round the house was a large beech-and-oak-planted park and a walled garden some way off from the house. A winding drive, called an avenue in Ireland, led to the lodge gates.

Adolphus Cooke had never liked his father, who had been a great sporting gentleman, famous for his dogs, horses and fighting cocks.

Adolphus had inherited from him a knowledge of livestock but he had been forced as a boy into the army and this was hardly congenial to him. He had fought in the Peninsular War under Wellington – this is rather remarkable when you reflect that there must still be many people who remember Adolphus Cooke – and later he was sent out on some mysterious military expedition to Africa. Here he was court-martialled for his humanitarian views. He was by no means a coward – indeed he was a very brave man – but he refused to shoot the natives. I have before me a photograph of the old man. It shows a beautiful old face with bright eyes, a high forehead, a mane of hair. A beard hides the chin. The figure is clothed in shapeless wrappings – a sort of exaggerated cloak. He certainly looks eccentric as he sits at a table, leaning on a stick.

Now for the trial. The occasion seems to have been one of public holiday. Even the judge enjoyed himself. He seems to have had a gay opinion of Mullingar:

'Is this town of Mullingar a very literary neighbourhood?' he said.
'I cannot tell, my lord.'
'There are fifty-two public houses in it. How many booksellers are there in it?'
'I don't know, my lord. There are not many.'

One witness says, referring to Adolphus Cooke:

'He was showing me the improvements he was making about the place at this time.'
Counsel: 'What were the improvements?'
'He showed me where they had collected a lot of brambles for the use of the crows, as they were losing their time.'
'Say what he said to you.'
'If you will allow me, I will. "Nulty," he says, "there's an improvement. I am getting the brambles cut down for the use of the crows. They are losing their time building their nests, striving to gather them up themselves. Don't you think that an advantage to them?" I said: "I think it is, if they will take them"; but I question whether they did.'

Another curious improvement to Cookesborough was made by Adolphus and it came out in this trial. He had some chairs with balloon-shaped backs – like half an hourglass – that he greatly admired. So he had the windows of his house made like them. They were sash windows, and those who are of a practical turn of mind will realize that, from being this shape, they would neither open nor shut.

He had another idea: to be buried in a cellar dug in the lawn, sitting up in a chair, surrounded by his books. The idea fell through, but this evidence of a builder, who produced a sketch of a marble chair, is worth quoting:

'Tell us what Mr Cooke desired you to do with reference to that sketch.'
'He desired me to get one of the best white marble chairs that could be got; but when he heard the price of it, he said he was not worthy of sitting in it.'
'For what purpose did he say he wanted it?'
'To sit in it.'
'Where was the chair to be put?'
'In the tomb.'
'Where was the tomb?'
'In the lawn.'
'Where was the lawn?'
'Before the hall door.'
'He was to sit in the marble chair?'
'Yes.'
'When he was dead?'
'When he was dead.'
'What else did he tell you?'
'He told me he would sooner stand.'

I could go on quoting from this trial, but you will be wanting to hear the result. Well, it transpired that Adolphus Cooke was a good landlord, infinitely kind to his tenants. Indeed at one time some men had attacked his house in order that he might think it was his servants, sack them and give their jobs to the attackers. He saw through this. He was a shrewd man of business. True, he had strange views about animals. A cow fell in a ditch and he told his men to leave it there that it might serve as a warning to the other cows. He had odd views, too, on sanitation. He wanted to install a water closet at Cookesborough, but it was to be two fields away from the house.

His personal opinions were very decided. He disliked missionaries; admired the Koran; did not dislike the Roman Catholics – odd in an Irish Protestant at that date. He wore strange clothes: all witnesses agreed to that. He was extremely learned and on his deathbed he read Sophocles in the original Greek to his doctor, who did not remember any Greek. He had beautiful manners and his last words were addressed to his butler: 'Give the doctor a chair.' His servants adored him. The judge, in summing up, said the whole story was very sad. Here was this poor old man, frightened of death, with all sorts of theories about his soul and anxiety about his estate and tenantry and servants and no direct heirs. So he left his property to a son of the man he thought the best landlord in the district. The jury agreed that Adolphus Cooke was right in the head. But when the seven-day trial was all over there could not have been much money left.

I have visited Adolphus Cooke's tomb and I have visited Cookesborough. The tomb in Reynella Churchyard is built in the shape of a stone beehive. As for Cookesborough, it is no more than the name for some ruined stables and small fields dotted with white cabins. The avenue is there, all grass-grown. I drove up it a year or two ago. A sham-Gothic gateway marked the entrance to the estate; the oak trees that Adolphus loved and refused to cut down were gone: a row of beeches, too old to be of any value, hung along the approach to the stables. The stables all had square openings. As for the house, only a grass platform marked the site of that odd building with its balloon-shaped windows. All that anxiety, all that money, all that kindness had been wasted and lost in the deep silence of Westmeath.

At one time Adolphus Cooke was said to have thought his spirit would enter the body of a screech owl. It was dark before I left Cookesborough. For all I know, it may have been the spirit of poor Mr Cooke that screeched in such a sad and terrifying way as an owl swooped over the ruined stables and disappeared into the tree-less expanse of what once was the property of Mr Adolphus Cooke of Cookesborough.

THE PARSON HAWKER
OF MORWENSTOW

From the series 'Western Worthies'

West of England Programme
Tuesday 7 February 1939
Producer: J. C. Pennethorne Hughes

• • •

About eighty years ago last October there was a violent storm at Morwenstow on the north coast of Cornwall, a remote sea-coast village below Hartland Point. A storm on these coasts is wonderful but terrible. Huge rollers from the open Atlantic curve into one another until they become the size of mountains and every seventh wave seems the highest mountain of all. It gathers up its strength, curls like a cobra to strike and then bursts in thunder on unyielding slate. The spray showers back from the cliff, surf collects in acres of trembling sponge on rocky shelves and ledges – the gale whips it up the cliff, three hundred feet high and over bleak fields and barren moor, so that after a storm you may find sea foam a mile or two inland, caught in slate hedges or lying in furrows. Feather-grey slate cottages grow black in rain. Light earth is pitted with rain holes. You are in a water world of blizzard, rain and spray.

Just such a storm as this was raging eighty years ago: the glass in the old Morwenstow church was rattling, so that Parson Hawker had to shout the evening service above the din. The wind had whipped the branches off slashed sycamores in the churchyard; slate headstones were knocked flat. Down below the church, the wind caused all the fires to smoke in the Parson's mock-Gothic vicarage. Through the night, doors rattled and windows flapped. Parson

Hawker slept through it all; he was used to storms. Now hear what he has to say:

> About daybreak I was aroused by a knock at my bedroom door; it was
> followed by the agitated voice of a boy, a member of my household –
> 'Oh sir, there are dead men on Vicarage Rocks.'
>   In a moment I was up, and in my dressing-gown and slippers rushed
> out. There stood my lad, weeping bitterly, and holding out to me in
> his trembling hands a tortoise alive. I found afterwards that he had
> grasped it on the beach, and brought it in his hand as a strange and
> marvellous arrival from the waves, but in utter ignorance of what it
> might be. I ran across my glebe, a quarter of a mile to the cliffs, and
> down a frightful descent of three hundred feet to the beach. It was
> indeed a scene to be looked on once only in a human life. On a ridge
> of rock, just left bare by the falling tide, stood a man, my own servant;
> he had come out to see my flock of ewes and had found the awful
> wreck. There he stood, with two dead sailors at his feet, whom he
> had just drawn out of the water stiff and stark. The bay was tossing
> and seething with a tangled mass of rigging, sails and broken fragments
> of a ship; the billows rolled up yellow with corn, for the cargo of the
> vessel had been foreign wheat; and ever and anon there came out of
> the water, as though stretched out with life, a human hand and arm.
> It was the corpse of another sailor drifting out to sea.
>   'Is there no one alive?' was my first question to my man.
>   'I think there is, sir,' he said, 'for just now I thought I heard a cry.'
>   I made haste in the direction he pointed out, and, on turning a
> rock, just where a brook of fresh water fell towards the sea, there lay
> the body of a man in seaman's garb.

Hawker and his helpers saved the man's life and Hawker had him to
stay at the vicarage till he had fully recovered. He gave the dead sailors
a Christian burial. Many other sailors he rescued, dead or alive, and
somehow he got his parish to work with him.

In those days there was a saying round those parts:

> Save a stranger from the sea
> And he'll turn your enemy.

Men had been known to push back a drowning seaman into the water,
such were some of the evil superstitions with which Parson Hawker
had to contend. Life was war for him: war against the Devil, who was

almost a tangible person in evil cottages where witches lived, witches who were consulted by his parishioners; war for the Church against apathy and hate; war against landlords; war against poverty; war against stupidity. I like to think of his reply to a silly person who asked him what were his views and opinions: 'Mr Hawker drew him to the window – "There", said he, "is Henna Cliff, there the Atlantic stretching to Labrador, there is Morwenstow Crag, here the church and graves. There are my views. As to my opinions, I keep them to myself."'

He was certainly eccentric: people who live in solitude, remote from anywhere – and Morwenstow is still miles from anywhere – are wont to grow eccentric. His clothes were odd for a clergyman. He didn't like black so he wore a claret-colour tailcoat, a fisherman's jersey with a cross embroidered on it over his heart, huge waders and a pink, brimless hat. He rode round his parish on a mule and in rough weather he wore a yellow blanket he had bought in Bideford with a hole in the middle for his head. He was an old-fashioned High Churchman, well in advance of his times. When he came to Morwenstow vicarage in 1834, he found the verger had burnt most of the old chancel screen by way of tidying up the church before the vicar's arrival. Hawker rescued the remains and fixed them up across the chancel arch. In this dusty chancel, Hawker conducted his services. He wore a yellow vestment and scarlet gloves. The effect must have been very strange when suddenly a pair of scarlet hands were thrust through the screen and Hawker's voice called 'Thomas!' and Thomas, the churchwarden, came up with the offertory bags. Hawker was among the first to introduce a weekly offering in church. This he did in 1843. In that year, too, he instituted harvest festival, another innovation.

Funny stories about Parson Hawker are endless. For instance, he was very interested in carrots and sent for some seeds from a celebrated catalogue. He was recommended to sow the seed with the best ashes procurable so he brought all his sermons out on to the vicarage lawn and burned them. When the carrot crop was a failure, Hawker decided that it must have been due to some of his father's sermons being in the heap. His father was an extreme Calvinist clergyman.

When Hawker was twenty-one he swam out to a rock at Bude wearing a seaweed wig and naked except for an oilskin wrap round his legs. There he started singing in an unearthly voice by the light of the moon, looking into a glass and combing his seaweed hair. The natives thought he was a mermaid. The next night he repeated the performance and quite a crowd collected. He then plunged into the sea and disappeared. On the third night there was a good crowd from neighbouring villages as well to witness the Bude mermaid. This time Hawker ended his performance with 'God Save the King' and plunged into the water.

Above the eccentricities of this stern-faced priest, above his humour, above his reckless generosity to the poor and sea-wrecked, above the noise of wind and waves which roars through his life and through most of his poetry, there is an upper stillness in which he really lived. You must know, if you don't know Cornwall, that it is not like England – not even now, with all its bungalows and tea places. You can stand on English downs and feel, 'These downs are pagan. Those villages below me are pagan. Christianity here is a matter of indifference. Its roots are shallow.' But you can stand in some parts of Cornwall – little valleys where there are old churches and the wells of Celtic saints who lived 1,400 years ago – and feel the land is soaked in Christianity. Other parts feel intensely evil. It is a kingdom of contrasts: it hasn't the comparative smoothness of England. Hawker felt this. Morwenstow was a holy place to him. In his dusty chancel he saw St Morwenna to whom his church was dedicated. St Morwenna lived so long ago that no one knows quite who she was or what she did to become a saint. But Hawker knew her. Hawker felt angels all around him. He wrote a poem:

> We see them not – we cannot hear
> The music of their wing –
> Yet know we that they sojourn near,
> The Angels of the spring.

[from 'Are They Not All Ministering Spirits?']

Praying in Morwenna's church he heard angelic hymns. His church was to him 'a chancel for the sky' – a phrase from one of his poems.*

Hawker held that each man lived in a spiritual element that clouded over him like a pool over one's head. And in this element angels and devils slid up and down. Soul-felt hate radiated out and

* 'Aishah Shechinah'.

affected everyone else whose soul was live enough to feel. So did soul-felt love. Such emotions were not perceptible to the senses, only to the soul – and then only to the souls of people spiritually alive.

I've been so busy talking about Hawker that I've forgotten to say where he was born and when he died, where he was educated, what he wrote and so on. He is such a great man that dates and time seem unimportant. Robert Stephen Hawker was born in 1803 just outside Plymouth. He went to Oxford and married, while an undergraduate, a lady twenty-one years older than himself and whom he dearly loved all his life. She died in 1863 and he married a second wife, a Roman Catholic, in 1864. Hawker died in 1875 in Plymouth. It is asserted that when he was unconscious, his second wife arranged for him to be received into the Roman Catholic Church. At any rate, he died a Roman Catholic, though there is much dispute as to whether he wished this final step to be taken. In his life it was the Celtic Church and not the Roman Church in which he was interested. He wrote several essays and his poems have been collected into a volume still in print called *Cornish Ballads*. His life was well written by Baring-Gould and is called *The Vicar of Morwenstow* (Methuen, two shillings).

His only well-known poem today is the adaptation of 'The Song of the Western Men', with its refrain:

> Here's twenty thousand Cornishmen
> Will know the reason why!

But I think the best ending to my talk is the last verse of his poem on the Boscastle bells, which never reached shore, for the ship was wrecked which was bringing them:

> Still when the storm of Bottreaux' waves
> Is wakening in his weedy caves:
> Those bells, that sullen surges hide,
> Peal their deep notes beneath the tide
> · 'Come to thy God in time.'
> Thus saith the Ocean chime,
> 'Storm, billow, whirlwind past,
> Come to thy God at last.'

> [from 'The Silent Tower of Bottreaux']

THÉOPHILE-JULES-HENRI MARZIALS

Third Programme
Sunday 24 December 1950
Producer: Eileen Molony

• • •

Cast your mind back, if it will go back so far, to gaslight burning either side of the chimney piece. A large coal fire is leaping in the grate; fans and watercolours are hung upon the walls; china is displayed on white enamel shelves rising tier above tier in one corner of the room. In another room is a piano and beside it a silk screen, Louis Seize style. The folding doors of the sitting room have been thrown open into the dining room to make the place bigger. We are warm, well fed and ready to be entertained.

It is a suburban evening in the 1890s and some friends have come in with their music. Mr and Mrs Pooter, Mr and Mrs Cummings, Gowing, Mr Patch, Eliza and her husband, and others. What harmonies shall we have, what arch looks will be cast between the palm leaves or above that vase of Cape gooseberries, and what are the songs that will be sung? I think it is very likely that some of them will be by Theo Marzials, the most famous songwriter of the eighties and nineties. We shall have 'Twickenham Ferry' – Mr Pooter, will you sing that? It is suited to all tenor voices and oh! the ripple of the air suggests the long, lazy wave of brown Thames water down where the river is nearly tidal and rowing boats must take care:

> 'Ahoy! and O-ho! and it's who's for the ferry?'
> (The briar's in bud and the sun going down)
> 'And I'll row ye so quick and I'll row ye so steady,
> And 'tis but a penny to Twickenham Town.'

The ferryman's slim and the ferryman's young,
   With just a soft tang in the turn of his tongue;
And he's fresh as a pippin and brown as a berry,
   And 'tis but a penny to Twickenham Town.

'Ahoy! and O-ho! and it's I'm for the ferry,'
   (The briar's in bud and the sun going down)
'And it's late as it is and I haven't a penny –
   Oh! how can I get me to Twickenham Town?'
She'd a rose in her bonnet, and oh! she look'd sweet
   As the little pink flower that grows in the wheat,
With her cheeks like a rose and her lips like a cherry –
   'It's sure but you're welcome to Twickenham Town.'

'Ahoy! and O-ho!' – You're too late for the ferry,
   (The briar's in bud and the sun has gone down)
And he's not rowing quick and he's not rowing steady;
   It seems quite a journey to Twickenham Town.
'Ahoy! and O-ho!' you may call as you will;
   The young moon is rising o'er Petersham Hill;
And, with Love like a rose in the stern of the wherry,
   There's danger in crossing to Twickenham Town.

And now that Mr Pooter has broken the ice, perhaps Carrie, his wife, will be brave enough to sing a duet with him – 'Go, Pretty Rose'. I remember how well my father used to sing it in the bath:

Go, pretty rose, go to my fair,
Go tell her all I fain would dare,
Tell her of hope; tell her of spring;
Tell her of all I fain would sing,
Oh! were I like thee, so fair a thing.

And now what about one of the ladies on her own? This roguish little piece, since we are all warming up and enjoying ourselves – 'The Miller and the Maid'. I see that the words are by Mike Beverley and the music by Theo Marzials. But, as a matter of fact, Mike Beverley was a name Theo Marzials liked to assume when writing some of his lyrics. I have no idea why.

'Can't you stay one tiny moment?'
Said the miller to the maid,

As she went along the shallows
In the twinkling alder shade,
'For I've so much to tell you,
'And you always say me "nay",
'And with such a pretty bonnet, oh!
'You take my breath away,

'For hey dear, you are so pretty.'
She turn'd and answer'd low –
'That's just what cousin Dobbin says.
'But brother Bob says "no."
'If you've nothing more to tell me then
'Oh! Miller, let me go
'For my mother's making girdle cake
'And waits for me I know.'

'Oh! but that's not it at all,' he said –
The miller to the maid, –
And he tried to see her pretty face
Beneath her bonnet shade,
'For oh! I'm so unhappy
'From that twenty third of May,
'When you came here for my wheaten best,
'And stole me heart away.

'For I love you, oh! so dearly'–
She turn'd and tried to go –
'That's just what cousin Dobbin says,
'To ev'ry girl I know;
'If you've nothing more to tell me then
'Oh! Miller let me go,
'For my mother's making girdle cake
'And waits for me, I know!'

'Bother Bob and cousin Dobbin!'
Said the miller to the maid,
And he saw her pretty face at last
Beneath her bonnet shade,
'I'm dying all for love of you,
'And what am I to do,
'If I cannot get the marriage lines
'And go to church with you?

'And it's now you know it all,' he said,
'So bless you dear, and go' –
'Oh! miller, miller, wait a bit,
'I need not hurry so,
'If you've something more to tell me,
'You can tell me as we go.'
And he'd nothing left to tell her,
Yet he told it her I know,

For one never tires of telling
'Oh! sweetheart, I love you so!'

I am afraid one of the palm leaves is a little too near the gasolier,
Mr Pooter. Would you mind? Thank you so much.

And there is one piece of Marzials' that is still sung at school concerts and village halls – 'Friendship'. The words really are by Sir
Philip Sidney: Sir Philip Sidney isn't another name for Marzials. The
melody, by Marzials, is Elizabethan in flavour for it was in Elizabethan
lyrics and music that Marzials took the greatest delight. I expect
that in somebody's drawing room, listening in tonight, there is a
copy of that big, oblong, orange-coloured book called *Pan Pipes*,
with decorations by Walter Crane and music arranged by Marzials
from Elizabethan and seventeenth-century lyrics. Eighteen eighty-
three: that was the date of the book. It looks like a stained-glass
window of that time as I open it before me.

My true love hath my heart,
And I have his,
By just exchange, the one to the other given.

My heart is his,
And mine he cannot miss.
There never was a better bargain driven.

His heart in me,
Keeps him and me in one,
My heart in him, his thoughts and senses guides.

He loves my heart,
For once it was his own.
I cherish his, because in me it bides.

I think I must tell you how it happened that I came to take an interest in Marzials and what a rewarding occupation it was finding out about this forgotten man. Many years ago I went into a second-hand bookshop at the foot of Highgate Hill, near Dick Whittington's stone, and I bought for one and sixpence a book of poems called *The Gallery of Pigeons* by Théophile-Jules-Henri Marzials. Eighteen seventy-three was the date but it was not the kind of poetry you expect to read of that date. No, it was bold, strange, arty stuff – a fore-taste of some of Swinburne's and William Morris's later work. I lent the book and I cannot remember where it is now, so I can only quote from memory. Here are some characteristic lines that I remember:

> I chased her to a pippin-tree, –
>   The waking birds all whist, –
> And oh! it was the sweetest kiss
>   That I have ever kiss'd.
>
> Marjorie, mint and violet
>   A-drying round us set,
> 'Twas all done in the faience room
>   A-spicing marmalet.
>
> On one tile was a satyr,
>   On one a nymph at bay
> Methinks the birds will scarce be home
>   To wake our wedding-day!

I imagine that last fantastic scene really means a room with William De Morgan tiles all round the walls and the table where some cherry-lipped maidens are putting spices into marmalade – a very daring fancy for 1873 or, indeed, for any age. Though I have quoted rather ridiculous lines of Marzials', he *was* a poet – there is no doubt about that. He was a stern critic of himself and I remember that my edition of his poems had comments that he had written in the margins: 'Naughty, naughty little Marzials', 'Pre-Lauberian period', 'Ridiculous but I like it' and things like that.

I started to look him up in books of reminiscences and I found tantalizing information. For instance, there was this by Ford Madox Hueffer* in a book he wrote called *Ancient Lights*, published in 1911:

* Better known as Ford Madox Ford, the name he adopted in 1919.

The mention of chocolate creams reminds me of another musician who was also a Pre-Raphaelite poet – Mr Theo Marzials. Mr Marzials was in his young days the handsomest, the wittiest, the most brilliant and the most charming of poets. He had a career tragic in the extreme and, as I believe, is now dead. But he shared with M. the habit of keeping chocolate creams loose in his pocket, and on the last occasion, when I happened to catch sight of him looking into a case of stuffed birds at South Kensington Museum, he had eaten five large chocolates in the space of two minutes.

I don't know whether Hueffer is a reliable informant but he is certainly interesting. He admired Marzials' poems and quotes one of his little tragedies★ in two verses, which I will read to you:

> She was only a woman, famish'd for loving,
>   Mad for devotion, and such slight things;
> And he was a very great musician,
>   And used to finger his fiddle-strings.
>
> For heart's sweet gamut is cracking and breaking
>   For a look, for a touch, – for such slight things:
> But he's such a very great musician,
>   Grimacing and fing'ring his fiddle-strings.

Then I remember in a book of reminiscences by Henry de Vere Stacpoole† there were some references to Marzials' genius and to his having been led astray in Paris.

Then came the great time two years ago when I spent a whole day with Max Beerbohm and I asked him about Marzials. 'Theo Marzials?' he said. 'Oh yes, wasn't he rediscovered by Henry Harland?' – *re*discovered, mark you, so he must have been well known as a poet and musician before the days of Wilde and *The Yellow Book* – 'And didn't he take stimulants in order to shine at Aubrey Beardsley's parties?' And then he told me how Marzials had been in the British Museum Library as a clerk at the same time as Edmund Gosse when the great Panizzi, the librarian who founded the British Museum Reading Room, was in command there. Marzials was always a highly

★ Marzials' poem 'The Tragedy' is now often quoted as the worst poem in the English language.
† Author of *The Blue Lagoon* (1908).

picturesque figure, with flowing moustaches, long hair and a silk tie that fell in folds over the lapels of his coat. When out of doors he wore a wideawake hat. He must indeed have been a picturesque figure in the British Museum Reading Room while Karl Marx was scratching away at *Das Kapital* and various mad antiquarians were hiding among pyramids of books. Anyhow, one day, Marzials was in the gallery of that enormous, silent Reading Room – and if you have not seen it, you can imagine it as something like the dome of St Paul's – when the great Panizzi came in. Suddenly, in a loud voice, Marzials leant over the gallery and said, 'Am I or am I not the darling of the Reading Room?'

With these titbits of information I went to see my friend Martin Secker, the publisher, who knows more about the nineties than most people, and he was so interested that he put a letter in the *Sunday Times* asking for information about Marzials, poet and eccentric. He had some fascinating replies. To begin with, Marzials was not dead in 1911 as the result of drink and drugs in Paris. No. He had spent most of the time in the West of England, living first in Blandford, Dorset, and then with his sister in Colyton, Devon. She predeceased him by many years and he died in 1920 at Mrs Power's farm at Elm Grove, Colyton. He was aged seventy. I wondered how he had gone on all those years between when he was a famous singer and poet, the flashing centre of bohemian parties and drawing-room concerts, and those last years when he was living outside a tiny Devonshire town as a paying guest in a farmhouse. Mr Zealley, who had been a boy at Colyton when Marzials was an old man there, has allowed me to make this extract from his letter:

He lived quite alone, and it is certainly true that he was a most eccentric and striking figure in the rural community in which he lived. His interest in music was the outstanding feature which made him known to the villagers. He attended all concerts that were held, and almost invariably caused consternation by standing up in the audience and declaring, in his very strong accent, most outspoken, not to say rude, criticisms of the efforts of the performers. This was particularly the case if he thought he detected any form of affectation or musical insincerity. I remember on one occasion a lady, who really sang quite well, and who had a great affection for Italy in which she travelled a great deal, singing a song to a village audience in Italian and in the operatic style of that country. Brushing aside (not without physical violence) all efforts to dissuade him, Marzials got himself on the platform and sang 'Madam will you walk?' in the Italian manner, with every sort of trill and musical exaggeration.

The most interesting letter of all, giving a vivid picture of Marzials, comes from Mr F. G. Skinner who had known him well in his declining years. Really, I must read you nearly all of it. Mr Skinner stayed with Marzials at Elm Grove farmhouse and says:

Theo had one fair-sized room on the ground floor with a single bed in one corner, occupying it day and night. By his bedside was a small table on which there always seemed to be a saucer containing sliced beetroot in vinegar so that the room continually smelt of this, together with the odour of chlorodyne (which he took to induce sleep), with, at night, the fumes of an enormous oil lamp. During conversation, he would often fish out a slice of beetroot on the end of a fork and drop it into his mouth most elegantly – it was almost a joy to watch him. In another corner of the room, he kept a huge stockpot on a stove, into which he threw all sorts of odds and ends so that he had a kind of perpetual stew. What he did with this I do not know, but we thought he gave it some of the poorer farmhands elsewhere.

He was certainly the most striking figure I have met – fairly tall and of huge girth. When he sat down at the piano he dominated it by his size as well as his genius. His hair was snow white, his complexion pink and clear as a healthy child's and, although his clothes were odd and often the worse for wear, his person was always very well groomed. When I used to call and ask him out for a drink, he would slide out of bed, put on a tie, boots with no laces, no socks (he seldom wore socks) and join me with gusto. He seemed to love it. If we went to one of the lesser pubs, he would go in with me to the bar-parlour and drink a pint or two of old-and-mild: but once I suggested going into the Colcombe Castle Hotel and he said 'All right' but made me go into the Lounge while he went into the Public Bar with the locals, I passing his beer through a kind of hatchway. He said he wasn't dressed for the Saloon Lounge – and he was the most important man in my mind for miles around!

He often seemed to have no money and would occasionally beg me, as I was a Christian, to give him sixpence or a shilling. I knew that he went later to the confectioner's and bought lollipops for the

village children. I believe that his income was sent directly to his landlady and that most of it went for board and lodging so that very little
was left for pocket-money.

We used to go mostly to Ye Olde Bear Inn, where I often stayed,
and where in an upper room he would play and sing, even when he
was nearly seventy, in a fine, rich, deep baritone – oh! splendid, splendid. His rich speaking voice too was a delight to hear – magnificently
rich and when he was roused in any way it was like thunder.

While speaking of his voice, I must mention another habit. He was
sometimes seen and heard walking bare-footed in the garden of Elm
Grove in the small hours – one or two o'clock in the morning. He
would sing in a very soft, low voice and now and then take a flower
between his fingers, bend down and kiss it, and murmur, 'O my
pretty!' Theo Marzials – poet and eccentric!

He was ravenous for reading matter and whenever I left Colyton
for London he would beg me to send him anything, 'from *Hansard* to
the *Family Herald Supplement* – or somebody's catalogue'. I did what I
could and he was grateful to excess.

In the books I have mentioned which he annotated are many interesting scribblings. Here is a sample – written under a picture of
George Meredith:

> He was audience to my first singing of 'Summer
> Shower'. Mrs H (No. 2) a tall, dignified, comely, sympa-
> thetic French woman, loving and by G.M. most beloved,
> used to be most kind about my speciality of French
> very old songs. I first met her at Mendelssohn's cousin's
> (Box Hill). I was the hired singer – 25gns. for 3 songs –
> a lot in the 70s.

I remember that sometimes after a long evening at Ye Olde Bear
Inn I would walk back to Elm Grove with Theo. He insisted on taking
my arm – no easy thing for me as I weighed only eight stone while
he must have turned fifteen stone – and although I could have walked
the distance in three minutes, it generally took us twenty minutes or
half an hour. He would keep on stopping and talking – books, music,
art, local gossip, anything.

Our conversation has always lingered with me. I started it by asking
him whether he had seen that Mr Alfred Noyes had written that he
(Noyes) considered the finest single line in English poetry was
Shakespeare's 'Following darkness like a dream'. That was enough to

keep us up till about two in the morning, with Theo quoting, quoting from Chaucer to Newbolt. He had a marvellous memory and could roll off passage after passage with ease and splendour. But what I most remember is that when I rose to go to bed that night, he put his hand on my shoulder and said, 'Well, Fred my boy, you can take it or leave it, but as far as my judgement is worth anything, *I* say that the finest single *verse* in English poetry, Shakespeare, Milton and all the rest of 'em included, is Mrs Alexander's

> There is a green hill far away
> Without a city wall,
> Where the dear Lord was crucified,
> Who died to save us all.

Théophile-Jules-Henri Marzials – poet, and *not* so eccentric, perhaps, after all!

The last person who wrote to us and whom I must mention is Mrs Belt. She is the daughter of Cyril Davenport, the great friend of Marzials' youth who drew the picture of him in the wideawake hat that I mentioned earlier. This letter to Mrs Belt is very touching. It was written from Colyton in 1918, two years before his death, and when he had had a stroke that paralysed him down one side:

I kept my voice almost intact until this last 'breaking up'. But who cares to hear an old man sing? This is a rambling dairy-farm. Folk come in summer and take rooms and some used to pay-guest or board, but since the war and ration &c. they don't. It is all very clean. The head is a wonderful old woman and she and I live here. She in her part and I in mine. I sup with them. The niece housekeeps. Her husband does for me – and in his way is very like Cyril and me – in fact it is very like the situation of when your mama and papa and me were all just married, as it were. Of the folk who come and go in the house I don't often mix with them. Cyril knows my fits of retirement and since all this dying and the war I make no new friends – oh, I couldn't. Cyril is a bit of me – of course, and always was and ever will be. We just meet and are side by side, arm in arm, heart to heart, as if he had gone into a shop and I was writing outside. Dear old Squirrel. This is a most beautiful place, of endless and immediate variety. I have never known a place like it, in this respect. Seaton is the ugliest seaside I have ever seen, too commonplace to be odious – but the seventeen odd miles of wild landslip, just off Seaton, is quite perfection – and

quite indescribable. And your wonderful letter. And oh what a gen-
tlewoman you must be . . .

On a lovely day in the spring of this year I went to Colyton to find
Marzials' grave. I had never been to this unspoiled and beautiful little
Devonshire town before. It is a huddle of cream- and pink-washed
thatched cottages collected round a silver-grey church tower and it
lies in a little lush Devonshire village with small hills around it. The
cemetery is high above the town and looks down towards the farm
where Marzials lived, over a landscape, as he describes it, 'of endless
and immediate variety'. There was the grave with his sister's name
above and his own below on a stone cross:

Théophile-Jules-Henri Marzials. Born at Bagnères de Bigorre,
Hautes-Pyrénées, France, December 20th, 1850. Died at Colyton
February 2nd, 1920. Fight the Good Fight of Faith.

Let us go back to that evening party where we started. The
refreshments are over and only one more song is to be sung. Let it be
that most famous of all his songs and lyrics, 'The River of Years' –
once sung by throaty tenors at village concerts and evening parties all
over the English-speaking world and even joked about in *Punch* by
the cartoonist Phil May. And as we listen, if it isn't too inappropriate
at a party, let us remember him whose body has been lying so long
forgotten in that Devonshire hillside and whose soul is, I pray, in that
fair daylight of his song.

> Stay, steerman, Oh! stay thy flight,
> Down the river of years.
> Turn, turn to the old sweet time,
> Far from sorrow and tears.
> Moor thy bark to the shelving glade,
> Where as children we laugh'd and play'd.
> Where we gather'd the crimson may.
> Stay! Stay! Stay!
>
> 'Nay' said Time, 'we must not bide,
> 'The way is long and the world is wide,
> 'And we must be ready to meet the tide.'
>
> Stay, steerman, Oh! stay thy flight,
> Down the river of love.

See, summer is waning fast,
Clouds gather above.
Moor thy bark to the twilight shore,
There to wander along once more,
Hand in hand the old sweet way.
Stay! Stay! Stay!

'Nay' said Time, 'we must not bide,
'The way is long and the world is wide,
'And we must be ready to meet the tide.'

Stay, steerman, Oh! stay thy bark,
The storm is here and the night is dark.
I fear the light and the foam afar
And the great waves dashing against the bar.

'Nay' said Time, 'we must not bide,
'Tho' storms may gather and seas divide,
'For daylight is fair,
'Daylight is fair
'Yet daylight is fair on the other side.'

TENNYSON AS A HUMORIST

Third Programme
Friday 7 July 1950
Producer: P. H. Newby

• • •

One bright summer day I went to see Tennyson's house, Farringford, in the Isle of Wight. I approached it by a back way, past thatched buildings of chalk and stone, down a hot, forgotten lane fluttering with peacocks and white admirals. And then round the corner was the grey, deserted house – it seemed to be some sort of holiday camp★ – with its southward view of cliffs and sea:

> For groves of pine on either hand,
> To break the blast of winter, stand;
>   And further on, the hoary Channel
> Tumbles a billow on chalk and sand;
>
> Where, if below the milky steep
> Some ship of battle slowly creep,
>   And on thro' zones of light and shadow
> Glimmer away to the lonely deep . . .†
>
> [from 'To the Revd F. D. Maurice']

Suddenly you feel the presence of Tennyson. You see the tall, bearded figure in cloak and wideawake hat striding on the lawn away from a trespasser, probably to say, when he reaches his Gothic study, hidden from visitors by a separate staircase – probably to say, as he

★ Changed to 'now a hotel' in the broadcast version.
† Extracts were read by Sir Charles Tennyson.

said to William Allingham, 'I saw a beast watching me! I saw his legs behind the ilex.' For Tennyson had a hatred of publicity. One of his last recorded sayings, which he made on his deathbed in 1892, was, 'O, that Press will get hold of me now!' So, since his death, Tennyson has had many set-backs: his dislike of newspapermen, the fact that he was a Victorian god and giant (a giant physically as well as mentally), the jealousy that other literary men had felt for him – for Tennyson was, I suppose, the last Englishman to make a decent living by writing poetry: all these things made it fashionable to run him down after he was dead. There is something very enjoyable about smashing idols. And now he is coming into his own again as the greatest and most melodiously observant nature poet England has ever known.

I would there were time this evening to convey to you some of my own delight in his poetry – not in those things like 'The Charge of the Light Brigade', 'The Revenge' and the *Idylls of the King*, which, good as they are in their way, are not the best Tennyson, but such poems as 'Audley Court', 'The Gardener's Daughter', the blank-verse passages in 'The Brook', lyrics in *In Memoriam* (to look in that poem for a connected philosophical argument is like looking for a haystack in a packet of needles; it is, of course, a series of lyrics) and those poems like 'The Progress of Spring' and 'To Mary Boyle'.

Instead, I am to correct an impression people have that he was a heavy, humourless, aloof man. On the contrary, Tennyson must have been delightful company and we know he was a good and loyal friend. You have only to read Sir Charles Tennyson's life of his grandfather, which is already a classic, or Hallam Tennyson's splendid life of his father or Edward Fitzgerald's letters or Harold Nicolson's *Tennyson* or William Allingham's *Diary* to see this. Moreover, I have been lent by Sir Charles Tennyson a manuscript record that Hallam Tennyson, the poet's son, made when he was a boy of his father's conversation.

Certainly the great poet had a lot to put up with. His name was often taken in vain, as in an advertisement for pills: 'Dear sir, like most literary men, I am subject to violent constipation. Your pills I find the greatest possible comfort, A. Tennyson.' And there was the man at Scarborough who wrote to him, 'There is to be a grand summer party here, my lord, gentlemen to appear in character, I having been requested to appear as "Lord Tennyson". Would your lordship lend me any outer clothing, by Thursday morning at latest – a cloak, etc? Then I should feel so thankful and fulfil the character better.' And there were the numberless ladies who, because the poet was always very good-looking in a Spanish and saturnine way, claimed to be his wife. To a shy man, this must have been embarrassing. If you would see him as strangers saw him, look him up in the index of any Victorian book of recollections and you will find that he always made an impression, if not a favourable one. Even the conventional Walter Crane in his *An Artist's Reminiscences* (1907) wakes up when Tennyson appears:

> The poet himself was brusque, almost rough in his manner, and had a strong burr in his speech and spoke in a deep voice, which occasionally became rather like a growl, especially when he objected to some dish that was served at dinner. He was rather taciturn at first, but melted by degrees, and even told stories (after the ladies had retired).

And his stories were endless and never told twice. He had a Commander Campbell-like★ memory and delight in the fantastic, such as:

> In Canada people see their toes dropping off with the cold, but it does not hurt them because there is no wind.

> I met a man in Exeter in an Oyster shop who said he had soaked livers of various animals in various spirituous liquors and found some less destructive than others, so always drank rum.

> In Chile people never drink milk when in a passion for fear it should turn sour.

> The man who came to a foreign inn and found a human nail in his meat and searched through rooms near him and found a dead man.

> A sailor travelled all over the world. 'And did you come to the edge of the world?'
> 'Yes.'

★ Commander A. B. Campbell was one of the regular panellists in the popular radio programme 'The Brains Trust'.

'And what was there?'

'A wall.'

'And what did you see over the wall?'

'A lot of old moons lying in a heap.'

This was conversation that appealed to his sons when schoolboys. With his adult friends he was adult. There was the very perceptive and rather catty remark he made to Allingham about the other giant, Browning: 'If the pronunciation of the English language was lost, Browning would be considered the greatest of modern poets.' He did not like Matthew Arnold and said, 'I was asked by someone in London, "Shall I ask Matthew Arnold?" I said I didn't much like dining with gods.' Frederick Locker-Lampson went on a tour with Tennyson to Switzerland in 1869 and he writes:

> We know that Tennyson's power of expressing himself in his writings was remarkable, and it is equally so in his conversations; he always, and without effort, uses the most felicitous epithets; they light up his sentences and are never pedantic. And reader, while reading these cheerful notes, you must always please to remember that my many-sided travelling companion was a humorist.

A friend of the later part of his life, Benjamin Jowett, the learned Master of Balliol College, Oxford, confirms this view: 'His humour was constant and he never, or hardly ever, made puns or witticisms, but always lived in an attitude of humour.'

How easy, then, it is to imagine Tennyson and his friend Edward Fitzgerald, the translator of *Omar Khayyam*, on a walk and trying to compose the weakest line in English blank verse, and Fitzgerald remarking that his sister was engaged to a Mr Wilkinson, a clergy-man, and Tennyson saying, 'There's a line like Wordsworth: "A Mr Wilkinson, a clergyman!"'

Most of all, Tennyson enjoyed the sardonic and laconic. Here is a story in his own words:

> A Russian noble, who spoke English well, said one morning to an English guest, 'I've shot two peasants this morning!' 'Pardon me, you mean pheasants.' 'No, indeed, two men – they were insolent so I shot them!'

And there is another about the hierarchy of the servants' hall and no one doing more than his duty:

> Mrs Russell's [the poet's aunt's] turban being on fire, she rang for the footman. The footman came in. 'I am on fire.' 'Very well ma'am,' says the footman, 'I will go and tell Amy.'

Then there is the tale of Tennyson driving through Winchester and saying to a coachman, 'What can you tell me about Winchester?' and his reply: 'Debauched, sir, debauched, like all cathedral cities.'

Many Victorians, Tennyson among them, thought lavatorial jokes funny and one of Tennyson's I find so amusing that I hope you will forgive me telling it. Macready was acting Othello – the last act, where he strangles Desdemona on the bed. The audience began to laugh. He looked and saw a plain white chamber pot under the bed. When the curtain fell he went out to complain to the property man. 'Please, sir,' said the man, 'the truth was I couldn't get a flowered one!'

We must never forget Tennyson's love of Lincolnshire, where he was born at Somersby Rectory, near Louth, in 1809, one of a large, happy family. To this day those hilly wolds – Sussex without the stockbrokers – are much as he knew them:

> Unloved, by many a sandy bar,
>   The brook shall babble down the plain,
>   At noon or when the lesser wain
> Is twisting round the polar star;
>
> Uncared for, gird the windy grove,
>   And flood the haunts of hern and crake;
>   Or into silver arrows break
> The sailing moon in creek and cove . . .
>   [from *In Memoriam A. H. H.*, CI]

From heights near the modest village you may still see:

> Calm and still light on yon great plain
>   That sweeps with all its autumn bowers,
>   And crowded farms and lessening towers,
> To mingle with the bounding main.
>
>   [Ibid., XI]

And, unless some devil has recently cut down the timbery hilltops of that sweet, intimate country, you may still look where

> Like some great landslip, tree by tree,
> The countryside descended

and where the

> . . . briony-vine and ivy-wreath
> Ran forward to his rhyming,
> And from the valleys underneath
> Came little copses climbing.

[from 'Amphion']

Lincolnshire, which inspired his best poetry, also inspired his humour. No man understands country people better than Tennyson. He delighted in Lincolnshire stories. Since I dare not attempt the dialect myself, Sir Charles Tennyson is going to tell some of Tennyson's Lincolnshire tales for me; but before he does that, here is a Devon one of Tennyson's.

> A farmers' dinner at Exeter. Lord F., speaking to some toast, had occasion to name one of the most important farmers present, and alluded with sympathy to 'a recent family affliction', the man's wife having died a short time before. The farmer having to speak by and by, thanked his lordship – 'As for my old woman, she was a teasy twoad and the Lord's welcome to her.'

> An' I reckons tha'll light on a livin' somewheers i' the Wood or the
>   Fen
> If tha' cottons down to thy betters, and keeäps thysen to thysen
> But niver not speäk plaain out, if tha wants to git forrards a bit
> But creeap along the ledge bottoms, an' thou'll be a Bishop yet.

That was the farmer who so disliked Baptists who practise total immersion, 'For they wash'd their sins i' *my* pond, an' I doubts they poison'd the cow.'

Tennyson appreciated the peasant directness of a maid who said to her mistress, wearing a bustle, 'If tha' Maäker had meant tha' to have a loomp there, tha'd have had one.' And a peasant's contempt for learning, as in this poem which describes a man of culture:

But I 'ears as 'e'd gie for a howry owd book thutty pound an' moor,
An' 'e'd wrowt an' owd book, 'is own sen, so I know'd es 'e'd coäm
   to be poor;
An' 'e'd gied – I'd be fear'd for to tell tha 'ow much – for an owd
   scratted stöan,
An' 'e digg'd up a kloomp i' the land an' 'e got a brown pot an' a
   boän,
An' 'e bowt owd money, es wouldn't goä, wi' good gowd o' the
   Queen,
An' 'e bowt little statues all naäkt an' which was a shaäme to be
   seen,
But 'e niver loöokt ower a bill, nor 'e niver not seed to owt,
An 'e niver know'd nowt but boooks, an' boooks, as tha' knaws,
   beänt nowt.

                      [from 'The Village Wife']

And never has there been a more scathing condemnation of the clannish materialism of some farmers than Tennyson's 'Northern Farmer (New Style)', where a father is advising his son against marrying the parson's daughter and threatening to cut him off if he does so:

Seeäd her todaäy goä by – Saäint's-daäy – they was ringing the bells.
She's a beauty – thou thinks – an' soä is scoors o' gells;
Them as 'as money an all – wot's a beauty? – the flower as blows.
But proputty, proputty sticks, an' proputty, proputty grows.

Do'ant be stunt; taäke time: I knows what maäkes tha sa mad.
Warn't I craäzed for the lasses mysen when I wor a lad?
But I know'd a Quaäker feller as often 'as towd me this:
'Doän't thou marry for munny, but goä wheer munny is!'

An' I went wheer munny war: an' thy muther coom to 'and,
Wi' lots o' munny laäid by, an' a nicetish bit o' land.
Maäybe she warn't a beauty: – I niver giv it a thowt –
But warn't she as good to cuddle an' kiss as a lass as a'ant nowt?

It is getting late and I can think of no better end to a talk on Tennyson's humour than to give you his description of a bore. Again it is a farmer – a breath of English scenery – and it makes you feel as though you were leaning over a rail prodding cattle in a country market with a smell of straw and cow dung about, the jingle of harness and

never a motor car or an atom of energy near to remind us of the blessings of the mechanical barbarism that is upon us. It is from 'The Brook':

> For in I went and call'd old Philip out
> To show the farm: full willingly he rose:
> He led me thro' the short sweet-smelling lanes
> Of his wheat suburb, babbling as he went.
> He praised his land, his horses, his machines;
> He praised his ploughs, his cows, his hogs, his dogs;
> He praised his hens; his geese, his guinea-hens;
> His pigeons who in session on their roofs
> Approved him, bowing at their own deserts:
> Then from the plaintive mother's teat he took
> Her blind and shuddering puppies, naming each,
> And naming those, his friends, for whom they were:
> Then cross'd the common into Darnley Chase
> To show Sir Arthur's deer. In copse and fern
> Twinkled the innumerable ear and tail.
> Then, seated on a serpent-rooted beech,
> He pointed out a pasturing colt and said:
> 'That was the four-year-old I sold the Squire.'
> And there he told a long, long-winded tale
> Of how the Squire had seen the colt at grass;
> And how it was the thing his daughter wish'd,
> And how he sent the bailiff to the farm
> To learn the price, and what the price he ask'd,
> And how the bailiff swore that he was mad,
> But he stood firm; and so the matter hung;
> He gave them line: and five days after that
> He met the bailiff at the Golden Fleece,
> Who then and there had offer'd something more,
> But he stood firm; and so the matter hung;
> He knew the man; the colt would fetch its price;
> He gave them line: and how by chance at last
> (It might be May or April, he forgot,
> The last of April, or the first of May)
> He found the bailiff riding by the farm,
> And, talking from the point, he drew him in,
> And there he mellow'd all his heart with ale,
> Until they closed a bargain, hand in hand.

Then, while I breathed in sight of haven, he,
Poor fellow, could he help it? recommenced,
And ran thro' all the coltish chronicle,
Wild Will, Black Bess, Tantivy, Tallyho,
Reform, White Rose, Bellerophon, the Jilt,
Arbaces, and Phenomenon, and the rest,
Till, not to die a listener, I arose,
And with me Philip, talking still; and so –

And so? And so you will admit Tennyson is a hit of a humorist. You'll agree, won't you, after all this, that the last lines of 'Enoch Arden' –

And when they buried him the little port
Had seldom seen a costlier funeral

– are not evidence of Tennyson's lack of humour; rather they are characteristic of the sardonic wit in which he delighted.

CHRISTIAN SOLDIERS

SABINE BARING-GOULD

From the series 'Western Men'

West of England Home Service
Friday 21 September 1945
Producer: Not known

• • •

S. Baring-Gould. Sabine Baring-Gould, spelled 'Sabine' and pronounced 'Saybin': the name appears on novels and volumes of
history, anecdote and description, mostly about the West Country,
France and Germany. And there is the name again in the index of
authors in my hymn books: he wrote the words of 'Onward,
Christian Soldiers' and 'Daily, Daily Sing the Praises'; he wrote the
words *and* composed the music of 'Now the Day is Over'.

With his friends Bussell and Sheppard and others, he hunted out
the folk songs of the West and published them before even Cecil
Sharpe was on the scene. To Baring-Gould the world outside Devon
is first indebted for the song 'Widdecombe Fair', which appeared in
his book *Songs of the West*.

I might as well give you here a description of how he used to collect these folk songs. You must imagine the tall young clergyman –
ascetic-looking, with a largish nose – driving up in a dog cart to a
Dartmoor cottage in the 1880s. No progress *then*; places really were
remote: white witches, the evil eye, ghosts and strange customs
survived in those lonely, unvisited West Devon hamlets.

Over cider of an evening in lonely inns or at open hearths, old men
would sing songs centuries old. The words were as broad as the Devon
they were singing; the airs were often descended from plainsong. Up
drives Baring-Gould one day, then, in his dog cart, and with him the
elegant clergyman F. W. Bussell, vice-principal of Brasenose College,

Oxford, Bachelor of Music and friend of Pater, that exquisite prose writer. Bussell himself is so exquisite that Baring-Gould tells the story of how he specially had orchids sent from London to match his clothes. (Bussell lived with his mother in a house Baring-Gould built and sang falsetto at village concerts to the amusement of the village and the distress of his mother.) 'We visited Huccaby,' says Baring-Gould, 'to interview old Sally Satterly, who knew a number of songs. But she was busy, she had to do her washing. Mr Bussell seated himself, inconsiderately, on the copper for the boiling, till she lighted the fire under it and drove him off. I had to run after her as she went about her work, dotting down her words, while Bussell followed, pencil and music book in hand, transcribing her notes.'

The energy that Baring-Gould threw into collecting folk songs he threw into everything else he did through the eighty-nine years of his life, from 1834 when he was born in Exeter until 1924 when he died in Lew Trenchard, a few weeks short of his ninetieth birthday. It has been the custom for the last twenty years to decry Baring-Gould as hopelessly inaccurate and amateur. That immense work of his, *The Lives of the Saints*, is mentioned by hagiologists with a superior smile; modern archaeologists with their horn-rimmed intensity and arid laboratory-like methods of research blench at the thought of Baring-Gould with a shovel and a few men off the estate opening up an ancient earthwork; historians despair of his facts. All the same, inaccurate though they may be, all his works are eminently readable, from the three-decker novels he wrote as a young man to the rather prolix reminiscences of his old age. And not only are they readable but they must have been the inspiration of many children and nourished the first love and pride in Devon and Cornwall that those children remember. I was one such child. I suppose *In the Roar of the Sea*, that tale of the smuggling on the north coast of Cornwall, was the first grown-up novel I ever read. Cruel Coppinger haunts me today. And as for *Strange Survivals* and his other books of antiquarian lore, they first stirred me to marvel at rough pieces of granite, hewn centuries ago, seen lying in tamarisk-sheltered churchyards or in similar manner on Bodmin Moor.

Baring-Gould brought to life for me the strange-named saints of little holy wells. He peopled high Cornish lanes with ghosts and hinted at curses and tragedy round some sheltered, feathery-grey-slate manor house of Elizabeth I's time, now a decrepit-looking farm. And I suspect that many of those archaeologists and historians who despise him today took up their careers on account of Baring-Gould's pioneering enthusiasm. So, even if the words of his hymns are known all over the world, his enthusiasm for Devon and Cornwall is why we love him in the West.

But I am going to try to make you see him as a man and, although I never met him, I will try to give you a sketch of him from what I have gathered by talking to those who knew him and by reading his books.

The Baring-Goulds are an old Devon family with landowning, military, naval and clerical branches, as have all such families. Baring-Gould's father, after a short career in the East India Company's army, came into his estate as a squire but preferred travelling in Europe to staying at home in Devon. He dragged his intelligent wife and little children round with him. Thus did Sabine learn languages and enjoy continually being on the move. Even when he restricted his orbit to law he was ever exploring within and beyond its boundaries. Baring-Gould Senior had strong views on education. He thought children's minds were blank pages on which the parents' wishes could be written. 'I was educated to be a mathematician,' says his son. 'At the present day I cannot do a compound addition sum.' The father disapproved of learning by heart. 'The only date, as a consequence, I can remember is 1066,' adds the son.

He admits too that he was never particular about accuracy but had the gift of rapidly getting a general impression of the main purport of a mass of facts. Finally, the father believed in repressing the imagination and refused to allow fairy stories to be told his children. The results on the son we know. If there is one thing Baring-Gould will willingly credit and write down in one of his books as the stark truth, it is a good ghost story or some unlikely but highly entertaining anecdote. And he has a marvellous gift of telling such a story.

I do not need to trouble you with his early career as a master at Hurstpierpoint, how much against his father's wishes he became a clergyman, was ordained curate at Horbury near Wakefield, found a wife there, went to Dalton in the same county of Yorkshire in 1867 and made great friends with Yorkshire millworkers. Then there were two years at Mersea on the Essex marshes where he did not like the place or people.

Baring-Gould the man, so to speak, completed himself when he had ejected an unsatisfactory tenant from Lew House in 1876 and with his wife and growing family – there were fourteen children when the family was complete – entered the village of Lew Trenchard as squire and parson in one – that is to say, as squarson. Lew Trenchard is a wooded kingdom on the western edge of Dartmoor. Motorists rushing over Lew Down on the road from Okehampton to Launceston would not suspect that the Baring-Gould kingdom lay within a few yards of them. It is sunk below the main road, out of sight. A meadow with a moorland millstream and a dower house, a slate building with granite mullions; unfenced roads running halfway up the valley slopes, on one side to farms, on the other to the manor house and church. It is a valley of luxuriant growths, huge blackberries, ropes of birdwood, thick woods of fir and larch and beech, and right in the middle of it – deep, blue-black and terrifying – a huge pond, cliff-surrounded, tree-shadowed, known as the Quarry Pool.

But the loveliest thing in the village is the church of St Petroc. Small wonder that Baring-Gould never sought church preferment, said what he liked to bishops and fellow clergy, avoided local clerical meetings – except to meet friends at them. He had come into an earthly kingdom that he loved. 'I felt I had a work to do, not like that of Newman in England at large, but at Lew Trenchard the small.' And at Lew he gave himself three objects: 'one, the moral and spiritual improvement of Lew Parish; two, the restoration of the church; three, making habitable and comfortable the houses on the estate, including my own'. He achieved the last object, for the manor house (at the moment let outside the family), and the few cottages and the rector's house bear the mark of Baring-Gould. They are slate buildings with Rhenish features, the sort of thing you would expect of someone imbued with the Scottish and German craze of Queen Victoria's later years. They harmonize well with the firs and that yawning Quarry Pool.

As for the church, it is almost overwhelming in its beauty. It is a small building – just a nave and north aisle and low tower on the woody hill slope. But when you open the door, the full glory of a great rich Devonshire screen bursts upon you. Encrusted with saints and vines and leaves, it cuts across the whole church and through it you may glimpse the altar and monuments. A lovely chandelier from Malines shines from the chancel like gold through the screen's elaborate tracery. The church is filled with carved benches, new and old, in the Devon manner. If, afterwards, you visit neighbouring Devon churches where the screens and benches have gone, they will seem empty and incomplete. This screen and the benches were put in by Baring-Gould. He fulfilled his second object, the restoration of the church.

It is not for me, a stranger twenty-one years after the squarson's death, to say what he may have done towards his greatest object in coming to Lew: 'the moral and spiritual improvement' of the parish. We only know that he was welcome in all cottages; that people said what they liked to him and he to them, as equals. Here he describes himself having a glass of metheglin with a gossiping old woman, Marianne:

> I reproved her once for never coming to church. 'Oh,' said she, 'I've got my Bible here,' pointing to one on a side table. I looked at it, the cover was thick with dust, so with my finger I scribbled on it *Marianne's Bible.* 'You may have a Bible,' said I, 'but it is never opened. If you read it you would find therein, "Thou shalt not bear false witness against thy neighbour."' 'Oh!' she said, 'I am so short of amusements. Men have horse races, foxhunting, shooting and cockfighting. What are we poor women to do for a little entertainment? To get a lot of women by the ears is rare sport!'

Such an equality as shown in this and hundreds more conversations and reminiscences is a true equality of humans. The fact that he was squire and parson was accepted without resentment as part of the divine order of things by both parties. Life was easier to live in those days.

There was no pomposity about him. He dearly loved jokes and stories in talks with parishioners. His friends were his neighbours and he was unknown in any 'literary' set. There he stood, every day, at a high desk, writing his books for love of Devon and Cornwall and to make money to improve Lew Trenchard and to educate his family.

He worked and lived for Lew Parish and House and snapped his fingers at the world. Bitterly would he have resented the form-filling life the state has imposed on us today. I can imagine he would have gone to prison rather than submit to the enquiries that the state now makes into our affairs. He was an intense individualist, and did not mind what he said or wrote about those with whom he disagreed – particularly Roman Catholics and Protestants – for Baring-Gould was a thorough Tractarian, an old-fashioned High Churchman. For instance, I find him writing this about a fellow undergraduate at Cambridge named Maclagan: 'He was a canny Scot, and a Scot, like a fox, sweeps his tail over his traces, lest in any way he might compromise his future prospects by anything he had said or by association. Maclagan buttered his bread well with ecclesiastical margarine. He became eventually Archbishop of York.' And this tale, told me by his former curate, the present rector of Lew, is characteristic of his humour and outspokenness. A Protestant bishop objected to the last two lines of the chorus of 'Onward, Christian Soldiers': 'With the Cross of Jesus / Going on before'. He objected to a cross as papistical. So Baring-Gould suggested altering it to 'With the Cross of Jesus / Left behind the door'.

Sabine Baring-Gould died on 2 January 1924, aged eighty-nine. He lies under a granite cross in Lew churchyard. After his death, a volume of his sermons was published called *My Few Last Words*. Like all his work, they are simple and direct such as would appeal to those who prefer deep things to smart and clever things, as children and old people do. His sermons were short and dramatic – his record short one, the present rector tells me, was two-and-a-half minutes at Easter. He also recalled how he banged the pulpit with his fist for the final words of one sermon, which were 'The thing is – do you want to be a cabbage or not?'

But the sentence with which I want to end my talk is from one of those last sermons where Baring-Gould pays an unconscious tribute to that life object of his, 'the moral and spiritual improvement of Lew Parish':

I do not know whether I ought to speak to you of myself and my feelings, but when the heart is full it must overflow.

What I want to say to you is, that I do not think I have had a happier time in all my life than this that is now fleeting away, carrying me into my eighty-ninth year. And what has made me so happy is this – never before have I had so many tokens of affection and of my teaching having been of good to souls.

There can be few who would not like to be able to say that should they reach the age of eighty-nine.

AUGUSTUS TOPLADY

From the second series of 'Literature in the West'

West of England Home Service
Sunday 23 June 1946
Producer: Unknown

• • •

Augustus Toplady is, to me, one of the most fascinating and attractive characters of the eighteenth century. Though he died at the
early age of thirty-eight of consumption, he has left behind him six
large volumes of writing filled with love of God, vituperation of John
Wesley and his followers and reflections on animals, history, philosophy, apparitions, devils, meteors, highwaymen and above all
Calvinism, that great uncompromisingly logical system of theology
of which Toplady was a violent upholder. So smoothly, poetically and
clearly does Toplady write, so forceful is his personality, so startling
and original his imagery, that even his most involved argument is a
pleasure to follow. Here and there where daylight strikes through
clear glass windows onto high pews and galleries of little old chapels
of the Independent and Strict Baptist denominations and, I believe,
in about half a dozen Anglican churches, the prose works of Toplady
are still quoted. But to the rest of the English-speaking world he is
only remembered as the author of the hymn 'Rock of Ages'.

(In parenthesis I should say that there is no evidence that the huge
piece of fissured rock at Burrington Combe, Somerset, is the origin
of this hymn. True, he was curate at nearby Blagdon in the neighbourhood for two years and the 'Rock of Ages' image occurs in a
sermon preached then but he did not write the hymn until ten years
after he had left Blagdon and when he was vicar of Broadhembury in
Devon. The question of where he wrote the hymn and what

particular rock in the world it describes seems to me unimportant and I am unwilling to discountenance tradition. I only say there is no evidence, except tradition, that 'Rock of Ages' was written about Burrington Combe. One further fact about the hymn, before going on to its author: in my hymn books the last verse has been revised to start:

> When I draw this fleeting breath,
> When mine eyelids close in death . . .

Toplady's words are far more vivid and less mellifluously Victorian: they are more characteristic of Quarles and the seventeenth-century poets Toplady loved:

> When I draw this fleeting breath
> When my eyestrings break in death . . .

I always sing that line myself, despite the rest of the congregation.)

Augustus Montague Toplady was born at Farnham, Surrey, in 1740. His mother was Anglo-Irish and had an estate in County Wexford. His father was a major in the British Army and he died of yellow fever in Spain a few months before his son's birth. He was taking part in one of those mysterious Peninsular campaigns in which we were involved in the eighteenth century. Toplady was not rich but he was what is called 'well-connected'. Lord Chesterfield was one of these connections. When Toplady was a young man, he asked that finished courtier for a chaplaincy or 'scarf' as it was termed. His lordship said, 'I am exceedingly sorry you did not mention it early enough. Had you asked me two days sooner, a scarf should have been at your service; but no longer ago than yesterday I gave away the only vacant one.' Toplady wrote again and asked for the honour of the next that fell. His logical mind was amused and angered by this illogical reply from Lord Chesterfield: 'The next is already promised but you shall certainly have the next after that.'

From a very tender age, Toplady kept a diary. It records his school-days at Westminster and I have only read a few printed extracts from it, being ignorant of the whereabouts of the original manuscripts. These reveal a rather priggish but remarkable child and I wish I could read more of them:

I am now arrived of the age of eleven years. I praise God I can remember no dreadful crime: and not to me but to the Lord be the glory. Amen

When he was twelve he says:

Went to my Uncle Jack's to dine. I ran the gauntlet sorely; for I carried two or three of my sermons to show to my cousin Kitty. My uncle took hold of them and read part of one and asked whose I got them out of? I told him, nobody. He shook his head and said he knew what children can do before now. I still urged that I really did not take them out of anyone. He bid me hold my tongue and not make it worse by denying it. He went on 'If you were my boy I would flay you alive' (a fine friendly expression from an own uncle!) 'for doing such things and fetch the truth out of you.' A little after this Mrs Bate came into the room, and Miss ——, and they were in a close whisper, and now and then looked at me.

Six months later he said of that aunt, Mrs Bate, 'She is so fractious, and captious and insolent that she is unfit for human society.'

He went to school at Westminster and then in 1755 to Trinity College, Dublin. He heard a preacher in a barn in Ireland who 'converted him' in 1758 and turned his mind towards Calvinism.

Toplady is associated with the West Country because he was curate at Blagdon and then Farleigh Hungerford, both in Somerset. He then held the benefices of Harpford and Venn Ottery in Devon. In 1768 he arranged an exchange of livings with his friend Mr Luce, who was vicar of Broadhembury, a lovely cob-and-thatch village under the Black Down Hills. While he was still at Harpford, but after the exchange had been arranged, he was standing on top of a hill and noticed smoke in the farm near his vicarage. When he reached the village, a man saluted him and said, 'Sir, your house is burned to the ground.' He rode to Exeter where the Sun Insurance agent told him that as the exchange had been made, Mr Luce would be the only sufferer. Somewhat baldly he records in his private diary, 'What a providential mercy was it that I resigned the living before this misfortune happened! O God, how wise and how gracious art Thou in all Thy ways.' Yet it is characteristic of him that he did not allow this almost smug fatalism to interfere with his well-doing. He went to a great deal of trouble to get the Sun Insurance Company to pay full compensation.

Toplady remained vicar of Broadhembury almost until his death in 1778. Much of his time he spent travelling to London and Bath. He was a close friend of the foolish blue-stocking Mrs Macaulay in Bath. He also knew Lady Huntingdon, that evangelical noblewoman. In London he talked with Dr Johnson – somewhat unsatisfactorily if you will look him up in Boswell – and in London too he preached in crowded chapels to such men as Sir Joshua Reynolds and David Garrick.

The mainspring of Toplady's feverish activity, the energy which kept him writing till two and three in the morning in the stillness of his country vicarage, the power which gave him such eloquence in the pulpit that the galleries of churches and chapels were as full as the pews with groaning and weeping multitudes, was primarily his glowing faith in God; secondarily it was Calvin's doctrine of Free and Sovereign Grace. I hesitate to define in a few sentences this grand system, yet it is necessary for you to know one aspect of it if you are to understand Toplady. Calvin held, and proved by Scripture, that since God was omnipotent he would not willingly allow a soul to be damned to hell. Therefore, logically, Calvin concluded that some are predestined to hell before they are born and others are chosen by God for salvation. Just going about and doing good is not enough to save a man: he must own his worthlessness, his total inability of his own free will to be saved, and must acknowledge that God alone is powerful and that God alone can give him the grace to save his soul alive.

Now this system, you must agree, allows for no compromise. Toplady was not a compromiser by nature. The last thing you would call him is 'all things to all men'. He was the very reverse of the modern jolly padre with a cheery word for all, who will sacrifice any amount of his belief if it is going to avoid unpleasantness. So when Toplady published a translation of a Calvinistic writing, John Wesley, who was by no means a Calvinist, published a mockery of it and put at the end 'The sum of all this: one in twenty (suppose) of mankind are elected; nineteen in twenty are reprobated. The elect shall be saved, do what they will, the reprobate shall be damned, do what they can. Reader, believe this, or be damned. Witness my hand. A. T. . . .' This was a gross calumny of Toplady by an older man. Toplady was furious and about half of his subsequent writings are devoted to attacking Wesley. He certainly did not mince words. He called Wesley a 'Methodist weathercock' and an 'Old Fox' and said that he would 'tar and feather' him.

> Where unto shall I liken Mr John Wesley? – and with what shall I com-
> pare him? I will liken him unto a low and puny tadpole in divinity,
> which proudly seeks to disembowel a high and mighty whale in pol-
> itics. I do not expect to be treated by Mr John Wesley with the can-
> dour of a gentleman, or the meekness of a Christian, but I wish him,
> for his reputation's sake, to write and act with the honesty of a heathen.

Nor did Wesley and his followers mince words either when writing of Toplady as 'a beardless bachelor of arts, just stept piping Hot out of a university'; 'This prancing coxcomb'. Nor was the charge without foundation for Toplady *was* a bachelor, though Thomas Wright of Olney, his able biographer, thinks he may have considered marrying Mrs Macaulay. Moreover, he was rather a fine gentleman, with his beautiful manners (even to his opponents when he met them in the flesh), his handsome face, his fine clothes, his snuff box with Calvin's portrait on it in enamel, his cane and his witty and elegant remarks. His Calvinism never made him gloomy. Mr Northcote, a friend of his at Honiton, said, 'Dr Toplady believes in absolute predestination and yet he is loath to ride on horseback for fear of breaking his neck.' 'True,' replied Toplady 'and perhaps that very fear may be an appointed means of preserving my neck unbroken.' And let me quote in Toplady's own words a humorous story of his, with his Calvinistic comment on it:

> At Worcester there was (and probably still is) an idiot, who was
> employed at the cathedral there in blowing the organ. A remarkable
> fine anthem being performed one day, the organ blower when all was
> over said, 'I think we have performed mighty well today.' '*We* per-
> formed?' answered the organist. 'I think it was I performed; or I am
> much mistaken.' Shortly after, another celebrated piece of music was to
> be played. In the middle of the anthem the organ stops all at once. The
> organist cries out in a passion, 'Why do not you blow?' The fellow, on
> that, pops out his head behind the organ and says, 'Shall it be we then?'
>   What are all our pretensions to free will, spiritual strength and
> self-righteousness, but the pride of our hearts, realizing the idiot's
> question, 'Shall it be we?'

Living in the deep-laned West Country, walking for miles cane in hand and dog at heels to visit parishioners, as he did most assiduously, it is not surprising to find him referring often and often to the grandeur of nature and to birds and animals. He was no Gilbert White. For instance, he believed, as did most people in the eighteenth century, that swallows 'betake themselves in October to holes and shelves, under the banks of rivers, where they very comfortably sleep away the winter . . . There they lie clustered together in great numbers, their beaks and claws interlocked with those of one another.' The natural world was always interesting him. But he firmly believed that animals have souls, as he asserts in his sermons and reasons in his essay on 'The Sagacity of Brutes'.

Politically, Toplady was a Whig and a Wilkesite. He was strong in his denunciation of Britain's war with the American colonists. 'Not slaughter but the olive branch', he said, 'must decide the fate of the British Empire. Subduing the bodies of the Americans will not subdue their minds.' But he never let politics interfere with good manners and he records, as an example of dear old Dr Johnson's boorishness, the latter's behaviour at Mrs Macaulay's table. This lady was a republican.

Mrs Macaulay's footman was standing, according to custom, at the back of his mistress's chair, when Johnson, addressing him, said, 'Henry what makes you stand? Sit down. Sit down. Take your place at table with the best of us. We are all republicans, Henry. There's no distinction here. The rights of human nature are equal. Your mistress will not be angry at your asserting your privilege of peerage. We are all on a level. Do take your chair and sit down.'

I have left to the last the profoundest and loveliest side of Toplady and will weave into it the dramatic story of his death as recorded so eloquently by Thomas Wright. Every day, for hours and long into the night, Toplady would commune with his Maker. His spiritual diary, which survives, records his intimate moments of prayer. There would be times of dryness when he believed nothing and the face of the sun was darkened and the silence of the Devonshire night brought no hope for him and his early death, which he foresaw, would project him, he felt, into blackness and oblivion. Then came the showers of mercy and assurance to compensate him when he was 'dissolved in wonder, gratitude and self-abasement'.

All the tenderness of his nature, which you have not seen till now, comes out in his glorious sermon 'Jesus Seen of Angels', which is an account of the life of Our Lord as witnessed by the angels. It will surely appeal to Catholics and Protestants alike, to all Christians and even to those who do not believe. Settle yourself down in mind in a baize-lined high pew in Broadhembury church, then hung with colour hatchments and walls silver grey in the December light of 1775. In the high pulpit stands Toplady, aged thirty-five, his face pale with consumption, his voice melodious, his three-cornered eyes bright above hectic cheeks. He has reached the final periods of his pulpit oratory and describes the Crucifixion.

> Surely all heaven was, at that dreadful moment, emptied of its inhabitants. Surely not angels only, but the spirits likewise of just men made perfect (who had been saved on the credit of that great sacrifice which was now offering up) started from their thrones and dropped their crowns, quitted for a while the abode of bliss, and, with pensive admiration and drooping wings, hovered round the cross of their departing Lord. If ever sorrow was in heaven; if ever the harps of the blessed were suspended, silent, and unstrung on the willows of dismay; if ever angels ceased to praise; if ever the harmony of the sky was, not merely interrupted, but if it be possible, exchanged for lamentation and mourning and woe – it must have been during the six tremendous hours (such hours as nature never saw before, nor will ever see again) that the dying Jesus hung upon the tree.

In 1778 Toplady went to London to die. He preached to crowded churches and chapels and then retired to his rooms in Knightsbridge to breathe his last. When he was on his deathbed, a rumour reached him that the followers of Wesley were saying that he had denied Calvinism and agreed with the Wesleyans at last. It was a Sunday morning and, ill as he was, he got up and was carried to Orange Street Chapel near Leicester Square. When the sermon was over, Toplady was helped up to the pulpit by two friends. The congregation thought they were seeing a ghost, for deathly white was the young man and he could hardly stand up. Then he most solemnly and publicly averred that he would have nothing to do with Mr John

Wesley or his teachings and that he would not take back one single word he had said about him A few weeks later he died, aged thirty-eight, assured in his faith to the last. His deathbed is recorded in considerable detail. As he himself said, 'The deathbed of a Christian is the antechamber to heaven, the very suburbs of the New Jerusalem.'

He was buried, according to his wish, since he could not be buried in faraway Devon, nine feet below the surface of the ground in Whitefield's Tabernacle, Tottenham Court Road, London. The Tabernacle was rebuilt at the beginning of this century and I have no doubt that Toplady's coffin was moved when they dug the foundations of the new building, for the coffin plate was preserved in the new chapel. In the Hitler war, the chapel was badly bombed. Once again, I have no doubt, Toplady's remains were disturbed. But what matter to him? For here is what he says of the Resurrection of the Body, as definite and full of faith as everything else about this fiery young man:

> Whatever changes their bodies may undergo by a resolution into their first principles, or even by incorporation with other beings, the constituent particles requisite to identity shall, when the trumpet sounds, be collected from every quarter of the globe, whither they have been scattered: or, more justly speaking, treasured up: for the world is but a vast store-house, wherein the dust of the saints is reposited . . . the grave is but a steward, entrusted with our ashes and responsible for the charge. Soon will the several elements resign their deposit and give back the loan; the hallowed dust of God's elect: O death! – no longer thine. While their souls are happy in the converse of Christ and angels, their bodies lie refining in the tomb, until the latter have slept away their dross, that both may be glorified together.

ST PETROC

From the series 'It Begins at Home'

West of England Home Service
Monday 11 July 1949
Producer: Rupert Annand

• • •

St Petroc died in Cornwall more than 1,200 years ago. The sixth and seventh centuries in which he lived are a sort of Bodmin Moor, an unknown territory. Worse than that, they are a no man's land between the archaeologists and the historians of early Christian Britain. Archaeologists, who are generally ardent unbelievers, dismiss the period as 'Late Iron Age'. Writers of our church history take an almost unchristian pleasure in contradicting one another's statements about those remote centuries. The late Revd S. Baring-Gould, the most readable and enjoyable writer on the Celtic Church, is, alas!, regarded as unreliable. To him I owe all my early enthusiasm. The late Canon Doble, a scholar who did more than any man to find out about the Cornish saints, wrote mainly for scholars. If it were not for his pamphlet about St Petroc (third edition 1938) we would know hardly anything of St Petroc at all. What I say tonight is little more than a condensing and rearranging of some of the finds Canon Doble made. If a wireless talk can be dedicated to anyone's memory, this should be to that of Canon Doble, vicar of Wendron.

Strange and sweet-sounding saints of Cornwall – Morwenna, Monofroda, Endoliontra, Ladoc, Cadoc, Kow, Cuby and Tudy and all the rest of you! – come to my aid and help me to present, here on the wireless, a picture of the greatest of your number, Holy Petroc, Abbot and Confessor! Thirty or forty churches in the West bear Petroc's name: Padstow, Little Petherick, Bodmin and Trevalga in

Cornwall, three churches in Wales, two in Somerset, twelve in Devon, many in Brittany. Here in his own kingdom, where he lived and died, St Petroc is rarely remembered. But in Brittany his cult survives: hymns are sung to him, he is a fisherman's saint and in one place his statue is taken out and whipped if the fishing is bad. One of his statues there shows him as a small, benevolent-looking, bearded man, in spotted vesture, holding a book in his left hand while with his right he pats a stag that has jumped up at him. In Brittany, too, the life of St Petroc has been preserved. Canon Doble translated it into English. In 1937 a British Museum official found another *Life of St Petroc* in the Ducal Library of Gotha in Germany. They were not all that different from one another, and neither of them was authoritative, because they were written hundreds of years after St Petroc's death, but they contain local Cornish folklore about our beloved saint.

Put very shortly, this is something of what they said. Petroc was the son of a Welsh king. When his father died, he could have become king himself. He decided instead to be a monk and called together sixty followers and friends and asked them if they wanted to join him. They agreed to do so and sailed together to Ireland, where in those dark ages of Europe the light of learning and Christianity burned brightest. There they stayed in the monasteries of the Church. A monastery was a street of little stone cells in a walled enclosure containing also an oratory for praying and a church for worship. All the buildings were made of unmortared stones, like a drystone wall, and roofed with a dome of balanced stones. They were set beside streams or wells, even on the tops of great island rocks rising hundreds of feet from the ocean.

After twenty years of study in Ireland, Petroc and his followers sailed to Cornwall and landed in the Camel estuary, stepping ashore at Trebetherick – the place of Petroc. Here they found some men harvesting who were rude to them and laughed at their funny clothes. Petroc himself carried a staff and a small bell like a sheep bell. Many missionaries had been coming to the heathen Cornish at this time. 'We're thirsty', give us fresh water,' said the harvesters, by way of testing his sanctity. Petroc struck a rock and a spring appeared before their eyes. So then he asked them where the nearest religious man was – for Celtic tribal life was in two parts, religious and worldly, each with its own enclosures and rules of life and working arrangements with its neighbours. The harvesters pointed to the other side of the river, where a hermit named Samson lived at Lolissick. Near him lived a bishop called Wethnoc. Bishops were humble men then, less important than abbots of monasteries and used for confirming and consecrating rather than for administration. Wethnoc gave his cell to Petroc and thus the monastery was founded known to this day as Petrocstow, which we now pronounce Padstow. Here Petroc lived a strict life. When he felt evil desires on him, he stood in a cold stream. He ate bread only – except on Sundays, when he had porridge. On fast days he ate ashes with his bread. He and his monks ground their corn at Little Petherick mill and built an oratory beside it.

One day his companions were grumbling about the weather. 'It will be fine tomorrow,' said Petroc. But it was not. So Petroc accused himself of presumption in thinking he could prophesy about the weather and decided to go on a pilgrimage to Rome as a penance for his presumption. Then he went to Jerusalem, to the Lord's Sepulchre, and the 'thirst, hunger, sweat and cold and night-watching which he had endured for the Name of Christ on the way, he counted as delights'. Then, sleeping by the seashore of India, to which he had gone, he woke to see a boat full of light floating towards him. This he entered and was carried to an island where he lived for seven years on fish. Then he returned to Cornwall and found his sheepskin cloak and his staff on the seashore and a wolf guarding it which accompanied him until he came back to his companions at Padstow.

A local king called Tendor kept poisonous snakes and horrible reptiles and centipedes in a marshy lake. But when this lake was no longer used for punishing criminals, the hungry monsters started eating each other until only one was left – a hideous creature of enormous size, its body swelled with all the snakes and centipedes it had eaten. It ravaged the neighbourhood. But Petroc boldly went up to it, bound it with his holy stole and led it away. As he was leading it along, a huge funeral came in view and the mourners were so astonished and terrified at the sight of this fearful monster, they fell on the ground. Petroc went to the coffin and brought the body of the young man who lay in it to life. He then released the monster and ordered it to hurt no more people and it went away beyond the sea.

One day when Petroc was praying, a stag came running towards him pursued by hounds and huntsmen. Petroc protected the animal and the huntsmen did not dare to touch it while it was being cared for by a religious man. Then Constantine, the chief of the huntsmen, appeared and raised his sword to slay Petroc but he was struck with paralysis and could move neither hand nor foot. Then the saint prayed and Constantine was released and he and all his men were converted to Christ.

A great dragon that lived near Petroc's cell on the moor got a piece of wood into its right eye. It ran to Petroc's church and laid its head on the entrance step for three days, waiting for a miracle. By Petroc's command it was sprinkled with water mingled with dust of the church floor and straight away the wood was removed and the dragon's sight restored and it returned to its accustomed wallowing place.

After sixty years in and about Padstow and Little Petherick, after performing many more kindnesses and miracles, Petroc commended his monks to the care of him whom he had chosen as his successor. Taking one companion, he journeyed to Bodmin and there in a remote wooded valley he found a holy hermit living alone whose name was Vuron. Vuron offered Petroc his cell and himself moved one day's journey southward. There, between two mountains and by a streamside, Petroc lived and prayed, visited by his monks and his successor.

When he felt that he was dying, Petroc set out to Little Petherick and Padstow to say goodbye to his monks there. But on his way from Little Petherick at a place called Treravel, where the footpath leaves the road and crosses the fields to Padstow, Petroc felt he could go no further. The man of the house took him in and there on the night of the fourth of June he died and his soul shone like a star in the room where his dead body lay. And they say that whoever was ill in the farmhouse of Treravel (the old building, not the present one) had to be taken out of the house before he could die.

St Petroc was buried at Padstow and his remains were taken to Bodmin in the tenth century when the Danes pillaged Padstow. There they were kept in the priory church until in 1177 an angry Bodmin monk stole them and took them to St Méen Abbey in Brittany. Henry II ordered the abbot of St Méen to return them to the prior of Bodmin. So they came back and at Winchester, Henry II and his court venerated St Petroc's relics and the monks returned with them to Bodmin, carrying them in a beautiful box that Henry II gave to them. This box survives in a Bodmin bank. It is ten inches by eighteen, faced with white ivory and bound with brass and on the ivory are engraved birds picked out in golden roundels. But St Petroc's bones are no longer there.

One last and thrilling discovery about St Petroc was made just lately by a monk of Downside Abbey. He has identified the beehive cell by the streamside of the empty farm of Fernacre on Bodmin Moor as the dwelling that St Vuron gave up to St Petroc. Whether it was the cell or not, I do not know. While historians and archaeologists fight it out, let us go in spirit, as last year I did in the flesh, to that lonely valley between Rough Tor and Brown Willy. Fernacre Farm is granite, its garden walls are granite and there, before short and deep-grown grass by a streamside, is St Petroc's cell.

It is made of granite boulders and stones, stuffed in between with grassy turf. Inside, one can stand upright in the middle, for the top of the dome is seven feet high. Sunset shone on the entrance of the cell – Rough Tor, sprinkled with sacred stones, on one side, Brown Willy's heathery slopes upon the other. Not a motor car, nor aeroplane, nor modern sound was heard, only sheep bleating and larks singing and the startled thud of a nearby moorland pony. A silence so deep and so long that the chirps and scurryings of nature only made it greater. Here, as to St Petroc, because nature was near, so was the Creator. Time disappeared. The Celtic Church tinkled in Cornwall with the bells of its saints expecting Christ at any moment. Here on Bodmin Moor it would be no shock to see the bearded form of Petroc, with stags, poultry and wolves following him, not bothering to eat one another, for devotion to the saint.

WILLIAM BARNES

From the series 'For Your Book List'

West of England Home Service
Tuesday 20 March 1951★
Producer: Rupert Annand

• • •

A friend of mine said the other day that he couldn't read Barnes because of the accent. This is the reason why many people who are not West Country do not read Barnes. It certainly looks formidable in print and if I had started to read it myself to you I should feel a fool – or like a Londoner singing 'Widdecombe Fair' at a Devon concert.

The truth is, Barnes will be resurrected by the wireless, for he is a man to be recited rather than read. And here's a Dorset man† who will recite one simple piece of his work by way of introduction. Imagine yourself sitting in an oil-lit village hall at a concert in, let us say, Whitchurch Canonicorum, on a rather hard chair, thirty years ago. An old man mounts the platform and recites 'The Two Churches':

> A happy day, a happy year,
> A zummer Zunday, dazzlen clear,
> I went athirt vrom Lea to Noke.
> I goo to church wi' Fanny's vok:
> The sky o' blue did only show
> A cloud or two, so white as snow,
> An' air did sway, wi' softest strokes,

★ Broadcast on the 150th anniversary of Barnes's baptism at Sturminster Newton. Geoffrey Grigson had just brought out an edited selection of Barnes's poetry.
† The poems were read in this broadcast by W. J. E. Brown.

> The Eltrot roun' the dark-bough'd woaks.
> O day o' rest when bells do toll!
> O day a-blest to ev'ry soul!
> How sweet she zwells o' Zunday bells.

You will notice that though it is in Dorset dialect, you can under-stand it. You will also notice that though it isn't sung, it sounds like bell music and it recalls hot days before there were motor cars, when Dorset villages really were remote and white lanes went up chalk hills from thatched village hamlets. No aeroplanes, no poles, no tarmac – just bells and footpaths. On weekdays the rumble of wagons and on Sundays the sound of bells and always the rustle of leaves and singing of birds and the sight of the clouds travelling over the parish. Real deep country. Mr Brown of Sherborne is going to read a bit more of 'The Two Churches' – and 'Creech' is the name of a hamlet.

> An' on the cowslip-knap at Creech,
> Below the grove o' steately beech,
> I heard two tow'rs a'cheemen clear,
> Vrom woone I went, to woone drew near,
> As they did call, by flow'ry ground,
> The bright-shod veet vrom housen round,
> A-drownen wi' their holy call,
> The goocoo an' the water-vall.
> Die off, O bells o' my dear peace,
> Ring out, O bells avore my feace,
> Vull sweet your zwells, O ding-dong bells.

I suppose I ought to say something about Barnes. He was born in 1801 in the parish of Sturminster Newton in the Blackmoor Vale of Dorset and christened a year later. His father was a small farmer. He went to a good dame's school and was later made a lawyer's clerk and when he was about eighteen he met a girl in Dorchester called Julia Miles. He saw her first climbing down from a coach in the high street. She had blue eyes and was wearing a sky-blue jacket. He mar-ried her in 1827 and she bore him six children. She died in 1852 and the rest of his life was lost without her. All his love poems are about her and he thought of her every day of his life and night after night he wrote her name – 'Julia' – at the end of the day's entry in his diary.

He was never rich. He ran a school at Mere in Wiltshire and then another in Dorchester. When he was forty-seven he was ordained a deacon and the next year became a priest. For the last twenty-four years of his life he was rector of Winterbourne Came, which is outside Dorchester. He was a mild-looking old man with a long white beard, a broad brow and a pointed head.

Those are some of the facts about the Revd William Barnes but they are not the man. There have been many English country clergymen who have written local verse; there are not many who were such true poets as Barnes. And Barnes's secret is this: so far as poetry was concerned, he was a humble craftsman. He was a man of endless activity, very keen about the origins of language and he taught himself Sanskrit and Persian and Anglo-Saxon. He was a musician and a wood engraver and an antiquarian. He regarded poetry as a relaxation at the end of a long day, like stamp collecting or fretwork.

Let us have one more bit of Barnes's craftsmanship and this time it will be one of his poems in ordinary English – or, as he called it, 'National English' as opposed to good old local English – and I shall read a bit of it, as I've got such a lovely English voice and BBC accent. And notice that not only does he use internal rhymes and echoing rhymes but he also uses alliteration in the Anglo-Saxon style.

> Or else in winding paths and lanes, along
> The timb'ry hillocks, sloping steep, we roam'd;
> Or down the dells and dingles deep we roam'd;
> Or by the bending brook's wide sweep we roam'd
> On holidays, with merry laugh or song.
>
> But now, the frozen churchyard wallings keep
> The patch of tower-shaded ground, all white,
> Where friends can find the frosted mound, all white,
> With turfy sides upswelling round, all white,
> With young oft sunder'd from the young in sleep.
>
> [from 'Shellbrook']

I said 'humble craftsmanship'. Well, *there* is the craftsmanship and the humility is in every word of Barnes's poems. He does not try to be fine or deep; he never tries to be poetical. He does not invoke his muse or attempt like Tennyson to scan the universe or like

Wordsworth to listen to the pulse of eternity. Barnes does not even describe anything so vast as the sea or the stars except to mention that they exist. No, he is content with his own parish and the nearest town. He likes a few fields and some trees and he likes to hear church bells. And he sets down what he sees and hears in his poems. And they are as though you and I were leaning on a gate looking out across the parish. Barnes is so simple and humble that that is why he was so long popular with country people. He was like them and he was of them. Here is Dorset for you, simply set down.

> Now the light o' the west is turn'd to gloom,
> An' the men be at hwome vrom ground;
> An' the bells be a zenden all dwon the Coombe
> From tower, their mwoansome sound,
> An' the wind is still,
> An' the house-dogs do bark,
> An' the rooks be a-vied to the elms high an' dark,
> An' the water do roar at mill.
>
> An' the flickeren light drough the window-peane
> Vrom the candle's dull fleame do shoot,
> An' young Jemmy the smith is a-gone down leane
> A-playen his shrill-vaiced flute.
> An' the miller's man
> Do sit down at his ease
> On the seat that is under the cluster o' trees,
> Wi' his pipe an' his cider can.
>
> [from 'Evening in the Village']

And of course there is 'Linden Lee', whose beautiful words are forgotten in Vaughan Williams's famous tune, but perhaps if we hear the first verse read in the original Dorset in which it was written it will help you to remember the poet as well as the composer:

> 'Ithin the woodlands, flow'ry gleaded,
> By the woak tree's mossy moot,
> The sheenen grass-bleades, timber sheaded,
> Now do quiver under voot;
> An' birds do whissle auver head,
> An' water's bubblen in its bed,

An' there vor me the apple tree
Do lean down low in Linden Lea.
[from 'My Orcha'd in Linden Lea']

Barnes was humble and simple but that doesn't mean to say that he was slight. His poems reach as high and deep as an oak tree. They are a part of nature.

Barnes did not describe scenes. He wrote touching love poems to his wife. And indeed, the only emotion that he ever shows in his poems is that of love.

All these quotations come from the excellent selection of Barnes's poems which has been made by Geoffrey Grigson for the Muses Library*. Most of the facts in this talk and most of the ideas are pinched from Geoffrey Grigson too. He has written an introduction that is a model of poetical appreciation.

---

* *Selected Poems of William Barnes*, ed. Geoffrey Grigson, (London: Routledge & Kegan Paul, 1950).

PUGIN: A GREAT VICTORIAN ARCHITECT

Midland and West of England Home Service
Monday 15 September 1952★
Producer: Eileen Molony for Paul Humphreys

• • •

Pugin was one of the most entertaining men of the last century. After his death, the doctors said that in the forty years of his life he had done enough work to last a man a century.

Pugin was an architect, and I am going to start with the least interesting thing about him – his buildings, and these were nearly all churches and convents. In the Midlands and the West I suppose these are his chief buildings. See if you know any of them: St Chad's Roman Catholic Cathedral in Birmingham; St Mary's Derby; St Barnabas Roman Catholic Cathedral Nottingham; St Osmund's Roman Catholic church at Salisbury; St Mary's Grange – a Gothic house he built for himself – at Salisbury; the Church of England parish church of Tubney near Abingdon in Berkshire; St Augustine's Kenilworth. His biggest buildings that I have seen are Scarisbrick Hall, Lancs; Alton Towers, Staffs; the Roman Catholic cathedral of St George's Southwark, now bombed out of recognition; the students' buildings at Maynooth, the famous college for training priests in Ireland; and the cathedral at Enniscorthy, Ireland. The two buildings Pugin himself liked best of all he built were St Giles's Cheadle and the church he built for himself with his own house beside it, St Augustine's Roman Catholic church, a flint-and-stone structure on the west cliff at Ramsgate.

★ Broadcast one day after the centenary of Pugin's death.

Now I don't think it matters very much to your liking of this great and remarkable man if you have never seen his buildings. All the same, if you do go to Cheadle or Ramsgate, have a look at his churches there. Whenever I am in Birmingham and have a little time to spare negotiating that awful and inconvenient change of stations from Birmingham New Street to Birmingham Snow Hill, I leave my luggage at Snow Hill and step across the few yards from the station to see Pugin's cathedral. It is of red brick with twin spires and it stands on a hilly site. It is not much to look at outside. But inside it fairly takes the breath away: it soars to the heavens; its long, thin pillars are like being in a mighty forest. The roof is a bit flimsy-looking – all Pugin's buildings are a bit flimsy-looking, as though he couldn't get away from the stage scenery in which he was so interested as a youth – but the flimsiness is redeemed by the brilliant colours. The stained glass glows like jewels; the great rood screen in front of the altar adds mystery to what would otherwise be a rather obvious place; the altars blaze with gilding and colour. I think Pugin liked the place very much, for he buried his second wife there. He buried his first wife in Christ Church Priory, Hampshire, but that was in the days before he became a Roman Catholic. His third wife survived him and indeed she had him buried in his own much-loved church of St Augustine, Ramsgate.

There is one more building ascribed to Pugin: it's one of the loveliest buildings in England and we all know it – the Houses of Parliament in London. I have said 'ascribed' to Pugin because I really don't think it is by Pugin at all. I am quite sure it is by the architect who was knighted for designing it, the great Sir Charles Barry. (There may be several people listening to this who remember the old King Edward School in Birmingham. Well, that was designed by Barry and it always seemed to me to be a foretaste of the Houses of Parliament he designed several years later.) People try to make out that Barry, who designed many fine Classical-style buildings that exceed in beauty many of the works of Wren, couldn't design a medieval-style building and had to call in Pugin to help him. But that is untrue. What is quite true is that Pugin helped over the details. He designed the shiny tiles made by Minton, the stained-glass enamel work made by the Birmingham firm of Hardman, the furniture and inkstands and locks and metalwork.

Pugin himself, always a truthful man, never claimed to have designed the Houses of Parliament. He liked Barry as a man and he admired his architecture. When Barry won the competition, Pugin said, 'Barry's grand plan was immeasurably superior to any that could at that time have been designed' – this was in 1836 – 'and had it been otherwise, the Commissioners' – they were the people who set the competition – 'would have killed me in a twelvemonth. No sir, Barry is the right man in the right place; what more could we wish?' And recently evidence has come to light to show that Barry did undoubtedly design almost all the Houses of Parliament.

And now we come to the most important things: Pugin as a man and as a writer and caricaturist. He was the son of a French émigré who had married a Miss Welby, known as the 'Belle' of Islington. His father was an architectural artist – he did the coloured plates of these beautiful books called the *Microcosm of London* and Rowlandson the caricaturist put in the human figures. Pugin's mother was a forbidding woman. She went to bed at nine and rose at four in the morning and rang the bell to rouse the maids. Then she rang a bell to rouse Pugin Senior's pupils, including young Pugin himself, out of bed. They were made to work before breakfast until 8.30, when they came in and bowed to Mrs Pugin. They ate in silence and bowed and went out to work until eight at night, with short intervals for meals. The only leisure allowed was between eight and ten in the evening. On Sundays Mrs Pugin took her son to hear long sermons by the celebrated Edward Irving. Old Pugin avoided going to chapel with them. He was a dear old man – very French and very humorous.

As soon as he was old enough, young Pugin seems to have shaken himself free from his mother's influence. He became very downright and unconventional. Beside his passion for the theatre, which his mother hated, he had a passion for the sea. This lasted all his life. He often made his drawings in an open boat. He would even etch on a copper plate in a choppy sea. (The motion of the boat never disturbed him.) He founded a home for destitute sailors at Ramsgate. He dressed as a sailor himself. His biographer Benjamin Ferrey tells us

He was in the habit of wearing a sailor's jacket, loose pilot trousers, jackboots and a wideawake hat. In such a costume, landing on one occasion from the Calais boat, he entered, as was his custom, a first-class railway carriage and was accosted with a 'Halloa, my man, you have mistaken, I think, your carriage.' 'By Jove,' was his reply, 'I think you are right; I thought I was in the company of gentlemen.' This cutting repartee at once called forth an apology. (The remainder of the journey was most agreeably passed in examining his portfolio filled with sketches just taken in Normandy.)

He was indeed a man who stood on his dignity and was no respecter of persons. Once Lord Radnor called on him at Salisbury when Pugin was standing in his partially built house. Lord Radnor didn't take off his hat, as the house was only half finished, and started to talk at once. Pugin looked at him in astonishment. Then he rang the bell and ordered his hat. Placing it on his head, he said, 'Now, my lord, I am ready.' He didn't mind whom he offended. His rebukes were sharp. Once a Roman Catholic bishop sent asking for designs for a new church of the following description: 'It was to be *very* large – the neighbourhood being *very* populous; it must be *very* handsome – a fine new church had been built close by; it must be *very* cheap – they were very poor, in fact had only £—; when could they expect the design?' Pugin wrote in reply, 'My dear Lord – Say *thirty shillings* more, and have a tower and a spire at once.'

So you see the sort of man Pugin was – unconventional, downright and humorous; not the sort of person who would do well for himself in a government department of the Slave State*. He was an intense individualist.

The one thing he loved more than the sea was architecture. From his earliest years he had been taught to draw it. The only style he liked was the ancient Gothic – Pointed arches, old churches, ruined abbeys and ruined castles, ancient cathedrals, and manor houses with mullioned windows. He hated anything new and anything he considered a sham. He hated workhouses and contrasted them with the almshouses attached to old abbeys for aged pilgrims. He hated Euston Station because it had a Greek portico: he said it ought to be Gothic and Pointed. He loathed St Paul's Cathedral because the flying buttresses that support its roofs are concealed from the outside: he

* Betjeman's term of abuse for the modern Welfare State.

thought this a pagan sham. He hated terrace houses in stucco or villas in stucco with little pointed windows – those graceful, cheerful little places we see in towns like Sidmouth, Cheltenham, Bath, Clifton and Brighton and admire because they are 'Regency': he liked things to be built of local materials and to be absolutely honest.

His two great principles of Pointed or 'Christian' architecture, as he called Gothic, were these: 'First, that there should be no features about a building which are not necessary for convenience, construction or propriety; second, that all ornament should consist of enrichment of the essential construction of the building.' And how forcibly and funnily he expressed himself. I must read you a bit of Pugin writing about the sham castles rich people used to build for themselves in parks and on hills and by the sea about 120 years ago:

> What absurdities, what anomalies, what utter contradictions do not the builders of modern castles perpetrate! How many portcullises which will not lower down, a drawbridge which will not draw up! – how many loopholes in turrets so small that the most diminutive sweep could not ascend them! – On one side of the house machicolated parapets, embrasures, bastions, and all the show of strong defence, and round the corner of the building a conservatory leading to the principal rooms, through which a whole company of horsemen might penetrate at one smash into the very heart of the mansion! For who would hammer against nailed portals, when he could kick his way through the greenhouse?

In his two most famous books, *True Principles* and *Contrasts*, both published at his own expense in 1841★, he illustrated his arguments with extremely funny caricatures. Mr Goodhart-Rendell has described *Contrasts* as the most entertaining book on architecture ever written. I am sure he is right. It is angry, prejudiced, eloquent and uproariously funny. Very unfair and very funny both books are. But it is impossible to describe them to you. Pugin chose the worst Classical-style buildings, in the manner of ancient Greeks and Romans, and stuck little chimney pots on them and fat, lazy ruffians lurking about in the foreground, and he pasted advertisements on them; then, with infinite care and with beautiful shading, he showed a contrasting

★ The first edition of *Contrasts* in fact appeared in 1836.

building of his beloved Middle Ages with knights in armour walking about. He loved good craftsmanship so much that he would not tolerate anything which was not made by hand.

Had he been just a funny man or just a dull pedant who liked dates and to put FSA after his name, Pugin would not have been the great man he is. And don't forget that there were architectural caricaturists as funny as Pugin before him. Pugin could not separate buildings from their use and from the people who lived in them. He loved the Middle Ages. He loved people. He lived at a time when narrow brick slums were going up beside gloomy mills where there was child slavery, before the Factory Acts were passed. He saw pale, dulled mechanics dazed by the monotony of their work, thinking only of wages and escape to ease from the grindstone. He saw belching smoke and steam trains and the growing wealth of the Midlands, the ostentation of the new rich, the worldliness of manufacturers, the heartlessness of employers, the enforced depravity of the employed. And then, away from the towns, in still quiet country where he sketched among grassy lanes the old churches of unpolluted villages, he saw the relics of the Middle Ages. He thought about his soul and how everything was under God and how machines were the Devil because they killed the joy of craftsmanship, so he idealized the Middle Ages. He did not copy them. He lived in his dream world, with the Church in charge of everything and all craftsmanship done by hand on looms, in smithies, in glass stainers', in carpenters' shops to the glory of God. He thought the Middle Ages were perfect and he wanted England to go back to his dream of what they were like.

He thought the Church of Rome was the True Church of those old days and in 1834 he joined – partly out of a desire to save his soul and partly out of disgust at modern industrialism and the laziness of many Church of England clergy in those days. At Ramsgate he lived a mediaeval life. His wife had to do his hair in a Gothic style. He ate off Gothic plates of his own design. He went to his chapel at six in the morning and said his prayers. He then worked in his library until 7.30 and then the bell tolled for morning prayers, which he said dressed in cassock and surplice. He heard mass at eight. He then worked till one when he dined very simply, without wine or beer, for quarter of an hour. Then he looked at his buildings and saw his one assistant, his son-in-law. He worked all the afternoon and then wrote letters until nine in the evening. He designed buildings till ten when he went to his chapel to say compline. Then he read theology till he went to sleep. It was a sort of RC version of his Protestant youth.

A man's religion colours his work. I only wish his buildings were as wonderful as his writings and drawings and as his own lovable, downright self. But they aren't. His colour and his detail are beautiful but he lacks that essential of all great architecture, a sense of proportion. Much of his work is a little unreal and dreamlike and not very solid, as though he was trying to bring an illuminated manuscript to life. His buildings are an escape rather than a challenge.

Pugin was a dreamer. He was shocked, as all sensitive artists were, by modern barbarism. He built himself a never-never land of the past, all colour and kindness and honest craftsmanship. He forgot the smells, disease, cruelty and injustices of the Middle Ages. He could only see modern evils. As Sir Kenneth Clark in his brilliant chapter on Pugin in *The Gothic Revival* realized, he was really a prototype of William Morris. Both invented false Middle Ages of perfection.

Pugin clung to his Church and I fear the Roman Catholic Church of those days did not think so well of Pugin as did the Church of England, to which in his later years he became increasingly friendly. Morris clung to aesthetic socialism. Both dreamed of an unreal Middle Ages. Both dearly loved what is beautifully made and honestly done. Both loved their fellow men. Both were intolerant of sham. Both were energetic and single-minded artists of great talent. Both had their enemies. Ruskin disliked Pugin. Many more than Ruskin have disliked Morris. The worst legacy that Pugin has left us is much dull copying, done in the name of 'restoration' and 'Gothic architecture' by his followers who believed the palpably untrue maxim that only Gothic is Christian architecture. And Morris has left us a legacy of dull economists. I don't know which is worse. The greatness of the two men survives in their love of the beautiful – something the vigour of Pugin's personality implants on everyone who sees his drawings or reads his books or the books written about him. I have only given you the briefest sketch in this talk of a man who set England reverberating a century ago with the church bells of his fancy. But if you can find any of his books or buildings, imbibe them and then go out into the world again, prejudiced maybe, but certainly invigorated and inspired by a man who loved God and his creatures.

ISAAC WATTS

From the series 'Sweet Songs of Zion'

Radio 4
Sunday 6 July 1975
Producer: David Winter

• • •

Hymns are the poems of the people. From 'Abide with Me' to 'Onward, Christian Soldiers', they provide us with memories of happier, more devout days of Sunday school and school assemblies, of weddings and funerals. They've given phrases to the language: 'change and decay', 'bright and beautiful', 'soft refreshing rain', 'all is safely gathered in', 'fir and foe', 'meek and mild', 'God moves in mysterious ways' and dozens of others.

Even today, when it is assumed that we've all given up religion, millions of people enjoy programmes on the radio and television that consist solely of people singing old, familiar tunes. And you can still catch milkmen and bus conductors whistling hymn tunes (especially if they happen to be West Indians).

We're starting this series on hymns and the people who wrote them with the man who's credited with being 'the father of all English hymnody' – Isaac Watts. Before him, singing hymns was regarded as a popish aberration, putting 'human words' on a par with Holy Writ. Even the Dissenters confined themselves strictly to the Psalter, albeit in a metrical version, and heavy going it was, as young Watts himself is reported to have observed to his father on the way home one Sunday afternoon from the Southampton chapel where they worshipped. 'Then give us something better, young man!' said his father, and was probably shocked to discover the following Sunday that Isaac had brought to chapel with him a brand new hymn: not a paraphrase of a Psalm but – horror of horrors! – a hymn of human composition. This is what Isaac Watts, then twenty-two, had written:

> Behold the glory of the Lamb
> Amidst the Father's throne;
> Prepare new honours for his name
> And songs before unknown.

Very prophetic, because the new honours and the songs before unknown poured from Watts's pen for the next fifty years and it is quite safe to assume that tens of millions of people this very day have been singing one or other of them.

They were very different from what had gone before – different in style, in content, in quality and, very strikingly, in cheerfulness. There was a sort of confidence and optimism about Watts, whose Calvinism was tempered with just a hint of the universalism that from his day became a feature of much Nonconformity. He had a splendid, universal vision. Just listen to one of his greatest hymns.

> Jesus shall reign where'er the sun
> Doth his successive journeys run;
> His kingdom stretch from shore to shore,
> Till moons shall wax and wane no more.

There's a rather lovely story about that hymn. When Tonga became Christian, the king of the island (George, in fact) arranged a national act of worship on Whit Sunday 1862 in the open air under the banyan trees, and it's said that many of the five thousand Tongans attending this service broke down and wept as they sang this hymn. 'Jesus shall reign' was one of Watts's 'Christian Psalms': he got around the prohibition of hymns other than those in the Psalter by asserting that all he was doing was re-expressing the psalms of David in a New Testament idiom. Indeed, the title of his collection published in 1719 is *The Psalms of David, Imitated in the Language of the New Testament*.

When Isaac Watts was born, in 1674, just three hundred years ago, his father, who was a deacon of their chapel, was in prison for his religious beliefs. Isaac himself was barred from Oxford and Cambridge and instead went to what was called a 'Dissenting Academy' in Stoke Newington, London. So you see, his Protestant 'dissent', his own religious beliefs, cost him a great deal. One of his hymns reflects this experience – one shared, of course, at different times in our history, by almost all the branches of the Church in Britain – 'I'm Not Ashamed to Own my Lord':

> I'm not ashamed to own my Lord,
> Or to defend his cause,
> Maintain the honour of his word,
> The glory of his cross.

Watts was a pioneer in another field too: poems and songs for children. He compiled a book of *Divine and Moral Songs for the Use of Children*, which included such immortal advice as this:

> Let dogs delight to bark and bite
> For God hath made them so;
> Let bears and lions growl and fight,
> For 'tis their nature too.

And in the same collection was another poem that enjoyed huge popularity, and I expect you'll recognize the opening lines:

> How doth the little busy bee
> Improve each shining hour . . .

It's a far cry from that to great national occasions like Remembrance Day at the Cenotaph but Watts manages to bridge the gap. He wrote a hymn that has almost acquired national-anthem status – 'O God [or as *he* wrote, Our God], Our Help in Ages Past':

> O God, our help in ages past,
> Our hope for years to come,
> Our shelter from the stormy blast,
> And our eternal home.

Interesting, isn't it, that at a festival of remembrance we sing 'They fly forgotten, as a dream / Dies at the opening day' – but hymn-singing is full of paradoxes like that.

Probably Watts's greatest hymn, and some people think the greatest hymn ever written, is 'When I Survey the Wondrous Cross'. Like many Calvinists, Watts was fascinated by the Cross and the whole concept of 'atonement'. But here he enlarges the vision – not only the love of Christ but our love in response, as broad as 'the whole realm of nature'.

Incidentally, in the first published version of this hymn, in 1707, the opening lines were slightly different:

> When I survey the wondrous Cross
> Where the young Prince of Glory died . . .

I wonder if our slightly more pedantic version ('On which the Prince of Glory died') is *really* an improvement?

> When I survey the wondrous Cross
> On which the Prince of Glory died,
> My richest gain I count but loss,
> And pour contempt on all my pride.

Dr Watts became minister of the renowned Independent Chapel in Mark Lane, London, but ill health forced him to give this up when he was only thirty-eight and for the rest of his life – thirty-six years in fact – he was the guest of Sir Thomas and Lady Abney in their big house at Stoke Newington. The site of the house became a huge public cemetery but Watts himself was buried in the Puritan burial ground, Bunhill Fields, just north of the City of London, and later on a monument was raised to this notable Dissenter in that shrine of the Establishment, Westminster Abbey.

As with many of his contemporaries, death was a frequent theme in his hymns – death and the fleeting nature of life and the continuity of praise in heaven:

> I'll praise my Maker while I've breath,
> And when my voice is lost in death,
> Praise shall employ my nobler powers;
> My days of praise shall ne'er be past,
> While life, and thought, and being last,
> Or immortality endures.

I hope heaven matches Watts's expectations of it, which were sublime.

Let's end with one of his 'heaven' hymns, the best of them probably: 'There is a Land of Pure Delight'.

> There is a land of pure delight,
> Where Saints immortal reign;
> Infinite day excludes the night,
> And pleasures banish pain.

THE COMFORT OF CHURCHES

HOW TO LOOK AT A CHURCH

West of England Programme
Wednesday 31 August 1938
Producer: J. C. Pennethorne Hughes

• • •

There's something much kinder about a house that has been lived in for generations than a brand-new one. Apart from the fact that, ten to one, an old house is better built than a new one, it's part of England, not a bright red pimple freshly risen on its surface. An old house reflects the generations that have lived in it – your mother's taste for frills and silk lampshades, your grandmother's passion for framed watercolours, your great-grandmother's needlework and heavy, well-made furniture. It may be a bit inconvenient and muddled but it is human.

But of all the old houses of England, the oldest and most interesting are the houses of God – the churches. Better still, they are open to the public, or they ought to be. Each generation has contributed to the adornment of the old church and the result isn't a museum of showpieces but a living thing, still in use. Old glass still diffuses the daylight on the latest hats as softly as it did on the wigs of the eighteenth century or the woollen hose of the people of the Middle Ages. Elizabethan silver is still used for the sacrament. And from the tower, a bell cast soon after the Wars of the Roses lends its note to the peal that ripples over the meadows and threads its way under the drone of aeroplanes. The magniloquent epitaph and well-carved bust of some dead squire look down in breathing marble from the walls and the churchyard is a criss-cross of slanting old stones. Here lies the England we are all beginning to wish we knew, as the roar of the machine gets louder and the suburbs creep from London to Land's End.

Nine out of every ten churches in England have been terribly mutilated by the Victorians. And I'm afraid that it's no good expecting to find much merit in Victorian work: sticky pitch-pine pews; church furnishers' horrors in the way of reading desks and stalls; cumbrous altar frontals; anaemic stained glass; and sharp, unyielding new-cut stone. The Victorians were downright ugly and had the courage of their ugliness but the present generation has not improved things: 'refained' unstained oak, powder-blue hangings and tidy little children's corners; gimcrack devotional objects; theatrical floodlighting; more stained glass, but now of a fearful sort; colour schemes thought out by 'artistic' religious people.

Yet under this mere surface decoration, the old church struggles on. Your great-great-grandfather would recognize it. The proportions are probably the same: some windows, some carving, some tombs, some woodwork would remind him of the place he knew, before he closed his eyes in the big box pew and slumbered away the parson's elevating sermon.

Looking at churches is really learning to look beyond the Victorians. Church architecture has been made incredibly boring by the antiquarians. In their anxiety to find a Norman window or to open up an Early English piscina, in their insistence on the difference between the varying modes of Gothic architecture, they've omitted to see the church as a whole. They've turned what should be the enjoyment of part of England's beauty into a wretched wrangle over mediaeval dates. Forget that old bore who lectured to you at school on Norman fonts; forget those long hours trying to distinguish between Early English and Decorated. I'll give you a rough-and-ready rule for all this. There's not enough Saxon architecture for you to bother about. Norman architecture, which went on until about 1100, consisted of round-headed arches, rounder, stubby columns and thick walls: it was a brave attempt to copy the architecture of the ancients. 'Gothic' architecture, which came along after the Norman, cannot be divided accurately into styles. You may take it that the more pointed an arch is, the nearer it is to the earliest Gothic; it gradually grew wider and flatter until by Henry VII's reign, the arches over the windows and arcades had become almost flat. And anyhow, much of the Gothic you see will be Victorian.

Don't imagine, as all the guidebooks do, that churches ceased to be worth looking at after the reign of Henry VII. Some of the most beautiful were built by Wren and the Dances and local Renaissance architects in the seventeenth and eighteenth and early nineteenth centuries. In those days too, our greatest sculptors and artists did most of their work for memorials in churches. Today that sort of thing is generally left to commercial-minded monumental masons. They in turn find it cheaper to buy tombstones already carved from Italy – to which they add a name in hideous lettering – than to use good local stone. Because of this, there's hardly a churchyard in England that hasn't during the last fifty years been defaced by staring white monuments in Italian marble.

Let us visit the church of Hagworthy St Philip. There isn't a church nor such a place but we'll invent one that stands for the typical English village church.

The guidebooks says, 'Hagworthy St Philip: Norm. with Perp additions. Note interesting E.E. pisc.' This gives you no idea of what Hagworthy church is like.

You'll have to use your eyes and your common sense. The country around Hagworthy is limestone of that grey, yellowy quality that is quarried in the Cotswolds and in parts of the Midlands – what few old cottages have been allowed to survive by 'progressive' local councils are built in it. So is the church. No one but a fool visits a church without looking carefully at the exterior. Hagworthy church is all of that yellowy-grey limestone but the chancel at the east end seems to be cleaner cut and sharper than the rest. The windows in it are full of elaborate tracery but the stonework is shallow and less delicately finished than that in the windows of the nave or body of the church. In fact it looks a little too good to be true. You may therefore conclude that the chancel is Victorian, especially since the roof is covered with bright red tiles and steeply pitched. This roof contrasts with that of the nave, which is almost flat and covered with lead.

The tower has some tiny windows with round heads to them – mere slits, and survivals of the days when glass was difficult to procure. These windows are Norman. Then take a look at the windows of the nave. You see that in the upper portions of some of them there are pieces of glass that have a feathery silver quality on the outside? These are bits of mediaeval stained glass. Now look at the stained glass on those Victorian chancel windows. They have no silver featheriness. The colour shows through on the outside. This spells Victorian or modern glass. You've only got to go inside to see how right you were. The little bits of mediaeval glass glow like jewels. They diffuse the light but they don't throw coloured light as Victorian glass does. The Victorian glass is thinner and more garish; it doesn't diffuse the light but blocks it out altogether. Mediaeval glass usually had a lot of white* in it; Victorian glass usually has none.

One more thing to notice before you go into Hagworthy church: all the best old tombstones – those covered with cherubs and urns – are on the south side of the church. On the north side, the entrance door is blocked and there are only a few hideous new white-marble tombs. This is because a legend grew up in mediaeval times that the Devil lived on the north side of the church. The north door was locked so that he couldn't get in and generally only disgraced people were buried in the shadow of the church.

Let us go in by the south door. There's some Norman zigzag carving over its round arch. When the door is open, the familiar smell of wet earth, hassocks and old hymn books reaches one. Hagworthy is fortunate in having only its chancel spoiled by the Victorians.

The first things you notice when you enter an old church are the walls. At the best, they are plastered and covered with a limewash beneath which, here and there, are the remains of mediaeval wall painting: the wing of an angel, the halo of a saint or the fearsome form of a devil carrying off a shrieking soul to hell. The Victorians liked to pull the plaster off the walls inside churches and thereby destroyed hundreds of hidden wall paintings. You'll notice this has been done in the chancel of Hagworthy. How dark, dull and characterless that chancel appears, contrasted with the white, light-reflecting walls of the nave.

Now notice the woodwork. Hagworthy is lucky. There is an old west gallery where the choir used to climb up with its old instruments of fiddles, serpent and flute. The old choir has been replaced by a

* Clear glass.

wheezy organ, played sincerely, if not accurately, by the vicar's wife. But the old gallery's still there. The new choir sits in the hideous chancel – a Victorian innovation. And then in odd corners there are still some of the old box pews with doors and even a fireplace, and baize lining to the seat backs and watered-silk cushions. Box pews are generally of pine and sometimes painted. Earlier pews are usually of oak and are no more than benches, often elaborately carved.

The pulpit may be a fine piece of Elizabethan woodwork with a sounding board above it and carved panels. All such woodwork exists at Hagworthy – in the nave. But in the Victorian chancel there are pitch-pine stalls for the choir and an oak reading desk for the rector, and it's hard to say which is uglier.

Then have a look at the monuments on the walls – all of them excellent up until the date of 1840 when they tail off and the lettering becomes ugly and the design is heavy. On the walls you'll be able to trace the rise and fall of the big family of Hagworthy: first the simple brass let into the floor, then the kneeling figures gaily painted of the Jacobean monument, then that disconsolate widow of Queen Anne's reign weeping among cherubs, then that chaste female of the reign of George III leaning elegantly on a half-draped urn, then the Victorian tablet to the squire's son who died in the Crimea, then the chancel, a hideous memorial to the good squire himself, and finally the ugly little brass tablet on the wall to the last of the squire's race to live in Hagworthy.

And here we'll leave Hagworthy and return to a general rule.

If there's a slight smell of incense and *The English Hymnal*★ is used and the church is open and easy to get into; if the altar has many candles on it and a carved and painted wood at the back called a reredos and a glowing frontal, then the church is 'High'.

If there are only two candles and a brass cross on the altar and a couple of vases of flowers and a non-committal frontal, then the church is 'Broad' or what is termed 'ordinary'.

If there is a bare table at the east end with an alms dish on it and a chair at the north side and a little reading stand on the table, then the church is 'Low'. Low churches are often locked.

★ First published in 1906 as an alternative to the sentimentality of Victorian hymns.

I've not had time to mention the many other things to be found in a church: the well-carved or painted royal arms, symbols of the union of Church and State; the commandments board and paintings of Moses and Aaron; the old organ cases; scratch dials, rewards of the mediaeval time system; ringers' rhymes; epitaphs; hourglasses; roofs; clerestories; and old brasses.

The old churches of England are the story of England. They alone remain islands of calm in the seething roar of what we now call civilization. They are not backwaters – or they shouldn't be if the clergy and people love them – but strongholds. I only hope I've shown you in this talk that a church is not just an old building which interests pedantic old brass-rubbers but a living building with history written all over it – and history that, with very little practice, becomes easy and fascinating reading.

ST PROTUS AND ST HYACINTH, BLISLAND, CORNWALL

From the series 'Three in Hand'

West of England Home Service
Wednesday 21 July 1948
Producer: Gilbert Phelps

• • •

Down what lanes, across how many farmyards, resting in how many valleys, topping what hills and suddenly appearing round the corners of what ancient city streets are the churches of England? The many pinnacles in Somerset, of rough granite from the moors in Devon and Cornwall, of slate by the sea coasts, brushed with lichen, spotted with saffron, their rings of five and six bells pouring music among the windy elm trees as they have poured their sound for centuries, still they stand, the towers and spires of the West.

They are still there as in the days when villagers still came to church and when footpaths were still left by farmers. There are about twenty thousand churches in England and of these quite a half are ancient. They are more in number than one could see in a lifetime. I have seen about five thousand and I hope I shall be spared to see as many more.

I know no greater pleasure than church-crawling. You never know what you are going to find: an eccentric incumbent, a derelict church, a live church, an ugly or a lovely one, or just a church. And even if it's 'just a church', there is always something about it for those who have eyes and ears and imagination.

Oh, if you have not taken to it yet, let me advise the hobby of church-crawling! It is the richest of pleasures: it leads you to the remotest and quietest country, it introduces you to the history of

England in stone and wood and glass, which is always truer than what you read in books. You meet all sorts of people on your travels. You learn to know where to find the key: to look under the mat, in the lantern of the porch, under the porch roof, behind the noticeboard, or to enquire at the nearest cottage – or perhaps it will mean a long bicycle ride to the parsonage.

In the days when food was plentiful, what teas I have enjoyed on rectory and vicarage lawns, what talks in book-lined studies, what friends I have made – and all because of church-crawling.

Some learn their faith from books, some from relations, some (a very few) learn it at school. I learned mine from church-crawling. Indeed it was through looking at churches that I came to believe in the reason why churches were built and why, despite neglect and contempt, innovation and business bishops, they still survive and continue to grow and prosper, especially in our industrial towns.

I'm afraid I'm like Sir Walter Scott (but not so good a writer): I take a long time getting to the point. This series of talks is about three West Country churches and this one is about Blisland in Cornwall. I must remember that.

But I'm not ready to start yet. You must have the instruments of the church-crawler. The first of these is a map. A one-inch Ordnance map: no others will do. That map tells you whether the church has a tower or spire, for it is marked with a cross and black square if it's a tower, a black circle if it's a spire. Then you can generally assume that a country church is old, even if it has no tower or spire, if the map shows the dotted lines of footpaths leading to it.

The next thing you need is an eye. Please notice that. An *eye*. Not knowledge of style of architectures, of squinches, squints, piscinae, aumbries and all the other jargon of the church guidebooks. Look at the church for what it is: a place of worship and a piece of architecture combined. You will read much nonsense in many guidebooks. They will tell you that something is in the 'debased' style, meaning that it was built in the sixteenth, seventeenth or eighteenth centuries. But it does not matter when it was built or whether it is 'pure' or 'debased'. What does matter is: do you like the look of it yourself? Instead of bothering about dates and what the guidebooks say is old, use your own eyes. Something is not beautiful simply because it is old.

But it is more likely to be than not, for there is no doubt that most of what is modern, especially in the way of church furniture, is ugly. We have emerged out of civilization into barbarism, so naturally we have a few barbaric objects to commemorate the times we live in – the gimcrack rubbish in 'children's corners'. (I always remember that story of a caustic old clergyman in Oxford who was asked what he thought was the best furnishing for a children's corner. 'A birch rod,' he replied.) Then there is that awful combination of unstained oak and powder-blue hangings so popular for side altars. There are the hideous floodlighting schemes, the mutton-fisted electric-light fixtures. Ideally, no old church should have electric lights at all: their glare is too harsh for the delicate texture of an old building. Candles are the best light of all or, failing that, oil lamps; and if it must be electric lights, as many bulbs as possible of the lowest power possible.

And now for Blisland. Of all the country churches of the West I have seen, I think it is the most beautiful. I was a boy when I first saw it, thirty or more years ago. I shall never forget that first visit – bicycling to the inland and unvisited parts of Cornwall from my home by the sea. The trees at home were few and thin, sliced and leaning away from the fierce Atlantic gales. The walls of the high Cornish hedges were made of slate stuffed in between with fern and stonecrop and the pulpy green triangles of mesembryanthemum, sea vegetation of a windy sea-coast country. On a morning after a storm, you might find the blown yellow spume from Atlantic rollers lying trembling in the wind on inland fields. Then, as huge hill followed huge hill and I sweated as I pushed my bicycle up and heart in mouth went swirling down into the next valley, the hedges became higher, the lanes ran down ravines, the plants seemed lusher, the thin Cornish elms seemed bigger and the slate houses and slate hedges gave place to granite ones. I was on the edge of Bodmin Moor, that sweet brown home of Celtic saints, that haunted, thrilling land so full of ghosts of ancient peoples whose hut circles, beehive dwellings and burial mounds jut out above the ling and heather. Great wooded valleys, white below the tree trunks with wood anemones or blue with bluebells, form a border fence on this, the western side of Bodmin Moor.

Perched on the hill above the wood stands Blisland village. It has not one ugly building in it and what is unusual in Cornwall, the houses are round a green. Between the lichen-crusted trunks of elm and ash that grow on the green, you can see everywhere the beautiful silver-grey moorland granite. It is used for windows, for chimney stacks, for walls. One old house has gable ends (sixteenth or seventeenth century, I should think) carved in it, which curl round like Swiss rolls. The church is down a steep slope of a graveyard, past slate headstones, and looks over the treetops of a deep and elmy valley and away and away to the west where, like a silver shield, the Atlantic sometimes shines in the sun. An opening in the churchyard circle shows a fuschia hedge and the vicarage front door beyond. The tower is square and weathered and made of enormous blocks of this moorland granite, each block as big as a chest of drawers. However did those old masons haul them up to the topmost stages? When I first saw it, the tower was stuffed with moss and with plants that had rooted there between the great stones. But lately it has been most vilely repointed in hard straight lines with cement. And the church itself, which seems to lean this way and that, throws out chapels and aisles in all directions. It hangs on the hillside, spotted with lichens that have even softened the slates of its roof. Granite forms the tracery of its windows; a granite holy-water stoup meets you in the porch.

The whitewashed porch, the flapping notices, the door! That first thrill of turning the handle of the door of a church never seen before, or a church dearly loved and visited again and again like Blisland – who but the confirmed church-crawler knows it?

The greatest living church architect, Mr J. N. Comper, says a church should bring you to your knees when first you enter it. Such a church is Blisland. For there, before me as I open the door, is the blue-grey granite arcade, that hardest of stones to carve. One column slopes outwards as though it was going to tumble down the hill and its carved wooden beam is fixed between it and the south wall to stop it falling. The floor is of blue slate and pale stone. Old carved benches of dark oak and a few chairs are the seating. The walls are white, the sun streams in through a clear west window, and there – glory of glories! – right across the whole eastern end of the church is a richly painted screen. It is of wood. The panels at its base are red and green. Wooden columns highly coloured, twisted like barley sugar, burst into gilded tracery and fountain out to hold a panelled rood loft.

There are steps in the wall to reach it. Our Lord and His Mother and St John, who form the rood, are over the centre of the screen. My eyes look up and there is the irregular old Cornish roof, shaped like the inside of an upturned ship, all its ribs richly carved, the carving shown up by white plaster panels. These old roofs, beautifully restored, are to be seen throughout the whole church, stretching away beyond the cross, down the aisles. I venture in a little further. There, through this rich screen, I can mark the blazing gold of the altars and the mediaeval-style glass, some of the earliest work of Comper. And here beside me in the nave is a pulpit shaped like a wineglass, in the Georgian style and encrusted with cherubs and fruit carved in wood.

I think I said when I started this talk that all you needed was an eye to see, not a knowledge of dates and history. That screen, the glory of this church, the golden altars, the stained glass and the pulpit are comparatively new. They were designed by F. C. Eden in 1897 and he died only a year or two ago. Mr Eden had a vision of this old Cornish church as it was in mediaeval times. He did not do all the mediaeval things he might have done. He did not paint the walls with pictures of angels, saints and devils in amber and red and he left the western windows clear that people in this reading age might see their books. He put in a Georgian pulpit. He centred everything on the altar, to which the screen is, as it were, a golden, red and green veil to the holiest mystery behind it.

Now what does it matter about dates and styles in Blisland church? There is Norman work in it and there is fifteenth- and sixteenth-century work and there is sensitivity and beautiful modern work. But chiefly it is a living church whose beauty makes you gasp, whose silence brings you to your knees, even if you kneel on the hard stone and slate of the floor, worn smooth by generations of worshippers.

The valley below the church was hot and warm when first I saw this granite-cool interior. Valerian sprouted on the vicarage wall. A castor-oil tree traced its leaves against a western window. Grasshoppers and birds chirruped. St Protus and St Hyacinth, patron saints of Blisland church, pray for me! Often in a bus or train I call to mind your lovely church, the stillness of that Cornish valley and the first really beautiful work of man that my boyhood vividly remembers.

ST JOHN THE BAPTIST, MILDENHALL, WILTSHIRE

From the series 'Three in Hand'

West of England Home Service
Wednesday 28 July 1948
Producer: Gilbert Phelps

• • •

Let me ask you – unless you are so foolish as to be listening to this while driving a motor car – let me ask you to shut your eyes. Feel, under your feet, an old stone floor as scrubbed and uneven as that of a farmhouse kitchen. Sniff the faint damp smell of wet earth, sweating stone, peeling plaster, dank paper, lavender, sweet william, hassocks, cassocks, candle grease and hay – all those faint old perfumes of the past that come when one opens the leaves of a forgotten leather-bound book – when one opens the leaves and sniffs. With your eyes still shut, remember that you are standing, in imagination, in the nave of a country church, a country church that neither the Victorians nor our own generation has touched.

There is only one in Cornwall: Launcells. In Devon I can think of West Ogwell, Branscombe, Molland. In Somerset there are Holcombe, Cameley, Swell, Sutton Mallet, Babington and a few more. In Dorset there are Easton on Portland, Winterbourne Thompson. And in Wiltshire there are Inglesham and Mildenhall (pronounced 'Minal'). Ah, 'Minal'! I shall be coming to that later. And you may be able to tell me of yet other un-'restored' churches of the West.

But for the moment, think yourself back into this dream church, which is not unlike 'Minal'. The five bells have been rung down and the treble only is going. Through the old clear glass of the window, the last villagers are seen streaming along under the elms, past the limestone headstones sculptured with cherubs, hourglasses and skulls and in at the church door. The box pews are filling. They are so high that only the bonneted heads of the women and bowed silver locks of the men may be seen above them. Inside, the high boxes are lined with red or green or blue baize. Outside they are painted white. One extra big one is the squire's pew in a special aisle all to itself. It was once the family chapel where mass was said for the souls of the squire's ancestors: this extra big pew has a fireplace. It is still empty and the service will not begin until the squire and his lady arrive.

Look about the church for a moment while we await their arrival. White ceilings are over the chancel and nave. The walls are of plaster, washed a pale pink or white and cream, and below the limewash you can still faintly see the traces of mediaeval wall paintings of saints and devils with which the plaster was originally decorated. Over the chancel arch where once hung Our Lord and Our Lady and St John is a huge royal arms symbolizing the alliance of Church and State.

Noble marble slabs are on the walls — memorials to dead squires — and the effect of their carving and colour is enhanced by a wide black border painted on the plaster surface around each monument. Some of the upper lights of the clear glass windows retain pieces of old stained glass, out of reach of the hammers of Puritan reformers who delighted in smashing stained glass because they thought it a symbol of popery. You can often tell old stained glass, by the way, from the outside. It is all spotted and pitted with a silvery carving that looks like lichen. And it is thick.

Beside the chancel arch is a huge three-decker pulpit approached by a flight of steps. Over the pulpit hangs a sounding board. How easily it looks as though it might come crashing down on the parson's head and silence him for ever. By the pulpit desk is an hourglass in an iron stand to time the service and below the pulpit is yet another pulpit, from which the prayers and lessons will be read before the minister mounts, in his black gown and white tabs, to preach. And below the second pulpit is a third where sits the parish clerk, who loudly says 'Amen' and leads the choir off in the metrical psalms, for this is the time before hymnbooks came into general use.

A certain amount of coughing and throat-clearing in the chancel indicates the presence of the rector. That is where he dons his black gown and if it is Sacrament Sunday (four times a year they have a communion service) he changes into a white surplice and black scarf.

On such special Sundays as these when all the village drains the chalice of the grapes of God in recognition of an all-serving Creator who makes the corn to grow, the birds to sing, the cows to give milk, who gives us the sweet air we breathe in this old church – on such Sacrament Sundays as these, the altar and its fine linen cloth will be decked with flagons, cup and patten and two candlesticks all of gleaming Georgian silver bright against the dark commandment boards and richer than the rich velvet with which the altar's sides and front are draped.

Ah! There they come, the squire and his lady, in through the special gate into the churchyard from the park. There is some turning and wheezing behind us and we see high up in a gallery in the west of the church six rustics with a variety of wind instruments: a bassoon, a serpent, two oboes, a clarinet and a pitch pipe. They are the village choir and they marked the melody for the psalms before the days of organs and harmoniums.

Now the service will begin and I know no better description of it than that which the Devon poet N. T. Carrington published in 1830 in his poem 'My Native Village':

> Ah, let me enter, once again, the pew
> Where the child nodded as the sermon grew;
> Scene of soft slumbers! I remember now
> The chiding finger, and the frowning brow
> Of stern reprovers, when the ardent June
> Flung through the glowing aisles the drowsy noon
>
> .   .   .   .   .
>
> Till, closed the learn'd harangue, with solemn look
> Arose the chaunter of the sacred book –
> The parish clerk (death-silenced) far-famed then
> And justly, for his long and loud – Amen!
> Rich was his tone, and his exulting eye
> Glanced to the ready choir, enthroned on high,
> Nor glanced in vain; the simple-hearted throng
> Lifted their voices, and dissolved in song;
> Till in one tide deep rolling, full and free
> Rung through the echoing pile, old England's psalmody.

How are the mighty fallen! It pains me to say that in all England there are probably hardly more than a hundred churches that have survived the tampering of the last ninety years. We talk of our churches as 'old' but they are mainly Victorian – at any rate in their furniture. The west galleries were cut down. The old choir was dismissed and went disgruntled off to chapel or to form a village band or to appear self-consciously and surpliced in the chancel. That chancel was blocked by an organ or harmonium, its width was cluttered up with choir stalls, the pulpit was removed, the plaster taken off the walls, the ceiling stripped, the high pews chopped down, the clear windows filled with coloured glass, the old floor paved with slippery and shiny brown tiles. All the texture and atmosphere of the past was gone, to be replaced by a sticky, grassy, dark hardness that was wrongly, if piously, thought to be mediaeval.

Of all the churches that remain almost untouched by the Victorians, the loveliest I know is 'Minal', near Marlborough. It stands in the Kennet water meadows, a simple four-square affair – three-storey tower, nave, aisles either side and a chancel.

But when you approach it you begin to see signs of the past – clear glass panes, patched and flaking outside walls looking like an old watercolour. And then the inside! You walk straight into a Jane Austen novel – into a forest of the most magnificent oak joinery, an ocean of box pews stretching shoulder high all over the chancel. Each is carved with decorations in a Strawberry Hill Gothic manner. The doors and sides of the pews take a graceful curve either side of the font and another curve above them is made by the elegant west gallery. Norman pillars just raise their sculptured heads above the woodwork of the aisles. Two huge pulpits stand one each side of the chancel arch. The old stone floors remain, the long cream-washed walls, the stone arch moulding picked out subtly in white to form a pale contrast. The chancel, as it should be, is richest of all: panelled, with elaborately carved pews for the squarson and his family, a carved canopy, black and purple curtain over the board behind the altar, delicate carved communion rails such as an admirer of Chippendale-style furniture would pay hundreds for. Even the red leather kneelers at these rails and the scarlet service books are the same date: 1816. For there it is, written in gold letters on shields that look down from the corbels of the nave roof: 'This church deeply in decay has been all but rebuilded generously and piously at their own expense by . . .' and then follow in six pairs the names of the churchwardens, who were probably rich sheep farmers of the downs who loved their church.

It is not simply that it is an old building that makes this church so beautiful (there are thousands of old churches); it is that it contains all its Georgian fittings. Though the date is 1816, the style and quality of workmanship is that of fifty years earlier. I believe the designer was one of the Pinch family, who must also have built the cross-shaped village school with its octagonal Gothic-style tower in the centre and who designed Hungerford church and later did some churches and houses in Bath. Whoever he was, he was an artist.

Through the clear-glass windows you can see the Kennet meadows, the brick-and-thatched cottages of the village and, to the south, the chalky green cliff fringed by overhanging beeches of Savernake Forest★. The rector before this one (he was the squarson – squire and parson) preserved eighteenth-century tradition in a way I have seen nowhere else. He talked in the chancel and his scarf and surplice hung over the communion rails during the week. One pulpit he used for the service and crossed to the other for the sermon. Grand and reposeful those sermons were in the oil lamplight (now, alas, replaced by gas) as one sat penned up in a box pew and saw his fine eighteenth-century figure towering above one in the tall pulpit. He was a great man, loved in the neighbourhood – and so no doubt is his successor, but I have never 'sat under him' as the old-fashioned phrase of sermon-tasters goes. My association with Marlborough has never afforded me that pleasure.

Mildenhall is a patriarchal church. It is the embodiment of the Church of England by law established, the still heart of England, as haunting to my memory as the tinkle of sheep bells on the Wiltshire Downs. It puts me in mind of Thomas Hardy's poem 'Afternoon Service at Mellstock', which we might call 'Afternoon Service at Mildenhall'†:

★ Pronounced 'Savernack'.

† The text of this talk, as published in *First and Last Loves*, ends instead with Betjeman being put in mind of Jane Taylor's poem 'The Squire's Pew', contained in *Essays in Rhyme on Morals and Manners*, 1840.

ST JOHN THE BAPTIST, MILDENHALL, WILTSHIRE

On afternoons of drowsy calm
We stood in the panelled pew
Singing one-voiced a Tate and Brady psalm
To the tune of 'Cambridge New'.

We watched the elms, we watched the rooks,
The clouds upon the breeze,
Between the whiles of glancing at our books
And swaying like the trees.

So mindless were those outpourings! –
Though I am not aware
That I have gained by subtle thought on things
Since we stood psalming there.

ST MARK'S, SWINDON, WILTSHIRE[*]

From the series 'Three in Hand'

West of England Home Service
Wednesday 4 August 1948
Producer: Gilbert Phelps

• • •

The train draws into the outskirts of a big town. There they are, pricking the skyline above suburban chimney pots, the spires and towers of Victorian churches. Clean-looking in seaside towns, smoke-blackened in industrial ones. Sometimes no spire or tower at all but a red-brick affair with a huge roof, built in the 1880s, bombed in the 1940s. Tinkle-tinkle in the early morning, the little billcote at the west end calls the faithful few to a weekday service – to the dark but half-repaired interior of a chapel of ease. One-two-three! Four-five-six! Over the housetops rings that lush, sweet-toned peal from St Luke's or St Mark's or St Michael and all Angels – the favourite saints' names for Victorian churches. One-two-three! Four-five-six! Softly the organist starts the voluntary; bright gleams the gas on tiles and shiny pews; ruby red and topaz and blue stained-glass windows interrupt an evening twilight; and when the bells are down the surpliced choir moves into the chancel to the strains of Ellerton's 'The Day-ay Thou Gavest, Lord, is Ended'.[†]

So were the Victorian churches of our youth. So are they today except that some have, alas, been floodlit and some are bombed –

---

[*] According to the current rector of Swindon New Town, David McConkey, St Mark's approached Betjeman to write its centennial history in 1945 but there is apparently no evidence to confirm that what later appeared was by his hand.

[†] Betjeman attributed this hymn to Sir Joseph Barnby (1838–96), a professional musician who strongly defended his right to compose hymns in a contemporary style.

forming far more picturesque ruins than many an older building – and almost all are despised as architecture except by the discriminating few, among whom are you who listen to me tonight. For who, who doesn't know it, wants to hear of St Mark's Swindon? Swindon is no beauty spot. St Mark's is not even the old parish church. It is not even an outstanding example, as Victorian churches go. But it is a famous church and a live one. I have chosen it because it calls to mind two things about English churches that I have not yet mentioned: Victorian architecture and parish life.

So forgive me for a moment while I take you on a church crawl round other Victorian churches of the West. Everybody is so busy running down the Victorians or laughing at them that this is a chance to speak up in their favour. 'Ho! Ho!' says the vicar when I go to get the key. 'You can't want to see *our* church. It's a Victorian monstrosity, my dear fellow,' and he gives me a look that suggests that I really want the key in order to burgle the offertory box. 'But I think your church is *beautiful*,' I say. And he thinks I'm mad. Ah, vicars who despise Victorian churches, churchwardens with 'artistic' leanings, advisory boards and art critics: listen a while to the praise of some West Country Victorians, and then we'll go back to Swindon and St Mark's.

Let's admit straight away that when they were restoring old buildings even the greatest Victorian architects were arrogant, heavy-handed and insensitive to all but some phase of Gothic architecture of which they approved. Cornish people will not willingly forgive Mr J. P. St Aubyn for his workmanlike but hideous 'restoration' of most Cornish churches. His signature tune is an iron foot-scraper by the porch. If you see that foot-scraper, you know J. P. St Aubyn has been at the church and there will not be much that's old left inside the building.

But when they were starting from scratch, Victorian church architects were often as original and creative and as beautiful as any who have built before or since them. George Edmund Street, that indefatigable bearded genius who died in 1881 from overwork on building the law courts of London – George Edmund Street was a brilliant artist, a scholarly and entertaining writer and the inspiring master of William Morris, Philip Webb, Norman Shaw and J. D. Sedding. Life in his office was fun. One of his pupils had a stutter and could only sing without stuttering and so Morris and Webb and Shaw used to talk to him in Gregorian plainsong through rolled-up tubes of drawing paper. George Edmund Street designed St John's Torquay in 1867, for which Burne-Jones later did some pictures. He designed Holy Trinity Barnstaple and All Saints Clifton and in 1874 the superb church of Kingston in Dorset, which sits so stately on a hill slope and gleams with Purbeck marble.

All Street's churches are built on rigid principles. These are they: plenty of light from the west so that people can see their books; local materials; no screen; the altar visible from all parts of the church; and every detail down to the door hinges specially designed and very practical. One of his last works was the splendid nave of Bristol Cathedral. Then Street's pupil J. D. Sedding designed that noble clean and soaring church of All Saints Falmouth in 1887.*

Perhaps the most amazing church in Devon was that designed by Butterfield at Yealmpton in 1850 — a mass of local marbles like that original font he made for Ottery St Mary. Other great Victorian churches of the West are Truro Cathedral and St Stephen's Bournemouth by J. L. Pearson — tall buildings these, with infinite vistas of vaulted arches cutting vaulted arches. Pearson was a vista man — vistas and variety. And I have always had a weakness for that late-Victorian church St David's at Exeter by W. D. Caroë. A pale green building it is, with all sorts of funny quirks in the way of stone tracery and woodwork and metal — a sort of ecclesiastical vision of the old Deller's Café of Exeter.

Then there are Victorian churches that later architects have made more beautiful, like All Saints Clevedon and Wimborne St Giles in Dorset. One more I must mention before I move on to St Mark's is an Edwardian affair built for Lord Beauchamp by A. Randall Wells — the new church of Kempley in Gloucestershire. It is a sturdy little thing in stone with an extraordinary and enormous west window whose tracery is just a large diamond pattern in stone. This place inside is a miniature cathedral of the Arts and Crafts movement: local

* The original text continued, 'His brother Edmund, I think it was, who designed the strange beautiful church at Shaldon,' but this makes no sense and was removed in a later printed version of the talk.

labour was employed on it. Edward Burnsley, the Cotswold cabinet-maker, made the lectern, that fine craftsman Ernest Garrison made the candlesticks and the last surviving carver of figureheads for the old clippers carved the figures of Our Lord, St Mary and St John on the beam. The woodwork itself in the church was painted by villagers in vermilion, ruby, golden ochre, yellow, chrome green and blue. From Yealmpton to Kempley, these churches of another generation are arresting in the extreme. They are not copies of mediaeval: they are thinking in Gothic. They are original, violent, surprising. They take some getting used to. But they are full of thought and care and were inspired by the faith of their architects and builders. There's nothing tame or mediocre about them. Do go and have a look at some of those I have mentioned, if you happen to be near them.

Now for parish life. The train draws into the outskirts of a big town. It is Swindon. One hundred and eight years ago there was nothing here at all but a canal and a place where two newly built railways joined, the Cheltenham & Great West Union Railway (the Gloucestershire line) and the London to Bristol line, known as the Great Western and which not rack nor thumbscrew will ever induce me to call 'Western Region British Railways'. On a hill above the meadow was the old market town of Swindon. Then New Swindon was built in the meadow by the Great Western. It was a convenient point between Bristol and London. It consisted of sheds and a few rows of model cottages with open fields round them. These cottages are of Bath stone taken from the excavations of Box Tunnel. They still exist and are called the Company's Houses. They must form one of the earliest planned industrial estates in Britain.

The parishioners of St Philip and St Jacob in Bristol entreated the Great Western to build a church for their workers. Directors stumped up money, subscriptions were raised, land was presented and by 1845 St Mark's church was built.

There it stands today, close beside the line on the Bristol side of the station – a stone building, all spikes and prickles outside, designed by Sir George Gilbert Scott who was then a young man and who lived to build St Pancras Hotel and the Foreign Office in London and to 'restore' many cathedrals. (I have written 'restore' in inverted commas. I hope you can hear them.) One cannot call it a convenient site.

Whistles and passing trains disturb the service; engine smoke black-ens the leaves and tombstones and eats into the carved stonework of the steeple. No matter: it is a great church and though it isn't much to look at, it is for me the greatest church in England. For not carved stones nor screens and beautiful altars nor lofty cascades nor gilded canopies but the priests who minister and the people who worship make a church great. If ever I feel England is pagan, if ever I feel the poor old C. of E. is tottering to its grave, I revisit St Mark's Swindon. That corrects the impression at once. A simple and infinite faith is taught: St Mark's and its daughter churches are crowded. Swindon, so ugly to look at to the eyes of the architectural student, glows golden as the New Jerusalem to eyes that look beyond the brick and stone.

For there's no doubt that Swindon *is* superficially ugly. That pretty model village of the 1840s has developed a red-brick rash that stretches up to the hill to Old Swindon and strangles it, and beyond Old Swindon it runs tentacles to the downs and it spreads with monotony in all other directions. It is now the biggest town in Wiltshire, sixty times the size of the original market town. But I would rather see a red-brick rash (and mind you, Swindon has few if any slums; it is only ugly architecturally) – I would rather see a red-brick rash like Swindon enlivened with Victorian towers and steeples sticking out of it than I would see a gleaming glass city of architect-designed flats with never a church but instead only the humped backs of super-cinemas, the grandstands of greyhound tracks and the bub-bling cocoa fountains of community workers – all these cathedrals of the modern barbarism.

For Swindon is largely a Christian town and much of the credit for that goes to the priests and people of St Mark's. It is not Sabbatarian and smug. It has its cinemas and theatres and an art gallery and library and sports grounds and good old Swindon Town Football Club – but its churches are part of its life. That is the unusual thing about Swindon.

In the Centenary book of St Mark's, which appeared in 1945, there is a photograph of Canon Ponsonby★ wearing side whiskers and a beard that ran under his chin but not over it. This saintly

★ Otherwise Lord de Mauley, who also funded St Augustine's personally.

Victorian priest (who died in 1945 aged nearly 100) caused St Mark's parish so to grow in faith that it built five other churches in New Swindon. Two of them, St Paul's and St Augustine's, became separate parishes. He also caused the Wantage Sisters to open their mission house in Swindon. The work went on under the famous Canon Ross, his successor, and continues with the present vicar, through whom the beautiful daughter church of St Mark's was built, called St Luke's. It was designed by W. A. Masters. I can safely say that, except for the railway works, which are awe-inspiring inside, St Luke's is the only fine interior, architecturally, in Swindon. But it's not about lovely St Luke's nor about little St John's nor about the missions that St Mark's supports abroad nor about the many priests who have been Swindon men that I want to end this talk. Up a steep hill going out of the New Town winds Old Swindon. There is a church built of wood and called St Saviour's. That was erected in 1889–90 in six months by St Mark's men, mostly railway workers. When you consider that they did this in their spare time and for nothing, that some of them sacrificed their holidays and that their working hours were from 6.00 a.m. to 5.30 p.m. in those days, you can imagine the faith that inspired them to go out after a long day's work and build a church. Of course, with foundations of faith like this, St Saviour's grew and in 1904 it had to be enlarged. Over a hundred men once again set to work and the church was extended entirely by voluntary labour and in spare time.

I don't know why it is that St Mark's parish hangs together and is a living community, full of life and spirit. Perhaps it is because Swindon is the right size for an industrial town, neither too big nor too small. Perhaps it is because of the sort of work men do in a railway works – 'inside' as they call it in Swindon. Perhaps it's because the men 'inside' do not do soul-destroying work such as one sees in motor factories where the ghastly chain-belt system persists. Perhaps much of the work in a railway works is really worth doing and not beneath the dignity of man. But whatever it is, I know that the people of Swindon first taught me not to be so la-di-da and architectural, not to judge people by the houses they live in, nor churches only by their architecture. I would sooner be on my knees within the wooden walls of St Saviour's than leaning elegantly forward in a cushioned pew in an Oxford college chapel – that is to say, if I am to realize there is something beyond this world worth thinking about.

The church-crawler starts by liking *old* churches but ends by liking all churches and of all churches those that are most alive are often those hard-looking buildings founded by Victorian piety – churches like St Mark's Swindon.

HOLIDAY ESCAPES

IN AND AROUND FRESHWATER

From the first series of 'Coast and Country'

West of England Home Service
Friday 3 June 1949
Producer: Rupert Annand

• • •

The Lymington ferry shuddered as she slid past the moored sharpies and dinghies of Lymington river, out into the cross waves of the Solent. For last week, when I set out for Freshwater, it was sunny but rough. And the Lymington ferry doesn't usually cross in rough water. We all felt it was a concession on the captain's part to take us over those four stormy miles at all. There wasn't a large crowd of passengers. The holiday season was only just starting. A baby staggered about the saloon bar; spray fell over the deck where the motor cars were.

In one horrible car like a sausage made of black plastic, a fleshy couple had the wireless on and read newspapers. They represent a type of visitor who'll not be listening to this talk. They represent those unseeing ones who swirl round the Isle of Wight in luxury coaches and never go off the beaten track. For them this western and remoter part of the island, for which we are bound, will be dull indeed.

A contrasting type were two geologists who sat exposed to the weather and enjoying it, both in mackintoshes and berets and with bronzed faces. One, a woman, carried a bucket; the other, a man, carried a knapsack. They talked loudly of 'lacustrine and fluviatile deposits and seashore shingle containing the water-worn fragments of the bones of reptiles'.

Though no geologist, I couldn't help thinking that these two old things were right to look for stones. For that is what impresses me most about the Isle of Wight each time I visit it: its stones. The stones and sands of the island seem brighter in colour even than the trees and flowers. And these rocks – bands of sand and half rock – are torn up into such shapes, such stripes and colours, such gorges or chines, that one feels that western Wight is an earthquake poised in mid-explosion and ready any day to burst its turfy covering of wild, distorted downs.

We are nearing Yarmouth. The little town spreads out along this flat north coast at the mouth of its tidal river. Old red-tiled roofs contrast with silvery-white stone walls; ilex and seaside elms and firs form a dark background. Yarmouth is mostly a Georgian town in brick and stone with a sixteenth-century church, uneven, rugged and beautiful. I see there's a regrettable plan afoot to strip it of its plaster.

One of the prettiest buildings in Yarmouth is a private house called The Mount, built in the late eighteenth or early nineteenth century, of white brick. Its beauty is all in its proportions – the relation of window to wall space – and in the planted clumps of trees around it, affording its owners a glimpse across the Solent to Hampshire and the New Forest. Most of the finest old houses and towns of Wight are inland or along this uneventful north coast. The worship of the sea and nature in the raw, where it faces the Channel, is at its earliest a late-Georgian cult. The old idea was to put your house as far away from the wind and sun as you could. Hence the older towns of Wight – Ryde, Cowes, Newport, Yarmouth – are all on the north coast. And there's yet another: Newtown, near Yarmouth, now only an oyster fishery and a few old cottages arranged in streets on an eminence in the salt marshes with estuary all round it. It sent two Members to Parliament until 1832. The town hall remains, a Jacobean building, but where are the mayor and Corporation? The market days and fair days? Ask of the seabirds that sail above its vast, deserted stretch of harbour water. 'Gone, gone', they cry. And certainly Newtown is now one of the most romantic and, thank heaven, least visited places in all the island.

I can't help noticing that this talk is called 'In and Around Freshwater' and that so far I haven't mentioned Freshwater with its red-brick villas so out of tune with the local styles and colours. Once it was no doubt lovely – a little straw-thatched village with cottages and church of honey-coloured stone on the most inland reach of the tidal river Yar. Still there are hilly lanes in it, and a few fields.

In its best days Tennyson knew it. His house at Farringford, now a hotel, is still the loveliest big house in Freshwater. It's a long, low Georgian building in a sweet and fancy Gothic style of the period, a good deal older than Tennyson. It has its little park of elm and ilex and its main views – as usual, away from the elements. It's an enlarged version of Somersby Rectory, Lincolnshire, where Tennyson was born. Even the scenery is somewhat similar, being chalk downland; but the sea, instead of lying beyond miles of Lincolnshire marsh and fen, is almost at your feet. 'Something betwixt a pasture and a park / Saved from sea breezes by a hump of down,' wrote Sir Henry Taylor, and that still describes Farringford; and that hump of down is High Down, with Tennyson's monument on top of it and white chalk cliff falling sheer for five hundred feet into the Channel.

To walk along High Down towards the Needles is like a thrilling and terrifying dream. Behind you stretches the coast of Wight to St Catherine's Point, a series of changing effects from this whitest of white chalk on which we walk (take a bit home and compare it with white paper or linen and both will look cream-coloured beside it) to the pink and honey and gold and grey of the points behind us. Probably this south-western coast of Wight is the longest stretch of unspoiled and colossal landscape in the south-west of England. The few houses visible along it are old thatched farms in hollows of the downs. Not even the convoys of luxury coaches bowling along the coast road take the remoteness from these stupendous stretches of coloured and distorted rock. And here ahead of you are the Needles. The turf narrows, till suddenly you are aware that there is sea on either side of you, milky green four hundred feet below, and the Needle rocks themselves glitter and lean sideways out of the sea. Then, just when the point might have narrowed to but a razor's edge of turf, there's a fence so that you have to turn back.

And this is the time, if it's afternoon, to take a look at Alum Bay, which is on the Solent side of the Needles. I came to it first the usual coach way, parking where the ice-cream kiosks stand among the gorse bushes – came from the villadom of Totland, which is like Bromley or Muswell Hill set down by the sea. Alum Bay. It was a well-known 'beauty spot' and I suspect such places. But of all beauty spots I've seen, Alum Bay is the most certainly entitled to be called beautiful. Picture an L-shaped bay, the long part of the L a pearly height of chalk cliff four hundred feet high, stretching out into the sea, no beach below it, and the great merciless cliffs of chalk glittering brighter as the sun moves round to west. And here above a shingly shore is a series of promontories not quite so high as the chalk. Walk along the shingle to the arm of chalk and then look back at these capes. One is brilliant gold; the next is white; the next is purple; the next grey; the next black – one is green. In great broad bands these strips of colour run down the cliffs, turning the sky pale with the richness of their colour. 'Alum Bay: one side of it a wall of glowing chalk and the other a barrier of rainbows,' says my good Victorian guidebook, and it doesn't exaggerate.

I'm torn in mind between the three great beauties of western Wight: (1) the silvery-green inland country along the railway line from Yarmouth to Newport, with its glimpses of old stone manor farms, thatched cottages and protecting hump of downs – Dorset without the flint; (2) the colossal untamed landscape of the south-west coast from the Needles to St Catherine's Point; (3) Alum Bay. Anyhow, the point about 'In and Around Freshwater' is, for me, not Freshwater but around it.

PORT ISAAC

From the first series of 'Coast and Country'

West of England Home Service
Friday 1 July 1949
Producer: Rupert Annand

• • •

Can it really be that a town is half a mile from here? I've walked between high Cornish hedges from St Endellion, once the parish church of Port Isaac. Its old granite tower has pinnacles which look like a hare's two ears sticking out above the hilltop. The tower dwindles. The lane winds. The slate of the hedges is overgrown with grasses, bedstraw and milky-pink convolvulus, pale purple scabious and every so often valerian. From several places, standing on a hedge or looking through a gate, I can glimpse the sea. The sea is there all right – the great Atlantic, emerald green when I saw it, wrinkled, glittering, sliding streaks of water, spotted dark blue here and there with reflections.

It was a full tide, tamed and quiet for the moment, sliding round this inhospitable coast of North Cornwall, with white crescents of surf floating close inshore. From here on these high-up fields, where blackthorn is sliced by the sea wind and leans inland, I can see all along the rocky cliffs to Tintagel Head. Behind me is an even grander coastline to Rumps Points and Pentire. Cliffs and ocean are fine to watch from these high, windy fields as cloud shadows race over them but where can there be a town? Less than half a mile and still no sight of it?

There's no doubt this is the way to approach Port Isaac, from St Endellion on the Polzeath side of the port. The final hill is very steep and there's only a disused quarry in which you can park a motor car if you are not on foot. Not until you round a corner do you see any sign of Port Isaac at all. Then you see it all – huddled in a steep valley, a cove at the end of a combe, roofs and roofs tumbling down either steep hillside in a race for shelter from the south-west gales. A freshwater stream pours brown and cold along the valley, under slate bridges, between old houses, under the road and out into the little harbour.

Port Isaac is Polperro without the self-consciousness, St Ives without the artists. The same whitewashed slate houses with feathery-looking roofs that have been 'grouted' (that's to say the old slates have been cemented over and limewashed); the same narrow, airless passages between whitewashed walls. One of the sights of Port Isaac used to be to watch the lifeboat being brought down Ford Street and missing the walls by inches as she was manoeuvred round the bend at the Golden Lion on to the Platt★.

Lost in rambling cliff paths between the walls, some so narrow that a fat man couldn't use them, is my favourite house in Port Isaac. It's called the Birdcage, an irregular pentagon in shape, one small room thick and three storeys high and hung on the weather sides with slates that have gone a delicate silvery blue. It's empty now and obviously condemned. For that is the sad thing about Port Isaac: it's the sort of place town planners hate. It's the quintessence of quaint. There are no boulevards, no car stands or clinics; the dentist calls once a week and brings his instruments with him in his car.

The community centre is all wrong by town-planning standards. It's not the public house but the Liberal Club, for anyone who knows Cornish fishermen must know that most of them don't drink and many are chapel-goers, so a Liberal club without an alcohol licence is just the sort of place where you'd expect to find them.

The trade of Port Isaac really is fishing. The promise of a dark night after a shoal of pilchards had been sighted; the sound of rowlocks and splashing of oars in harbour water, then boarding the fishing boat from the dinghy; the outside roar of the sea; the dark cliffs fading in twilight and dropping away as we move out to open sea; letting down the nets and drifting – those were the times! Unless,

★ The local name for the harbour, where fishermen land their catch.

like me, you were a shocking sailor and sick all night and thanking God for dawn light and the nearing cliffs of Varley Head as we made for home and harbour.

There they are, the fishermen's houses, clinging by their eyelids to the cliffs. Sparkling quartz known as Cornish Diamond is cemented into garden walls; figs and fuchsia bushes grow in tiny gardens; big shells from the Orient rest on window sills; brass and front-door paintwork shine; and every window that can looks out to sea so that even as they die the old fishermen of Port Isaac may watch the tides – though I expect the old people will all soon be moved to some very ugly council houses being built on the windy hilltop from those hideous grey cement things called 'Cornish blocks' (so local, don't you know).

Across stupendous cliffs, as full of flowers as a rock garden, is another little fishing port: Port Quin, an empty Port Isaac, mournful and still. And beyond Port Quin what caves, what rocks there are between here and Pentire Point, what shuddering heights of striped slate, what hidden beaches and barnacled boulders, what pools where seals bask. All picturesque and grand, as blazing with colour as the strange rock pools themselves on a summer day. But in a storm or in a mist, how infinitely horrible and mysterious this coast can be as the rollers smash and suck, the blowholes thunder and caves syphon out fountains of sea water a hundred feet and more into the air. The sea is an army always fighting the land, as the men of Port Isaac know.

But let's forget the winter thunder and since this is a summer tourists' series, let's end with a summer picture of Port Isaac. I like to stand by that bit of wall in Fore Street and lean over to look down at the harbour and inland at the little town below me. It's evening, harvest-festival time. The small Victorian church has been hung with lobster pots and dressed with crabs and seaweed – a harvest festival of the sea. Church is over but chapel is still on. As I stand on this viewpoint high above the town, the seagulls are crying and wheeling, the flowery cliffs take the evening sun, the silvery slates of the old town turn pale gold. Above the wail of gulls and thunder of the sea beyond the headlands comes the final hymn from the Methodist Chapel across the green and gently lapping harbour water.

CLEVEDON

From the first series of 'Coast and Country'

West of England Home Service
Wednesday 10 August 1949
Producer: Rupert Annand

• • •

Clevedon is by far the pleasantest seaside place I've visited on this tour. It has the most character, the widest diversity of scenery, the fewest really hideous buildings. It's quiet, mild, medium sized. Its churches are full, its shops are polite, the same families come to it year after year – the same type of people who like peace and who mistrust so-called 'progress' – and they walk among its ilex-shaded roads. Upon that slender cast-iron pier, built in 1869, strode T. E. Brown, the Clifton schoolmaster and poet. Here he composed a poem about the salmon rushing up the Severn from the sea. To Clevedon the body of Arthur Hallam was brought in 1833 – Arthur Hallam, Tennyson's friend and the inspiration of *In Memoriam*. You remember the famous lines about Clevedon:

> The Danube to the Severn gave
>   The darken'd heart that beat no more;
>   They laid him by the pleasant shore,
> And in the hearing of a wave.
>
> There twice a day the Severn fills;
>   The salt sea-water passes by,
>   And hushes half the babbling Wye
> And makes a silence in the hills.

Not thirty years earlier Coleridge had brought his young bride to Clevedon, to a small cottage that still survives:

Low was our pretty cot: our tallest rose
Peep'd at the chamber window. We could hear
At silent noon, and eve, and early morn,
The Sea's faint murmur.
[from 'Reflections on Having Left a Place of Retirement']

Now he would only hear bus engines, for a big garage is opposite his cottage.

Great writers have come to Clevedon ever since the Elton family bought Clevedon Court in Queen Anne's reign. Successive Eltons, who seem always to have been men of taste and vision, improved the town throughout the last century. Clevedon Court, where the Eltons still live, is said to be the oldest inhabited house in England. Most of what one sees from the Bristol Road looks Tudor, Jacobean and later, but parts of it go back to Edward II. Terraced gardens rise to oak and ilex and ash woods. These form a dark and satisfying background to the house, which is of weathered limestone, honey and silver coloured, battlemented and irregular.

Much of Clevedon looks as though it were a continuation of the private park of the Court – thanks to skilful planting and planning in Victorian times. Roads wind among trees; there is plenty of open space. Skylines are often left undisturbed by building. Elton Road and Hallam Road leave little doubt about who the original owners were; Albert, Victoria and Alexandra Roads give one a good idea of the dates of others. The earliest development is to be found in simple late-Georgian houses of stucco-washed cream or white and set down below the crest of Dial Hill, where they peep from myrtle bushes and ilex trees. What a comment on our civilization it is that these modest houses actually *beautify* the hillside while, a few yards above them, a row of pre-war villas, commanding fine views no doubt, ruin the skyline for miles with their shapelessness and alien red brick among all this silvery stone. Such vandalism would never have been allowed under the benevolent liberalism of Elton control.

The prevalent style of house in the older, mid-Victorian parts of Clevedon is Gothic or Italianate, built of local greyish-blue stone, sometimes flecked with pink or honey-yellow. Bargeboards adorn gables, roofs are slated, trees surround lawns and hang over garden walls. It's all as though many comfortable vicarages had been set down here among trees within sound of the sea. Well-designed Victorian lamp-posts, instead of these frightful new boa constrictors in concrete, adorn the streets. Walks and shelters and flowering shrubs and parks decorate the seafront. Only the sea itself is a bit of a failure. It's often muddy with that chocolate mud one sees at Weston and which seems to clog the waves and dye their thin tops a pinky-brown. This mud lies upon the rocks. Bathing in the marine lake at Clevedon I accidentally touched some with my toe: it had the feeling of a dead body.

But stand on Castle Hill three hundred feet above the town, in the octagonal ruin of Stuart times, and view the landscape round. The gables of Clevedon rise from the spur of hills below us. Clifton is only twelve miles away behind us. Backbones of hill leading home to Bristol are dark with waving woods. Beyond the town and on to Weston run flat and pale-green moors till they meet the blue outline of the Mendips. Blue-green Somerset hills – all looking like the background of a Flemish stained-glass window. The Bristol Channel is a bronze shield streaked with sunlight. Flat Holm and Steep Holm are outlined to the west and to the north the coast of South Wales stretches out of sight. What was a tidal river has become a huge dividing sea. This wonderful view from Castle Hill is all Georgian enjoyment of the picturesque, especially when seen through an ivy-mantled arch. And the ruin has not yet been tidied up.

But at the other end of the town, where the old parish church stands sheltered between two grassy hills at the sea's edge, the atmosphere is older and even Celtic. The cruciform church built of dark-grey slate with storm-resisting central tower, the windy grave-yard, the low bushes blown landward, the brown grass, cliff paths and nearby thud and thunder of water all make me think I'm in Cornwall.

Clevedon is saved by being on the way to nowhere. The dear old light railway that connected it with Weston and Portishead has been ripped up by modern progress. Now only a Great Western branch line from Yatton serves the town. And buses of course. But buses don't go with Clevedon, any more than do modernistic arcades of shops and the new post office at the crossroads in the town. Let the char-à-bancs and megaphones and multitudes roar down distant main roads to Weston and to Cheddar Gorge. Clevedon will still be left as it is, a civilized, decorative seaside town, shunned – thank heaven – by modern barbarism, a refuge for civilization in Somerset (except on public holidays) in time of trouble, a beautiful haven of quiet.

ILFRACOMBE

From the first series of 'Coast and Country'

West of England Home Service
Wednesday 24 August 1949
Producer: Rupert Annand

• • •

Ilfracombe is the end of everything. The express train that had wound so long and crowded out of Waterloo had only three carriages left. Parts of it had been dropped off at Exeter and Barnstaple. Here at Ilfracombe Station, the end of the line, we seemed to hang in air on a clifftop, with the town two hundred feet below us, silvery slate cliffs, sea and the far-off coast of Wales beyond.

I hadn't been able to believe there was going to be a town after all those miles of bleak North Devon fields with their high stone hedges, blackthorns and foxgloves, and hardly a house in sight. A village perhaps – quite a big village – but not a town. By contrast with North Devon moor and farmland, Ilfracombe seems enormous. It has several churches, lines of Welsh-looking lodging houses, hills and valleys filled with houses, shops, cinemas, and loudspeakers giving off crooning – possibly giving off this talk! It's the Blackpool of the West, the Douglas of North Devon. The noise and the glitter dazzled me at first so that I couldn't sort out Ilfracombe nor discover why it had ever been built; and if it had to be in North Devon, why not at some more spectacular place like Heddon's Mouth or Lynton, where Exmoor rises to nearly a thousand feet and cascades in rocks and bracken or oaks and ash woods to cliffs above the Bristol Channel? Why is Ilfracombe *here* where there is no sand and these great hills – grass on the landward side, slate on the seaward – hide much of the town from the sea?

My son and I went up Torr Walks and from 450 feet looked back on the town. It's a wonderful view. We set off in a speedboat, swirling past the caves and cliffs to glimpse between gaps in spray and rock the terraces of the town. Leaving him to take more trips on the speed-boat, I climbed to airy suburbs where boarding houses flew bathing dresses from upstairs windows. I visited the Museum – quite the nicest and most old-fashioned provincial museum I've ever seen, crowded with all sorts of objects: old tickets, stuffed crocodiles, heathen gods, local photographs and prints and playbills, butterflies, moths and birds, drawers of dried seaweed, and shells arranged to look like flowers. Indeed this museum must be almost the last unspoiled one left in England. It has no horn-rimmed experts in it cataloguing and killing things with their erudition and asking you not to touch.

From walks and drives and cruises, and chiefly from this museum, I began to piece together the growth of Ilfracombe – and really, as an epitome of seaside development, the place is so interesting that I must tell you how I think it grew. Until 150 years ago, nobody cared about living by the sea unless they were fishermen or sailors. In those days Ilfracombe consisted of a harbour naturally guarded by Lantern Hill, on the top of which is an old chapel of St Nicholas, possibly Celtic in origin. Nearly a mile further up the brook that poured into the har-bour was an old village and parish church. If you go into that large and lovely old church today you can feel this West Country Ilfracombe about you, for it's a singularly countrified church for so large a town. It has grandly carved barrel roofs of wood, and wall tablets, and low West-Country style columns. And not far off are old houses with slate-hung sides, yellow stucco fronts and Georgian windows. In a place called Cuddeford's Passage, off the High Street, I found Clovelly-like cottages built of slate and whitewashed. This is all real old Devon.

Then you can see what happened. In Georgian days the harbour was extended. Ilfracombe grew as a fishing port. Then in about 1830, someone saw its possibilities as a watering place. Mild, warm, almost as sunny as Nice, it was a fuchsia-shaded ilex-waving paradise. Indeed the poet Charles Abraham Elton of Clevedon thus described it in 1835:

> Thy craggy coves, O Ilfracombe!
> The outline of thy ridgy hills,

> The ash-tree dell's sun-quivering gloom,
> And pebbled dash of viewless rills . . .

You will now understand why many attractive Georgian houses were built above the harbour and set snugly down in the grassy valley between harbour and church.

Still later, this mild climate and these mildly beetling rocks (not *too* rugged and wild) and these well-spoken Devon sailors (not too rugged and wild either) round the little harbour – all were just the thing for mid-Victorian merchants and their families. So next came stupendous hotels erected in the turfy hollow: St Pancras Station in white brick; the Louvre in red and white bricks. These hotels are the most impressive buildings in the place and the most prominent is the now empty Ilfracombe Hotel, built in 1867 in the French Gothic style in coloured bricks.

Since those mid-Victorian days, Ilfracombe has changed in character. Rich West Country and London merchants ceased to come. The Welsh arrived by steamer from Barry, Swansea and Cardiff. The railway opened in 1874 and made the journey less adventurous and the place less what used to be called 'exclusive', so the combe filled up not with the noble isolated villas proclaiming the riches of their occupants but with large hotels and rows upon rows of boarding houses designed to get plenty of bedrooms into the smallest possible space. Ilfracombe became what it still is: the people's playground.

My last picture of Ilfracombe is not of sea nor of Devon but of that peculiar and exotic thing known as 'seaside'. I stand on a steep hill on the way to the station. Warm salty air is round me and I can smell the sea but cannot see it. There rises in front of me a row of Victorian boarding houses in shiny yellow brick relieved with shiny red, a style very popular in Ilfracombe. The roofs are of blue slate and red tiles pick out the ridges. The cast iron railings are painted silver and the garden behind them is bright with lobelias, geraniums and hydrangeas. A palm tree rises as high as the first-floor window. The piers of the front gate are topped with pieces of white quartz. Ilfracombe, with your chapels, evangelical churches, char-à-bancs and variegated terraces, long may you lie embedded in your gorgeous cliffs and hills! Nature made you lovely. Man has not improved you. But on a sunny summer evening you are lovely still.

SIDMOUTH

From the first series of 'Coast and Country'

West of England Home Service
Tuesday 27 September 1949
Producer: Rupert Annand

• • •

A silvery mist of heat hung over Sidmouth when I came into it. A silver mist of heat was over it when I went away. The climate is so dominant in Sidmouth, you can almost touch it. In Connaught Gardens, a modern piece of Italian-style gardening on a clifftop, with views through arches of red cliffs five hundred feet high – in Connaught Gardens if you and I were tropic plants and sheltered from the sea breeze, we would flower and flower as high as the cliffs themselves if only the wind would let us. For that is one of the first things I noticed about Sidmouth: as soon as I was out of the gentle sea breeze, I was in a hothouse where wonderful West Country bushes filled the air with scent and enormous butterflies lit on asters and on antirrhinums, themselves twice as large as life. Fuchsia bells seemed three times the size of those anywhere else in Britain. If it were not for the sea, Sidmouth, I thought, would be tropic forest. Devon hills protect it on all but the seaward side. Peak Hill and Salcombe Hill guard the town west and east. Woods and little Devon fields climb their slopes. Other hills, blue-wooded, rise far far inland. And here is the little valley of the river Sid – a brown moorland stream that disappears in shingle by the site of the old gasworks (now a car park) at one end of the seafront.

And on a piece of level ground saved from inundation by a pebble beach stands Sidmouth. Wooded glens rise to the hills inland. Huge cliffs, shaved down almost sheer, stretch pinkly to the east until they change to the white chalk of the Dorset coast. Westwards to Devon there is a mile-long beach below Peak Hill where at low tide the stretch of sand changes from pink to gold as it goes further west. I could say that of all the seaside resorts I have seen on this tour, Sidmouth has the best sea, from the children's point of view. The pebble beach is only a high-tide affair. At low tide there is accommodation west of the town for all the population of Devon to play rounders by the salt sea waves. And ah! – to bathe as I did in warm summer water and swim towards the great pink cliffs and creamy stucco esplanade!

Despite these ample sands and hothouse garden walks, there are few chars-à-banc – I think we can safely use the correct plural 'chars-à-banc' instead of 'charabangs' – in Sidmouth. The crowds are neither vast nor noisy. No giant wheels nor kursaals intrude; no pier takes iron strides into the sea. The roads to Sidmouth are twisty and the streets of the town itself are far too narrow even for private motors to move with ease, let alone chars-à-banc. Sidmouth is indeed an exclusive place. It excludes the vulgar throng. No hideous jazz nor chain-stores nor gimcrack concrete cages defile the conscious quaintness of its older quarters.

The town is mostly Georgian, with few newer additions than those put up in Good King Edward's reign. You know the style of the newest Sidmouth, you who know Devon: a sort of red-brick Baroque with green copper domes and several hideous terraces of yellow and red brick near the gasworks. You know the older and more gracious Sidmouth too, you who know Devon: low, two-storey stucco villas with green ironwork verandahs, some with pointed windows, some houses all Greek, little show Parthenons among ilex trees with hydrangeas by the front doors. Devon Georgian – the simplest, gayest, lightest, creamiest Georgian of all. I doubt if anywhere on the south coast there is a prettier Georgian stucco crescent than Fortfield Terrace, which overlooks the cricket ground and sea, nor a more romantic fairy-tale-Gothic seaside house than Royal Glen a few hundred yards away. And round the parish church of St Nicholas (mediaeval and fairly High) and the newer church of All Saints (Victorian and very Low) are many stuccoed and barge-boarded villas and beyond them villas of a later age and Bournemouth in style, and many rare trees, wide gardens, flowering shrubs and care-fully concealed tennis courts.

Ah, what a place to live in in the winter! Those old people I saw in the shops were clearly living on in a calm and civilized world that still lingers throughout the year in this equable climate. How they or anyone else have the money to keep up these big villas among the wooded glens, I don't know. Perhaps great sacrifices are made. If it is so, I am glad it is, for they make Sidmouth civilized. What I am *certain* of is that in summer it is the hotel life that counts in Sidmouth. It is a town of vast hotels. From our table, what beautiful buttoned-nosed blondes I saw smiling secretly at young men in club blazers at neigh-bouring tables. Tennis-girl queens of Sidmouth! What romances must have started over coffee in basket chairs in the lounge or on the hotel court during a strenuous single. What last walks there must have been at the end of the holidays while he walks up the steps of Salcombe Hill and she pretends the climb is a little difficult – he has to take her hand – and all the time in one of the glittering hotels in the valley below their parents are trying to like one another over a rubber of bridge. Sidmouth, silvery-pink and creamy Sidmouth, sadly I say farewell!

LYNDHURST

From the second series of 'Coast and Country'

West of England Home Service
Friday 4 August 1950
Producer: Rupert Annand

• • •

Lyndhurst! Lyndhurst Way, Lyndhurst Grove, Lyndhurst Drive, Lyndhurst Crescent – the suburbs of England are full of the name. And was it not Lord Lyndhurst, the Chancellor, who invented the Deceased Wife's Sister Act? I cannot think why so small a place (the population I shouldn't think is more than three thousand) should so have taken the public fancy.

I believe Lyndhurst means 'Forest of lime trees' but a more truthful description would be 'Forest of Douglas firs' or even 'Forest of oak and beech'. Lyndhurst is the capital of the New Forest and it is up at the northern and wildest end, where Rufus was killed by an arrow.

The original New Forest, the Norman forest, was of oak. Then there were plantations of beech and later, in Victorian times, these miles and miles of fir. People say you cannot properly see the New Forest from the main roads and they are quite right. But on a warm evening you can smell it between the wafts of petrol and scent that linger on the tarmac – the resin scent among the conifers, the coconut smell of gorse on an open heath, the tropic scent like the Palm House at Kew under oaks and beeches where the holly shines and the bracken is a young green.

Outside Lyndhurst, the forest begins to look less wild. Victorian brick cottages peep about among the trees. Lodge gates stand guard to winding drives of laurel and azalea at the end of which – how deep, how far, who knows? – are the country houses of the formerly rich. Five or six times a year the verderers come to the swainmote that is held in the King's House at Lyndhurst. But don't let them bother you with a description of the ancient governments of the New Forest – the strange rights of turbary, pannage and smoke money that go with certain old freehold cottages. Enough to know that the forest laws are administered from Lyndhurst and it is as well to know some of them. For instance, if you are an entomologist you must apply to the King's House for a permit to catch moths and butterflies. And you are not allowed to sugar the trees. No licence is required, on the other hand, to be stung by flies among the oaks of the New Forest. These flies, called stouts, seem to carry small poisoned swords and draw blood. Hornets abound. When Tennyson, his wife and children and William Allingham, the poet, were swimming through bracken in July 1866 on their way to the great beeches of Mark Ash, Tennyson paused midway and said solemnly, 'I believe this place is quite full of vipers.' Of course he said this to frighten Allingham. And I am saying this to frighten you! He stopped again and said, 'I am told that a viper bite may make a woman silly for life or deprive a man of his virility.'

Despite the main road and the modern houses and the luxury coaches of Lyndhurst, wild life comes right into it. When I was there, three wild New Forest ponies and two colts were waiting outside the National Provincial Bank. Later that afternoon I saw one at the cross-roads, right in the middle of the traffic.

If I said Lyndhurst is like Aldershot without the army I would not be far wrong. Most of the houses are two storeys and the only old and remarkable one is the gabled King's House near the church. But I can imagine that before motors came into existence, before the 'caffs', 'kiosks' and guest houses ('guest house' is hotel language for 'We have not got a licence'), before the petrol pumps, wires, poles and signs that follow the motor car – before all these things, Lyndhurst, lost in the forest and its nearest railway station three miles away, must have been a paradise to stay in. Now it is a suburb for Southampton business people and there are cricket grounds around it and a golf course.

Fifty years ago, artists, poets and musicians booked lodgings in the district. The huge Crown Hotel, rebuilt in 1897 in a half-timbered style opposite the church, is a sign of those times. In fact Lyndhurst was the home of Victorian romance – wild nature after the smoke of towns; fir trees with a faintly Rhineland look; oak woods that took one back to the Forest of Arden; cultivated people instead of the vulgar throng. Ah! what a paradise it must have been to those rare Victorian souls! They expressed their gratitude in the huge church they built of red and yellow brick. Lyndhurst parish church was designed by William White and is in the most fanciful, fantastic Gothic style that ever I have seen – and I have seen a good deal. The spire itself is of brick – a remarkable feat. Inside, the brick columns have pipes of Purbeck marble round them and their capitals were carved by Seale with leaves of New Forest trees. Unexpected dormers and gables jut out from the huge roof. The tracery of the windows is as strange as tropic plants. Some of the stained-glass windows are by Morris and Burne-Jones and Rossetti. And the prevailing colours are red and yellow. But of course Victorian stained glass and Victorian coloured brick does not go with frescoes. And Lord Leighton came to stay with Hamilton Aidé, the songwriter, and he painted the fresco over the altar of the church free of charge. It shows Our Lord in white in the middle, with the foolish virgins on one side and the wise ones on the other.

I like Lyndhurst church inside and out tremendously. It is full of originality and thought and care. It expresses the courage and conviction of the Victorians. It is their lasting monument, towering on its mound above the gables of the Victorian houses and the oaks and beeches and fir trees of the New Forest. Lyndhurst is worth seeing for its church, the forest for itself.

VENTNOR

From the second series of 'Coast and Country'

West of England Home Service
Friday 1 September 1950
Producer: Rupert Annand

• • •

Far too few people on the Isle of Wight have the sense to go by its railways. These delicious single lines wind through most of the best scenery of the island. Oh, let me advise you, instead of sitting half asleep in the luxury coach with your arm round your girl and the wireless on and the petrol pumps passing and the gear-clashing and brakes squeaking at dangerous corners – oh, let me advise you to go by train. And of all lines on the Isle of Wight, the fairest, the wildest, the most countrified, the most romantic is that which runs from Cowes, not Ryde, to Ventnor West, not the main station of Ventnor.

It was by this line that I, almost the only passenger, first came to Ventnor. It is by this line that I would first have you see Ventnor too. And if the Southern Railway had any sense it would put observation cars on this part of the line.

We glide through alder-bordered meadows, past the thatched farms and greeny-grey stone cottages of inland Wight, little streams and meadowsweet, shorthorns and Friesians – an inland agricultural county that might not be an island at all, which is yet like neither Hampshire nor Dorset. Then the chalky downs grow nearer, high and golden brown with grass – suddenly the blackness of a tunnel – half a mile of it – and we are out in the jungle of the Amazon, or so it seems. For here at St Lawrence Halt and all along the sea coast to Ventnor West are strangled shrubs, luxurious undergrowth. Sycamores and ash trees wave above us and below us, old man's beard and bindweed clamber over broken stone walls. Damp-looking drives wind down to empty stables and huge houses turned into holiday camps or left to ghosts and centipedes. And all the time, between the ash-tree branches, an unexpected silver, shiny sea.

Ventnor! Here we are at Ventnor West! Not a sign of a town. The explanation is simple. Most of Ventnor is a park. The shopping streets are tucked away in a hollow. There are more steps than there are roads, for the town climbs up the hill for four hundred feet from the sea and for four hundred feet above the top of the town rises the wooded height of St Boniface Down. A little adding up will show you that Ventnor is eight hundred feet in all of wooded cliff. Most towns are horizontal; Ventnor is perpendicular. It is all trees and steps and zigzag roads and above all beautiful gardens, public and private.

This is how Ventnor came about. Some thousands of years ago, with a roar and a crunch or maybe more slowly and less dramatically than that, six miles of these chalky cliffs eight hundred feet high subsided into the Channel. But these six miles did not quite sink into the sea. What with streams and falling earth and nature, these fallen cliffs became a luxuriant land of their own. Today they are known as the Undercliffe. Artists came to see them more than a century ago when the sea and rocks and huge chasms were beginning to be appreciated. Many books were published with steel engravings of the Isle of Wight. The nobility and gentry built themselves marine villages of enormous size upon the Undercliffes – 'cottages' they called them, but we would call them 'palaces'. They bought their crabs and lobsters from the fishermen who lived in squalid cots beside the sand at Ventnor Cove. Then Queen Victoria and Prince Albert came to live at Osborne so the Isle of Wight was all the rage – and no place more the rage than Ventnor. *Little* Osborne was built on every available piece of cliff, every ledge and cranny, and each little Osborne had its garden of palms, myrtles and hydrangeas and its glimpse of sea.

And there they are today, unchanged. I bought the parish magazine of St Catherine's (the parish church of the town) and saw that the vicar pleads for more permanent residents. 'I wish the many people anxious to make their homes in Ventnor would join the church,' he says. Count me in, vicar, though I think St Alban's, up 350 steps, would be my place of worship so long as my heart would stand it. In that mild air, which is not heavy, how gladly would I live and die.

Of all seaside towns I have seen, Ventnor looks after its outward appearance best. The public gardens are amazing. The cascade down rocks that divide the seafront is always a mass of flowers: orange, pink and purple seem to be the favourite colours. The park is wild on the seaward side but on the landward-leaning slopes it is red, white and blue with municipal gardening that suits so well this Victorian town.

The sudden valleys in Ventnor between one bit of cliff and the next are so hot and still and so full of flowers that one almost expects a bird of paradise to flit from prunus to prunus or an alligator to slither out from underneath a palm. And then in another hundred yards is open cliff and familiar chalky-cliff flowers. Swinburne lies in Bonchurch graveyard here by Ventnor town. No one made the sea hiss and clang in English poetry better than he. The sea he sang keeps Ventnor fresh, for all its tropical vegetation. The sound of its waves on chalk and sand is never long out of your ears. The sound of the sea travels upward in this amphitheatre of wooded and tremendous hills.

HIGHWORTH

From the second series of 'Coast and Country'

West of England Home Service
Friday 29 September 1950
Producer: Rupert Annand

• • •

We had our tea in the lee of the goods shed. May I take this opportunity to apologize to the stationmaster at Highworth for our trespassing. But – my hat! – the wind and the rain! Even *you* would have trespassed. And it was Sunday, so Highworth Station was shut. With every gust of the storm the whole wooden goods shed – about the size of a tithe barn – creaked like a yacht under full sail. My son, who was sitting propped up against one of its walls, suddenly sprang up as the whole wooden length of the shed lurched over towards him.

Why, you ask, go for a picnic in a storm to a country railway station? The answer is simple. I like railways, and branch railways. And of all branch railways in Wiltshire, Berkshire, Gloucestershire and Dorset I like the Highworth branch best of all. Silly pseudo-progressives up at the impersonal railway headquarters in London are trying to shut the 'Highworth Bunk' for ever. May that dark day never come.

Curve after curve the little railway winds from Swindon, through willows and poplars, through delightful stations like Hannington with its grassy goods yard and disused ticket office till it comes to an end high up here in a field to the north of Highworth town.

Whew! The wind shook the goods shed as the black storm cloud raced away north-eastwards and streams of sunlight flowed behind it, lighting fields of elms below us and upper-Thames country.

A rainbow glowed brighter against the black sky than the pinks and snapdragons here in the station garden. We were in a kingdom here on the top of this Wiltshire hill – kings of a land of farms and limestone churches, hunting country and trout streams, and the chalk downs of Marlborough away behind us to the south.

I've never seen Highworth given its due praise in guidebooks for what it is – one of the most beautiful and unassuming country towns in the West of England. It is unspoiled by the vulgar fascias of chain stores. Concrete lamp-posts don't lean above its houses like seasick giants spewing orange light at night that turns us all to corpses. The roaring hideousness of main roads has left Highworth undisturbed. The only ugly things about it are some fussy red modern villas on the outskirts and too many telegraph wires zigzagging across its high street.

Now this is the extraordinary thing about it. It's most unusual but Highworth is about the only town I know where there are more beautiful buildings than there are ugly ones. It is mostly a Cotswold-coloured place of silvery-grey stone gathered round its church high on a hill, with a high street and market place, a street at right angles, a Georgian doctor's house in red brick with a fine white wooden porch and doorway, and one more grand brick house – and these old Georgian brick houses looking as beautiful and ripe as autumn apples among all this silver stone of the streets.

Then Highworth is full of old inns with bay windows and swinging signs and arches for coaches to go under into cobbled yards; there is a pleasant late-Georgian Congregational church; wisteria and vines trail over some of the houses; high garden walls show glimpses of fruit trees rising above them. It wouldn't surprise me to see periwigged men in knee breeches and ladies in silks and countrymen in smocks walking about in Sheep Street and in High Street or down Vicarage Lane. They would not look out of place.

Even the matting factory, Highworth's chief modern industry outside agriculture, is tucked away out of sight. So, for that matter, is the church. You can see its tower everywhere but you have to look through an arch under a house in the High Street to glimpse the porch and the lime-shaded churchyard. The church has a fine painted royal arms, a huge parish chest with three padlocks, some Norman work and much later work, and much too much late-Victorian work.

Highworth may be just on the border of the two regions of the BBC in which this programme is heard – the West of England region and the Midlands – but to you and me it is the centre of some of the loveliest country round its feet: Coleshill House in Berkshire, that four-square masterpiece of stone built in Charles II's reign with its lantern and moulded chimneys rising mightily from surrounding elms; Great Coxwell Barn, the oldest and loveliest tithe barn in Britain, beating, in my opinion, those at Abbotsbury in Dorset and Harmondsworth in Middlesex; Inglesham church down by the Thames, the church that William Morris saved from so-called 'restoration' – there it is: clear glass, box pews, old screens and wall paintings, a stony, lichen-crusted country church among the whispering grasses. These are some of the sights of the country round Highworth. Countless unknown lanes lead up the hill to Highworth.

When I am abroad and I want to remember what is the most typically English town – if anything is typically English – then I think of Highworth. It is the sort of town read about in novels from *Cranford* to Miss Macnaughten. Ah, Highworth as a whole! Churches and chapels; doctors' houses; the vicarage; walled gardens with pears and plums; the railway station; inns; the distant cemetery; old shops and winding streets. We walked down one of those narrow lanes between garden walls that lead under archways into the High Street. (The only way to see a town is to go down every back alley and see the *backs* of the houses.) Ivy-leaved toadflax with its little purple flowers hung over the stone; an uneven line of stone-tiled roofs and slate roofs, stone and brick chimney stacks, leaded windows under eaves – all these formed a base for the church tower. There was a sound of tea being cleared away in a cottage just near us. And suddenly, with a burst, the beautiful bells of Highworth church rang out for evening service. As though called by the bells, the late sun broke out and bathed the varied roofs with gold and scooped itself into the uneven panes of old windows.

Sun and stone and old brick and garden flowers and church bells. That was Sunday evening in Highworth. That was England.

ALDERNEY

From the third series of 'Coast and Country'

West of England Home Service
Thursday 28 June 1951
Producer: Rupert Annand

• • •

They said, 'I shouldn't go to Alderney if I were you. You'll be dis-appointed.' They said, 'It's flat and uninteresting. And anyhow the Germans occupied it during the war and blew everything up.' They said, 'Go to Sark. Now that really *is* beautiful.' And standing in the ancient town of St Peter Port in Guernsey – a town that is a blend of Cheltenham and Brittany – standing by the attractive daffodil-and-cream telephone kiosk and looking out across the shipping, I could see Sark and Herm and Jethou. But there was no sign of Alderney, that dim and most distant of the Channel Islands, twenty-seven miles north-east of Jersey and only seven from the coast of France.

Always disobey well-meant advice and you will be rewarded. It was Alderney for us. The aeroplane started from Guernsey at 8.10 in the morning. It was a tiny machine, a biplane, with seats for seven. Angry water crawling below us flecked with white worms of wave-tops on it. Twenty minutes and shadowy cliffs rose out of the sea. A long grim island, sloping eastward; here at the western end, high and terrible. Would there be room to land? We touched down on a windy field. A tiny airport. A customs official who was obviously a retired army officer.

Alderney is neither England nor Guernsey. It uses the Guernsey coinage but it has its own judge (recently renamed 'President'), system of government, flag, coat of arms and courthouse. It's an ancient Norman island under the King of England in his capacity as

Duke of Normandy. It is on foreign soil, hence the customs. And here we were, my son and I, alone on Alderney, a gale blowing and much too early in the morning for many people to be up.

Alderney is about three miles long and rarely more than a mile across. The only town, St Anne, is in the centre of the island. Wherever you are, you are unlikely to be more than half an hour's walk back to St Anne.

Ah, St Anne, St Anne! Surely the only European capital without a single ugly building except a concrete tower. The houses are mostly two-storeyed Georgian, washed white or pink or blue and with square-paned windows. The roofs are tiled like French houses and the streets have French names. All the roads in St Anne are cobbled with oblong setts of red granite (the pavements are cobbled blue and red). The chimneys are of all shapes and one chimney had a window in it. Wind-lashed seaside trees lean over high-walled gardens. A square and storm-resisting church by Sir George Gilbert Scott – quite the best work of his I have ever seen – rises over the rooftops. The country creeps right into this sheltered, hilly capital. And the country of Alderney has its valleys, its hedges like Cornish hedges, its few farms, and hundreds of flowers. It is not a bit flat but full of interest.

The wonder of Alderney is its coast. And the wonder of its coast is the forts. I must explain to you about them. Lord Essex, Queen Elizabeth's favourite, built one but most of them were erected by the Prince Consort and Queen Victoria. When the people of Alderney were evacuated by the British during the war, the Nazis came in. They made use of these old forts and tunnelled under them. And now, if you know where to find them, there are, on the coast of Alderney, discreet openings in ferny, gorsy places on the cliffs, steps down, and then room after room, concrete and air-conditioned, with German notices painted on the walls. In some you will find a small window and, looking out, you will see the waves tumbling on the rocks below. What horrors went on in the concentration camps on the island we can only imagine. People will show tourists a concrete wall with bullet holes in it and a cemetery a few yards away. What comfort the Germans lived in we can see for ourselves: all they had to do when we bombed the island was to shut the doors of their underground forts and wait until we had gone away. But up on the heather outside the forts there are still long fences of that extra-thick German barbed wire. And here their prisoners shivered.

Between the forts are bays and beaches with sandy places to bathe. There's a huge harbour looking towards England and a bombed harbour tower that has now been most beautifully rebuilt in the local style by the English Ministry of Works. And among the rocks you may find 'ormers' – those mother-of-pearl shells whose fish is as delicate to eat as oysters and as large as scallop.

Now, with the sun shining and a light breeze blowing and flowers waving and low trees leaning and the sea all striped with sapphire, lapis and emerald, Alderney must be one of the loveliest islands in the world. Peace has come back to it and its people – about twelve hundred of them and twelve public houses. Peace, but not yet plenty. The last thing one wants to see is Alderney turned into a glassy lake of greenhouses punctuated by bungalows as so much of Guernsey has become. Somehow this island must be allowed to support itself in its own way. How? By cutting down the Civil Service? I do not know. I am no economist.

Do you remember Swinburne's poem 'Les Casquets' about those rocks round Alderney: 'As flowers on the sea are her small green realmlets'? And those sharper, more desolate rocks still looked down upon by the gannets:

> With never a leaf but the seaweed's tangle,
> Never a bird's but the sea-mew's note,
> It heard all round it the strong storm's wrangle,
> Watched far past it the waste wrecks float.

Alderney is green and calm and sheltered among those rocks and racing waters. It is symbolic. Small enough and remote enough to remain civilized and beautiful among all the criss-crossing tides that surround it.

THE ISLE OF MAN

Third Programme
Sunday 7 August 1949
Producer: Eileen Molony

• • •

Only a week or two ago I was stepping out of an Edwardian electric tramcar on to the grassy height of Snaefell, two thousand feet above sea level. The day was clear, with Snowdon visible seventy-three miles away to the south-east and, much nearer, the peaks of Cumberland, the Mull of Galloway and, in the west, the Mountains of Mourne: four countries in bluish outline beneath a sky of mother-of-pearl and a wrinkled sea all round us, cloud-patched with streaks of purple. Four countries seen from a fifth, this ancient kingdom of Man, which once included Sodor or the southern islands of Scotland.

The tramcar returned down the mountainside. Many who had been landed at the top went into the café for tea or a beer and I had for a moment the whole island to myself, thirty-two miles long and twelve wide. There it was at my feet: brown moor and mountain in the middle, tiny fields on their lower slopes, green slate and blue slate, silver limestone and red sandstone, Cornish-looking hedges, and whitewashed cottages thatched with straw and drowned in fuchsia bushes. It is a bit of Ulster set down in the sea, a bit of England, Scotland, Wales and Cornwall too, a place as ancient as them all, a separate country, Norse and Celtic at once.

Here in the south of England, I find that when I say I have been to the Isle of Man, people regard me as a returned explorer. 'What's it like?' 'Isn't it lines of boarding houses and so full of people there's no room to move?' 'Isn't it all motor bicycles?' It would be useless to deny that between June and September – 'the season', as it is called – something like half a million Lancashire people cross to Douglas, whole towns at a time. But the crowds confine themselves to Douglas and to queuing for the various trips round the isle by motor coach. They leave miles of farmland undisturbed.

Each time I have visited the Isle of Man it has been at the height of the season and each time I have been able to lose myself in real country. One morning I tramped knee deep in blackberry bushes on the wild west coast looking in vain for the ruins of a Celtic chapel and not seeing a soul, not even when I turned inland and walked down rutty farm lanes between foxgloves and knapweed to the narrow-gauge railway. Then, on that very evening, I was able to lose myself again in the crowds on Douglas front, to see Norman Evans in variety at the Palace and afterwards to watch a thousand couples dance in one of the big halls. All this in so small a kingdom: such wildness and such sophistication, such oldness and such newness. The trams, the farms, the switchback railways, the mountain sheep, the fairy lights and the wood smoke curing kippers – how can I cram them all in?

The clearest way of describing the island is to divide it into the two peoples of which it consists: the Manx and the visitors.

And the Manx come first. They are there always. When the last boat of holidaymakers has steamed out of Douglas Harbour, back to Lancashire, about fifty thousand Manx are left behind. Their names seem mostly to begin with C, K or Q: Quayle, Christian, Crellin, Kewley, Caine, Kelly, Clucas, Cregeen. The guidebooks will advise you to read Hall Caine's *The Deemster* in order to learn about the Manx and I must say that reading that once-so-famous novel, I found it a very good story – much better than I thought it was going to be. But the Manx themselves will tell you that the writer who best understands them is not Hall Caine but T. E. Brown, the Victorian schoolmaster who wrote that hackneyed piece 'A garden is a lovesome thing, God wot!'

Brown's *Fo'c'sle Yarns* are long verse stories written in dialect and therefore a shut book to most people. On the island with the dialect about you and the way of life they describe still going on (if you stay in one of the older and truly Manx towns like Castletown or Peel), these fo'c'sle yarns seem at their best. They are about sailing, fishing, violent passions and stern Methodism and through them all is the misty melancholy that haunts the Isle of Man.

The Manx are a Celtic people in origin. Their language is a form of Gaelic. The look of the land is Celtic: many small farms and a field system unlike southern England. Antiquities lie about all over the place: ruined oratories, crosses, standing stones. As in all Celtic countries, there are more antiquities than architecture. Architecture that is beautiful, not just interesting, came along later with the English.

Poor Isle of Man! Its history is just a series of invasions. Celtic first, then Norwegian until 1266, then Scots, then vaguely English – a sort of private island belonging to the Stanley family. It was indeed a mysterious, little-known kingdom until a century ago. Smuggling went on, morally secure under Manx law. Regency rakes from England and Ireland who could not pay their debts escaped to Douglas. Two of the fine sham castles above Douglas Bay were built by such men as these. Exasperated, in the end we bought the island 120 years ago for half a million pounds. This was an immense sum for the period but England gained in the long run on the bargain. The only people who did not at the time do well out of this sale over their heads were the Manx.

Yet still they keep their independence. Invaded for centuries, Man is still a separate country. Indeed the very fact that it is another country, with its own parliament, laws, licensing hours, flag and language, is one of the chief delights of going there. Right in the midst of the season, on 5 July, the Manx assert their Manxness on their chief annual holiday, Tynwald Day. Imagine it as I saw it this year – a hollow in the hills in a natural meeting place of roads and valleys called St John's. That delightful Isle of Man railway has a junction there – a junction for its lines when old narrow-gauge rolling stock is drawn past creamy meadow and brown stream. Clouds on all the surrounding mountain tops but a hole in the sky above our heads, for it is always fine at St John's on Tynwald Day. The sun shines down on a terraced mound of grass with a silken canopy on top of it. A short grass avenue strewn with rushes – offerings to a pagan sea god even older than the Viking Tynwald mound itself – leads to an original and pretty Victorian Gothic church. Either side of the avenue fly alternately the Manx and British flags. It is eleven in the morning and Manx from all over this island have come to hear their land ratified by the Governor on the top of the mound while the red-robed Deemster or judge will read out the words of ratification in English and a priest will repeat them in Manx.

The members of the House of Keys and the Legislative Council, who together make up the Tynwald or Manx parliament; mayors; clergy – they will be there. The Bishop of Sodor and Man – that luckless bishop whose cathedral is a ruin and who has a seat but no vote in the British House of Lords; the Sword of State; the Lieutenant Governor himself – all will soon pass out of the church, over the rushes, between the flags, and ascend to Tynwald Mound. It is an immensely impressive ceremony. No wonder the Manx from farms and sycamore-shaded glen, lush primeval marsh and lovely mountain, from Ronague on the slopes of South Barrule where Manx may still be spoken, from the stately ancient capital of Castletown or the old and winding lanes of Peel – no wonder the Manx come to witness this ceremony. It is a symbol of their exis-tence as a separate nation.

And now for the chief industry of the island – the visitors. Their centre is Douglas. Douglas was once a sort of Brighton set on a cres-cent of wooded cliffs above the sands. Many fine old stucco terraces survive and among them – delicious contrast – many a sham castle that makes you think of Sir Walter Scott. But this romantic watering place cannot originally have been designed for half a million North Country folk; more likely for a few hundred half-pay officers eking out their pensions here where taxes are low.

I think the man of genius who turned Douglas into a people's holiday resort was a Victorian, Governor Loch. He improved the harbours and had the Loch Promenade built in the 1860s and '70s. Thereafter Douglas-style boarding houses appeared in rows wher-ever there were gaps between the older terraces. They are innocent enough five-storeyed, bay-windowed, gabled buildings – gloomy behind, sea-gazing in front – rows and rows and rows of them so that the distant effect is of white paper folded into a concertina and perched here and there and everywhere along the shore. They are not disfiguring as are the modern bungalows and clumsily arranged electric-light poles that ruin so much of the country ports of Man.

And now, what with the TT, the motor races, the improved harbours, the way everybody is out to be gay however gloomy they are feeling, you cannot be ill-humoured in Douglas. The boats arrive; the aeroplanes come down. Young men and old in open shirts, sports coats and grey flannels – young girls and old in cheerful summer dresses – queue for ices, queue for shrimps, crowd round bars for glasses of delicious dry champagne, gaze from horse trams over municipal flower beds to the Tower of Refuge, that romantic sham castle that rises on a rock from the sea. They travel in luxury coaches round the island, half asleep in one another's arms, till the sun sets behind the boarding houses of Douglas and all the lights go up and the dance halls begin to fill.

So on our last evening let us take a stroll in Douglas, somewhere among the boarding houses. It is nine o'clock. There is still light in the sky. Father and mother are sitting in chairs on the steps of the boarding house, basking in one another's love. Behind the front door peeps the inevitable castor-oil plant in its china pot. Beside the parents sit the younger children, unnaturally good and quiet for fear they shall be sent up to bed while it is still light and while the moon rises huge and yellow above the purple bay. The elder children, grown up now, are off to the dance halls. The girls wear white dancing shoes and that is how you know whither they are bound. Let us follow them along the front while a few rejected young men sit sadly on the steps among the ancients and the infants. Two shillings or 4s. 6d., somewhere round that, is the cost of a ticket to dance. I like the Palace dance hall best. It has a parquet floor of sixteen thousand square feet and room for five thousand people. It is in a gay baroque style, cream and pink in colour inside, and from the graceful roof hang Japanese lanterns out of a dangling forest of flags. A small and perfect dance band strikes up – ah, the dance bands of the Isle of Man! Soon a thousand couples are moving beautifully, the cotton dresses of the girls like vivid tulips in all this pale cream and pink, the sports coats and dark suits of the men acting as a background to so much airy colour. The rhythmic dance is almost tribal so that even this middle-aged spectator is caught up in mass excitement, pure and thrilling and exalting.

Let us leave the Isle of Man with one last picture. At the same time as the dance bands are playing in Douglas and the yellow moon is rising in its bay, here off the western, wilder coast, the herring fleet is setting out from Peel. The sun sets behind the outline of the castle and the ruined cathedral and round tower enclosed within its walls. A stiffish west wind is blowing and the sea beyond the breakwater is dark green and choppy. Here they come, the little drifters – over a hundred of them. (Alas, only nine are Manx-owned and manned; the rest are mostly Scottish.) Out of the harbour, round the castle island, the dying sun shines gold upon their polished sides. I stand alone upon a rock by Peel Castle. The herring fleet is disappearing into the sunset. The smell of salt and wet earth is in my nostrils; the dark-green slate of those old castle walls is at my side. Inland, the last rays of sun are lighting the winding lanes of Peel, the red sandstone of its church towers and the soft protecting mountains behind it. Here, salt spray, seagulls, wild rocks and cavernous cliffs. Beyond those mountains, the dance halls of Douglas and the dance-band leader in his faultless tails. An isle of contrasts! A miniature of all the Western world.

ESSENTIAL VIEWING

PADSTOW

From the series 'Buildings and Places'

Third Programme
Sunday 6 February 1949
Producer: Basil Taylor

• • •

Some think of the furthest-away places as Spitsbergen or Honolulu. But give me Padstow, though I can reach it any day from Waterloo without crossing the sea. For Padstow is further away in spirit even than Land's End. It is less touristy than other fishing towns like Polperro and St Ives; less dramatic than Boscastle or Tintagel; only just not a village for it has, I think, more than two thousand inhabitants. It is an ancient, unobvious place, hidden away from the south-west gales below a hill on the sandy estuary of the river Camel. It does not look at the open sea but across the tidal water to the sand dunes of Rock and the famous St Enodoc golf course. There is no beach, only an oily harbour, and remarkably large prawns may be netted where the town drains pour into the Camel. But would the prawns be safe to eat?

I like to think how annoying it must be to tidy-minded civil servants to have to put up with the green Southern Railway engines coming right into this brown-and-cream Great Western district of Cornwall to reach Padstow, Launceston, Egloskerry, Otterham, Tresmeer,★ Camelford, and so on down that windy single line. I know the stations by heart, the slate- and granite-built waiting rooms, the oil lamps and veronica bushes, the great Delabole Quarry, the little high-hedged fields; and where the smallholdings grow fewer and the fields

★ In fact Tresmeer comes between Egloskerry and Otterham.

larger and browner, I see the distant outline of Brown Willy and Rough Tor on Bodmin Moor. And then the train goes fast downhill through high cuttings and a wooded valley. We round a bend and there is the flat marsh of the Camel, there the little rows of blackish-green cottages along the river at Egloshayle and we are at Wadebridge, next stop Padstow. The next five-and-a-half miles beside the broadening Camel to Padstow is the most beautiful train journey I know. See it on a fine evening at high tide with golden light on the low hills, the heron-haunted mud coves flooded over, the sudden thunder as we cross the bridge over Little Petherick creek, the glimpses of slate roofs and a deserted jetty among spindly Cornish elms, the wide and unexpected sight of open sea at the river mouth, the huge spread-out waste of water with brown ploughed fields coming down to little cliffs where no waves break but only salt tides ripple up and ebb away. Then the utter endness of the end of the line at Padstow – 260 miles of it from London. The smell of fish and seaweed, the crying of gulls, the warm, moist West Country air and the valerian growing wild on slate walls.

The approach to Padstow I like most of all is the one I have made ever since I was a child. It is by ferry from the other side of the estuary. It was best in a bit of a sea with a stiff breeze against an incoming tide, puffs of white foam bursting up below the great head of distant Pentire and round the unapproachable cliffs of the rocky island of Newland, which seems, from the ferry boat, to stand halfway between Pentire and Stepper Point at the mouth of the river. We would dip our hands in the water and pretend to feel seasick with each heave of the boat. And then the town would spread out before us, its slate roofs climbing up the hillside from the wooden wharves of the harbour till they reached the old church tower and the semicircle of wind-slashed elms which run as a dark belt right around the top of the town, as though to strap the town in more securely still against those south-west gales. Sometimes we would return on a fine, still evening, laden with the week's shopping, and see that familiar view lessen away from the ferry boat while the Padstow bells, always well rung, would pour their music across the water, reminding me of Parson Hawker's lines

'Come to thy God in time!'
Thus saith their pealing chime.

'Youth, Manhood, Old Age past!
Come to thy God at last!'
[from 'The Silent Tower of Bottreaux']

Padstow is a fishing port and a shopping centre. There is an ice factory, an attractive Georgian-style customs house, a hideous post office, an electric-light company founded in 1911 and a gasworks founded in 1868 – this last beside sad and peeling Public Rooms of yellow stucco dated 1840.

If I were talking to town planners and economists and not to you, I would try to explain the decline of the boat-building industry, the amount of fish sent by rail to London, the economic and social effect on the town of the vast numbers of service people who pour in from a desert that has been made in the neighbouring parishes of St Eval and St Merryn – a form of desert known as an aerodrome. I would touch on the tourist trade and the corn trade. But the chief fact about modern Padstow to interest fact maniacs starts with a mermaid. She was combing her hair and singing in the estuary when a Padstow youth went walking along the cliffs towards open sea. He shot at her and in her rage she plunged down below the water and picked up a handful of sand which she threw towards Padstow, and that was the start of the Doom Bar. This bar is a bank of sand that for centuries has been slowly silting up the estuary. In all this long stretch of rocky coast, fierce and inhospitable, from Tintagel to Perranporth, Padstow is the only port of any size. If the channel silts up altogether, her trade will be gone.

It must have been a solemn conference that the Urban District Council called last November to discuss the future of the harbour. 'The council realized,' said Mr Brabyn, its chairman,

that unless something was done to make the harbour more navigable, Padstow as a port would become extinct. Less than a century ago there were regular sailings of passenger-carrying ships from Padstow to America and Canada and it was within the memory of many present that there was a fortnightly sailing from Bristol Channel ports of steamboats carrying flour and merchandise. This was continued for many years. As many as sixty or seventy trawlers use the port during the fishing season.

Then a letter was read from a Yarmouth firm of shipowners:

> We have always been in the habit of sending our boats to Padstow, as
> we did last year, and we intend to do so again in 1949 during February,
> March and April. Like everyone else, we are concerned about the silt-
> ing up of the estuary, making it extremely difficult to manoeuvre our
> ships in and out of port, and if action is not taken very soon we shall
> be unable to use the port at all, to our mutual detriment.

So there are hundreds of thousands of tons of good agricultural silver
sand increasing and increasing. I can well remember how as a child
I could see the hulks of ships that had been wrecked on the Doom
Bar sticking up black out of the yellow sand. These are now all
covered over. Who will take the sand away? And how will they do it?
Miracles are always happening. In Padstow they are easier to believe
in than in most places, because it is so ancient a town. So probably
the port of Padstow will be saved, even if it is a government department that performs the miracle.

While I sit here, I stand in memory on the old quay. I see between
the rigging of a sailing ship the slate-hung houses in a semicircle
round the harbour. Padstow looks all slate, though here and there the
silver-blue tiled buildings are diversified by an old rose-coloured
brick house and near me is a building called The Abbey House with
granite fifteenth-century quoins. A boy standing up in a dinghy pro-
pels her backwards across the calm, oily water by working an oar to
and fro in the stern.

I turn into the quiet square of the Ship Hotel and notice that
Miss Tonkin's boot shop is no longer there though her house with its
ferns in the window and lace curtains, its lush, enclosed front and
back gardens, still stands. I see that a jeweller's shop has been transformed into a souvenir haunt of tourists, that new diamond-leaded
panes look odd in the window and that wooden beams – unknown
in Cornwall – are fixed on to the outside walls. The main streets are,
thank goodness, little altered. There's not much grand architecture in
Padstow. It is all humble, unobtrusive houses, three storeys high. Yet
as soon as one of them is taken down, the look of the town suffers.

In order to avoid a concrete cinema and café, erected out of scale
and texture with the town in 1921, I take another of the many narrow

roads that lead up the hill. And as I reach the upper air near the church I realize what a lot of gardens and houses there are in Padstow, though the place looks so small from the waterside. From here one can look down at the roofs of the houses, on palms and ilex trees and bushes of hydrangeas peeping above slate walls. Narrow public passages pass right through houses under stone arches and lead past high garden walls, down steps under other houses to further streets. And I begin to notice that this slate is not grey, as we are inclined to think is all Cornish slate, but a beautiful pale green stained here and there with reddish-brown. This is all hewn locally from the cliffs: slate roofs grouted over with cement and then lime-washed, slate walls, slate paving stones and, as I near the churchyard gate, slate hedges as high as a house on either side of me, stuffed with ferns and pennywort. I saw the little purple flowers of ivy-leaved toadflax on these hedges blooming as late as November last. Above these stone hedges are holly bushes and, beyond the holly, the circling belt of Cornish elms.

A wrought-iron gate opens into the churchyard. In tree-shaded grass are slate headstones with deep-cut lettering of the eighteenth and early nineteenth centuries and cherubs with ploughboy faces and Victorian marble stones to sailors with carved anchors and cables. The parish church of St Petroc is built of a brown-grey slate and its large fifteenth-century windows are crisply carved out of dark blue-black catacleuse stone – a most beautiful hard stone for carving that lasts all centuries of weather. The church is unusually large and lofty inside for a Cornish building. It was pleasantly restored in the last century. The windows are mercifully nearly all of clear glass looking out into the green churchyard and embellished in the upper lights with gay heraldic shields which match a golden, red and purple east window of startling early-Victorian beauty – probably by the great stained-glass artist Hedgeland, who worked at St Neots, King's Cambridge and Norwich Cathedral. Alas, there is no screen across the church's three broad aisles. That has gone. But there is a fifteenth-century font standing on four pillars and carved with the twelve Apostles – all of this in the same, beautiful, hard catacleuse stone.

A huge monument with kneeling figures painted in reds and whites and yellows and blacks commemorates Sir Nicholas Prideaux (died 1627) and leads me to mention Padstow's great house, Prideaux Place. It stands on a grass clearing among elms, firs and ilex trees (that specially West Country tree) not far from the church, near the higher part of the town where late-Georgian houses with ilex- and palm-shaded gardens and glasshouses with geraniums and grapes in them suggest the land agent, the doctor, retired tradesmen and old sea captains. A sign saying 'No through road' encourages the sort of person I am to walk through and I come to a low, castellated slate wall in a toy-fort, Gothic style, with a genuine Gothic door let into it. Behind this, in full view of the road, is the E-shaped manor house – surely the prettiest Elizabethan building in this island. The eastern front, which we can see, looks over the road to its little planted park and on to the distant low sand hills across the estuary. The feathery slate walls are battlemented on top. Over the entrance porch, in the wings and in the spaces between them, are noble granite windows. Even the old lead rainwater heads are there with the Prideaux crest and initials on them. A large magnolia shelters in one fold of the house and a Georgian semicircular bay is just seen on the south wing, looking across another part of the park. The inside of the room is said to be full of panelling and wood carving and plasterwork and fine furniture – but I've never seen it.

All this is sixteenth and seventeenth century; and the church and the houses I have been describing in the town are mediaeval or Georgian. They seem comparatively new. What strikes one at once about Padstow is that it is even older than its oldest buildings. And on its ancientness I mean to end this talk. You must know that when the river Camel was narrower, and when woods now covered with sand waved in the estuary thirteen hundred years ago – that is to say, in the sixth century – Petroc, servant of God and son of a Welsh king, crossed the sea from Ireland in a coracle and landed at Trebetherick on the other side of the water. And then he crossed the river and founded a monastery which was known as Petrocstow or Padstow. Many miracles are recorded of him and tales of his kindness to animals and of his long prayers standing in a stream on Bodmin Moor, where to this day his little beehive cell, made of turf and granite, survives. He raised the dead, cured the sick and tamed a savage, serpent-eating monster.

A mediaeval life of St Petroc was discovered recently in Germany. I must read you the last story in it and its ending:

A woman, feeling thirsty one night, drank water out of a water-jug and swallowed a small serpent, [in consequence of which] she was for many years in bad health. As no physicians benefited her, she was brought to the holy man. He made a mixture of water and earth, which he gave the sick woman to drink, and immediately she had swallowed it she vomited a serpent three feet long, but dead, and the same hour she recovered her health and gave thanks to God.

After these and many such miracles, Blessed Petroc, continually longing for heavenly things, after afflicting his body with much rigour, full of days, departed to God on the day before the nones of June. The sacred body, therefore, worn out with fastings and vigils, is committed to the dust and the bosom of Abraham receives his spirit, the angels singing to welcome it. At his tomb miracles frequently take place and his bones, albeit dry, retain the power of his virtues. May his glorious merits intercede for us with Christ, who with the Father liveth and reigneth world without end. Amen.

I do not know whether St Petroc's Day, 4 June, is still celebrated in Padstow church. It is in Bodmin parish church and in most of the other thirty or so churches in Wales, Devon and Cornwall that are dedicated to him. His cult has survived too in Brittany – and at Loperec (really Locus Petroci, the place of Petroc) they have a statue of him, a more lively one than the little stone one in Padstow. It shows a benign, bearded man in a spangled cloak. In one hand he holds the Gospels and with the other he strokes a thin, nobbly little deer that has jumped up to him and put its forepaws on his breast. Blessed St Petroc! He was the chief of all Cornish saints, a man of pervading gentleness that has never been forgotten – not even in Padstow, for I went into a souvenir shop there last year and said, 'Have you got a statue of St Petroc?' 'No,' said the shopman. 'A picture of him then?' 'No.' 'Have you heard of St Petroc?' 'Yes, I've heard of him. But there's no demand.' Perhaps this talk will help to create a demand – at any rate for his help. Padstow port certainly needs it.

St Petroc may be neglected but the Padstow Hobby Horse is not. Whether it came in with the Danes, who sacked the town in 981 and drove St Petroc's monks to Bodmin, or whether it was a pagan rite that St Petroc himself may have witnessed with displeasure, I leave to antiquarians to dispute. The Padstow Hobby Horse is a folk survival that is almost certainly of pagan origin. Moreover, it is as genuine and unselfconscious as the morris dancing at Bampton-in-the-Bush, Oxfordshire, and not even broadcasting it or an influx of tourists will take the strange and secret character from the ceremonies connected with it. This is what happens. On the day before May Day, green boughs are put up against the houses. That night every man and woman in Padstow is awake with excitement. I knew someone who was next to a Padstow man in the trenches in the 1914 war. On the night before May Day, the Padstow man became so excited he couldn't keep still. The old 'obby 'oss was mounting in his blood and his mates had to hold him back from jumping over the top and dancing about in no man's land.

Now imagine a still night, the last of April, the first of May. Starlight above the chimney pots. Moon on the harbour. Moonlight shadows of houses on the slate walls opposite. At about two in the morning the song begins.

> With a merry ring and with the joyful spring,
>   For summer is a-come unto day.
> How happy are those little birds which so merrily do sing
>   In the merry morning of May.*

Then the men go round to the big houses of the town singing below the windows a variety of verses:

> Arise up, Mr Brabyn, I know you well afine,
> You have a shilling in your purse and I wish it were in mine.

And then on to a house where a young girl lives:

> Arise up, Miss Lobb, all in your smock of silk,
> And all your body under as white as any milk.

Morning light shines on the water and the green-grey houses. Out on the quay comes the Hobby Horse – it used to be taken for a drink to a pool a mile away from the town. It is a man in a weird mask,

---

* Betjeman continued, 'Here's the tune. I can't sing in tune, so I've asked my cousin Miss Elsie Avril to play it.'

painted red and black and white, and he wears a huge hooped skirt made of black tarpaulin, which he is meant to lift up, rushing at the ladies to put over the head of one of them. The skirt used to have soot in it. A man dances with the Hobby Horse carrying a club. Suddenly, at about 11.30 in the morning, there is a pause. The Hobby Horse bows down to the ground. The attendant lays his club on his head and the day song begins — a dirge-like strain:

> Oh where is St George? Oh where is he, O?
> He's down in his long boat, all on the salt sea, O.

The he jumps the hobby horse, loud shriek the girls, louder sings the crowd and wilder grows the dance:

> With a merry ring and with a joyful spring,
> For summer is a-come unto day.
> How happy are those little birds which so merrily do sing
> In the merry morning of May.

Farewell, Padstow! Forgive me, a stranger, for telling some of your secrets outside your little streets. I have known them and loved them so long, I want others to enjoy, as I have done, your ancientness and beauty.

KELMSCOTT MANOR

From the trio of programmes called 'Landscapes with Houses'
in the series 'Three in Hand'

Home Service
Sunday 4 May 1952
Producer: R. E. Keen

• • •

The best way of all to approach Kelmscott is the way William
Morris, the poet, craftsman and socialist, used to come to this
house of his dreams – by river. Kelmscott Manor House – it's pronounced 'Kemscot' – is on the banks of the upper Thames. It's not
the sort of Thames of Boulter's Lock and Maidenhead nightclubs,
not those used and wide waters, but a Thames that is almost a stream
up between the last locks. There are more kingfishers than boats, and
many dragonflies like gleaming aeroplanes, and meadowsweet and
willows and irises, and flat, almost Lincolnshire, landscape on the
Oxfordshire bank where Kelmscott stands. And gentle elm-covered
hills on the Berkshire bank opposite, and only a mile and a half away
you see the elegant spire of Lechlade church in Gloucestershire with
the meadows of Wiltshire across the stream. The roads round here
are like streams themselves, winding among unfenced or low-hedged
fields past greyish-golden cottages of stone and barns and dovecotes
and little churches. It is all like England was in 1871 when William
Morris and Rossetti first rented Kelmscott Manor House from the
Turner family for £75 a year. And it is like England was in the sixteenth century when the Turners first built themselves this gabled
manor house. Their descendants, the Hobbes family, still farm most
of the land round it.

What I have to tell you about Kelmscott is best told by other people's writing. The house is at the end of the village in a lane to itself and you can see it from a long way off because of the gigantic elms by which it is surrounded. (How sad it is to think that in twenty-one years, if the elm disease continues at its present rate, there will not be an elm tree left in England except the Cornish elms, which are not subject to the disease.) Now here is William Morris coming to the house as he describes it in *News from Nowhere*:

> Through the hawthorn sprays and long shoots of the wild roses I could see the flat country spreading out far away under the sun of the calm evening, till something that might be called hills with a look of sheep pastures about them bounded it with a soft blue line. Before me, the elm-boughs still hid most of what houses there might be in this river-side dwelling of men; but to the right of the cart-road a few grey buildings of the simplest kind showed here and there.
>
> . . . We crossed the road, and again almost without my will my hand raised the latch of a door in the wall, and we stood presently on a stone path which led up to the old house . . . My companion gave a sigh of pleased surprise and enjoyment; nor did I wonder, for the garden between the wall and the house was redolent of the June flowers, and the roses were rolling over one another with that delicious super-abundance of small well-tended gardens which at first sight takes away all thought from the beholder save that of beauty.

Before we go in, let's walk round this grey-stone-walled garden among the box borders, the cut yews and the roses. It's not a very big house and I think that why everybody likes it so much is that it is small and something they feel they could live in and love themselves. If you weren't sure, you would say that this old stone house, purple when wet with rain, gold in sunlight when seen against dark-green trees or approaching storm clouds – if you weren't sure, and like me you were someone who thought he knew about architecture, you would say it was mostly Tudor. But I believe it is later – more like Charles I's time, for the tradition of stonemasonry lingered on in this remote place even until well into the last century. And you will notice that one wing on the north is grander than the rest of the house, with carvings on the outside that are a hundred years later than Tudor. And while we are outside, look at the farm buildings: barns as big as churches, all in the local stone; high stone walls; and from the west side of the house a view across an apple orchard to huge meadows. They all seem to have grown with the landscape. 'If you touched them,' Janey Morris said to Rossetti, 'you would expect them to be alive.'

I think you ought to hear what a great Victorian architect, Philip Webb, the friend of Morris and designer of his tombstone, has to say about Kelmscott:

> From my earliest recollections this general kind of house was familiar to me, where the coarse oolite stone of the Thames valley gave the peculiar character to the old buildings in and around Oxford. There are still remaining, in more or less perfect state, many houses of the same quality, though some are more architecturally marked than at Kelmscott . . .
>
> For so late a time of genuine native building, and from the modesty of the house altogether, it was singular how the regular *plan* of the old English form, of all degrees of importance, was enclosed in the earlier part of it. There was the entrance doorway in the front wall leading through to the opposite doorway in the back wall, with the hall on the right hand, cut off from the passage by the screen, with kitchen and other offices on the left: the parlour (or *solar*) at the other end of the hall, by the side of the stairs, with cellar under; all of which was of the smallest and least pretentious work. Then, a comparatively few years later, the large square parlour was built with the tapestry room over, in loftier range, and in a style clearly showing the Renaissance influence, chiefly marked by the two large fireplaces, and small classically shaped windows in the gables of attics in the roofs.[*]

The house inside is very much as it was, except that there are water closets, and two bathrooms with immersion heaters, and electric light has been introduced. As Morris said in *News from Nowhere*, 'Everywhere there was but little furniture, and that only the most necessary, and of the simplest forms . . . [one wall] was still hung with old tapestry, originally of no artistic value but now faded into pleasant grey tones which harmonised thoroughly well with the quiet of the place and which would have been ill-supplanted by brighter and more striking decoration.'

And I must say that today you could not say Kelmscott was dis-

[*] From J. W. Mackail's *The Life of William Morris*, vol. 1 (Oxford: Oxford University Press, 1950), pp. 231-2.

appointing inside, for everything, according to the terms on which it was left to the Oxford University Chest which administers it, is as the Morris family left it. The furniture is solid stuff, some of it heavily handmade and painted by Morris and Rossetti; some of it Elizabethan, and there is a great four-poster Elizabethan bed in which William Morris used to sleep – an inconvenient place to sleep, for anyone passing into the tapestry room had to go past William Morris lying in his bed. The bed has a beautiful cover embroidered by Morris's daughter May and round the posts at the top of the bed is an embroidered border which begins like this:

> The wind's on the wold
> And the night is a-cold,
> And Thames runs chill
> Twixt mead and hill,
> But kind and dear
> Is the old house here,
> And my heart is warm
> Midst winter's harm.

The ornaments in the house are mostly blue pottery, collected I believe by Rossetti. There are numerous drawings of Mrs William Morris by Rossetti – Janey or Jenny Morris, with her long, long neck and chin, her full lips and sleepy eyes and flaming hair, who was so adored by Rossetti from the day he first met her at Oxford, when he and Morris and others were painting the roof of the library of the Oxford Union.

I suppose the grandest room is the drawing room, with its white Georgian panelling, on the ground floor in that north wing of the house I described when we were outside. And about equally grand is the tapestry room above it, though I could, like Rossetti, do without the tapestry, which has been there since the seventeenth century. It shows the life of Samson and one particularly nasty bit shows Samson having his eyes gouged out – not an ideal wall decoration.

The rooms I like best are the older ones at the west end: the ground-floor one which Rossetti moved into for a studio when he painted Janey Morris – his palette and paints are still there – and above it a bedroom all papered in the green willow-pattern paper Morris designed, which is so like the willowy lanes round here and seems to be made almost of living branches. Throughout the house there are Morris papers and Morris chintzes (The Strawberry Thief, The Daisy and so on) – flowered chintzes and papers that make it seem as though the beautiful garden outside had walked into the house and stylized itself on the walls and chairs and curtains. I wish Morris designs and chintzes were easily obtainable and not so expensive. They are miles pleasanter to live with than the dull cream walls and hygienic whites and greens with which we have to put up today. Morris would have liked them cheap and available to everyone. As it is, they are the perquisite of the very few.

I have not bothered you with a detailed tour of this uneven and rambling little manor house. What you cannot fail to notice, and what is worth mentioning last and emphasizing most, is its atmosphere. It haunts one. I know of no house with so strong an atmosphere. There is no other place which is kept as it was and yet so clearly is not a museum but a house. Come up to the first floor and look out of one of the windows over the tops of the yews and the flowering trees, through the great elms and into the wide upper-Thames meadows. Winter and summer for three centuries while the Turner family lived here this stone grew lichened and from those water spouts the heavy rain fell onto the deep green grass of the garden from between the gables. Never did you hear such a noise of English wet as when the rain pours off Kelmscott Manor roof and splashes on the grass and garden paths! And sometimes the Thames would rise and flood the front garden.

Yet I think the chief atmosphere here is of those Pre-Raphaelite tenants William Morris and Dante Gabriel Rossetti. They took the house. Rossetti went to live in it first and this annoyed Morris, so he went to Iceland. Rossetti, in love with Mrs Morris, remained at Kelmscott, getting more and more moody and thinking there were plots against him, staying awake till five in the morning and taking chloral, and only going out when he would meet few villagers. But he had his moments of loving the place and, since he was in love, produced some fine poems. I always like those stanzas he wrote at Kelmscott which, standing here looking out of the windows, so call to one's mind the trees and birds around us:

Sun-steeped in fire, the homeward pinions sway
    Above the dovecote-tops;
And clouds of starlings, ere they rest with day,
Sink, clamorous like mill-waters, at wild play,
    By turns in every copse.

Each tree heart-deep the wrangling rout receives, –
    Save for the whirr within,
You could not tell the starlings from the leaves;
Then one great puff of wings, and the swarm heaves
    Away with all its din.

[from 'Sunset Wings']

In 1877 Rossetti left Kelmscott, never to return. Thereafter Morris came back but used it chiefly as a retreat – a holiday house for his wife and children while he remained in London at his Hammersmith house, which he called Kelmscott House after his country manor. There in Hammersmith he did his printing and made his socialist speeches and tore bits out of his black beard when he grew angry.

I like to think of him in the summer of 1880 setting out with three near friends and his wife to row from Kelmscott, Hammersmith, to Kelmscott, Oxon. The boat looked like a horse bus on water with a pair of oars in the prow. They reached Oxford after seven days:

Janey the next day (Monday) went on by rail to Kelmscott: while we got up early and by dint of great exertions started from Medley Lock at 9 a.m., with Bossom and another man to tow us as far as New Bridge, where we sent them off, and muddled ourselves home somehow, dining at a lovely place about a mile above New Bridge, where I have stopped twice before for that end. One thing was very pleasant: they were hay-making on the flat flood-washed spits of ground and islets all about Tadpole; and the hay was gathered on punts and the like; odd stuff to look at, mostly sedge, but they told us it was the best stuff for milk. Night fell on us long before we got to Radcot, and we fastened a lantern to the prow of our boat, after we had with much difficulty got our boat through Radcot Bridge. Charles was waiting for us with a lantern at our bridge by the corner at 10 p.m., and presently the ancient house had me in its arms again: J. had lighted up all brilliantly, and sweet it all looked you may be sure.*

Sixteen years later in the early autumn of 1896, William Morris died. His body was carried to the little churchyard from Kelmscott Manor House in a yellow farm wagon with red wheels, wreathed with vine and willow boughs.

My own happiest memories of Kelmscott date from as late as the thirties, when May and her friend Miss Lobb lived in the Manor House. My wife and I used to drive by pony cart to tea there and were always welcomed with a huge tea and a feed for the pony, for May Morris loved anything that was not to do with this mechanized age. She used to show us the beautiful vellum books her father decorated, and to give us roses from trees he had planted in the garden. At any moment one would not have been surprised to see the burly form of Morris himself and the thin-bearded Burne-Jones beside him and perhaps William De Morgan walk in over the sunlit flagstones into the drawing room. They were about the house and their memory was loved by dear May Morris. And then the aerodrome came and the pylons and wire of electric light and the noisome dredging of the upper Thames by the Thames Conservancy, and she and Miss Lobb liked being alive less and less. Just before the war they went to Iceland together – Morris, you will remember, always went to Iceland – and soon after they returned May Morris faded out of life and Miss Lobb soon followed her. The manor house was left by May to Oxford University as a memorial to her father.

One final story I heard from a recent tenant of Kelmscott. She was sitting, on a still autumn night five years ago, up on the first floor in the room with Morris's bed in it and which leads to the tapestry room. She was alone in the house. In the silence, she heard two men talking amicably in the room. She opened the door of the tapestry room to see who they were. There was no one in it. Morris? Burne-Jones? Rossetti? Philip Webb? Who knows. The place is haunting and haunted, for it has been loved as only an old house can be loved.

* From *The Letters of William Morris to his Family and Friends*, ed. Philip Henderson (London: Longmans, 1950), pp. 137–8.

CARDIFF CASTLE

*From the trio of programmes called 'Landscapes with Houses'
in the series 'Three in Hand'*

Home Service
Sunday 18 May 1952
Producer: R. E. Keen

• • •

I have left the most amazing house for this the last of my talks.
'Amazing' is the word. It is amazing that it should be in the middle
of Cardiff; it is amazing in itself. I don't know how to start about it,
there is so much to say. But I will tell you this at once: it is worth
journeying from anywhere, however remote in these islands, to see
Cardiff Castle. Caernarvon and Windsor have richer associations;
Kenilworth is more famous; but for quaintness, learned ingenuity,
gorgeousness of colour, jokes, excitement and splendour, Cardiff
Castle has them all beaten.

The first amazing thing about Cardiff Castle is that it should still
be there. Cardiff is a new town. In 1801 there were only just over a
thousand people in it. Today there are nearly a quarter of a million.
It is the first coal port of the world and the administrative centre of
Wales – though not the capital, for Wales has no capital. Perhaps the
capital should be some ancient city. And Cardiff has many worlds in
it, only some of which are Welsh. There are the docks and that
crowded town of coloured people cut off geographically by railways
and water from the rest of Cardiff; there is a classy part on the road
to Llandaff Cathedral; there are other suburbs; and there are miles and
miles of council estates and little houses. The main shopping streets
are the usual hotchpotch of chain stores relieved by a great many
glass-covered arcades, so that shopping in Cardiff is comparatively

dry. And then bang in the middle of this industrial muddle, which might be Wolverhampton or Birmingham or anywhere – bang in the middle there is a green heart, still, spacious and seeming to stretch on in all directions. A great part of it is laid out as a civic centre. It is the finest civic centre in these islands and as it has something to do with Cardiff Castle, I must show it you for a minute.

You know what the huge head offices of banks are like. You know what Whitehall looks like. Well, imagine some really handsome buildings in this official, rather heavy Classical style set down in plenty of space among trees: the City Hall with its nobly sculptured steeple and its dome, and the Law Courts in a similar style – both by Lanchester and Rickards. (It was smart a few years ago to laugh at buildings of this sort and call them 'Commercial Queen Anne'.) See in your mind's eye the beautiful columned and domed Museum by Smith and Brewer, the Classic colonnade of Sir Ninian Comper's War Memorial, the County Hall and the University – imagine these public buildings all gleaming in a wonderful white stone, whiter than Portland and quarried locally at Lydney. See them as I saw them last week among blossoming trees and emerald elms and wide lawns. You feel you are in Paris, in something really monumental – and 'fine' you say to yourself. Yet within living memory this was the private deer park that adjoined Cardiff Castle. And there, west of us, rises the high creamy-grey stone of the Castle, the origin of it all, the origin of the city of Cardiff, for this site was fortified by the Romans – as Professor William Rees tells us – in about AD 75. Then the Normans built a castle on its site; and of course the place was stormed during the sad, brave story of the Welsh wars. By the eighteenth century it had become the property of the Stuart family, eventually Crichton-Stuart, who are now Marquesses of Bute.

Now let us imagine ourselves seventy years ago driving into Cardiff from Llandaff Cathedral in an open victoria. It is, let us say, the year 1878. Down the road from Llandaff our eye is caught by a tall, creamy stone tower, and as we come to the bridge over the broad Taff we would say we were coming to an ancient French town. The river water is rather black with coal washings, it is true, and there are not the poplars and the fishermen you see along river banks in France, but it winds like a French river and has spits of pebbles stretching into it, and the French effect is completed by this high creamy-grey wall and the tower of the Castle – a very French kind of tower, with a clock in it and coloured statues round and a pyramidal slated roof. Along the battlemented walls are wooden shutters pierced with holes and swinging on enormous hinges. You expect an armoured soldier to lean out and shoot you with an arrow. The tower and the Castle walls dominate the city of Cardiff. And here I should mention that the lords of Bute would not allow any Cardiff buildings to appear above the castle walls. This cost the Corporation a good deal of money earlier in this century when the civic buildings were being put up. But it was a wise rule: today a new office building that has just grown up spoils the effect from inside the castle walls.

We will get out of the victoria here below the Castle, and by magic – for the place is severely walled in and nowadays some of the battlements have stone animals carved on them: eagles ready to peck our eyes out, dogs slithering down to bark, wolves to bite and pelicans to swallow us in their bills – by magic we will transport ourselves from the victoria into the park by the river. This was laid out beside the Taff in Georgian times by the famous Capability Brown, landscape architect. Even today, despite mistaken municipal planting of straight avenues, the park retains its designer's winding, endless effect of trees and meadows, stretching away upstream from the Castle walls and backed by the wooded hills of far Glamorgan. In this park two gentlemen are walking, followed by two dogs; you will still see those dogs portrayed in tiles on the entrance floor of the Winter Smoking Room in the Clock Tower. The bearded man is the lord of the place, the third Marquess of Bute, who in 1868 threw over the Presbyterian Church of his birth and became a Roman Catholic. The other has a long moustache which merges into mutton-chop whiskers, but his chin is clean-shaven. He is a bohemian, jovial fellow, laughing and talking and caressing the animals. This is William Burges, the great London architect, who keeps a parrot in his office and draws on vellum in oak-gall ink and believes there is no salvation except through the thirteenth century. The third Marquess thinks along the same lines and adds his religion to it. He is a scholar and antiquarian, an authority on breviaries. They both live in a mediaeval world of their own making. They are discussing further alterations to the

Castle. Lord Bute has the cash and Mr Burges has the skill to translate their dreams into glass and stone and wood and painted walls and
hangings. I wish I could see the letters these two remarkable men
must have written to each other – if they still exist. But to see the
realization of their dreams is better than any letters, and this we can
do and will, for the present Lord Bute generously gave the Castle and
its park, his father having already given the Deer Park, to the people
of Cardiff. We can now go in for a shilling and take a conducted tour
of this glittering wilderness of wonder.

Out of the roar of Castle Street, and we are in the walled enclosure of the Castle – high stone walls, a wide raised stretch of green
with a moated keep in it, an entrance tower still kept by Lord Bute,
and on the left the fifteenth-century castle building and the Victorian
work of Burges. At once you notice the silence in this place, the fresh
grass and flying clouds and the graceful outline of the City Hall
steeple above the walls. When I was there some students were rehearsing theatricals – Shakespeare I should think from the look on their
faces and the way they stood. It was an appropriate setting.

The castle you are going to see is not as big as you would think
from the outside. It is a long building diversified by towers and a lead
steeple. It lies along only a short stretch of the old Roman and
Norman walls – a sort of private house, one room thick, whose chief
windows look onto the inside of the large enclosure. Now William
Burges was a good constructor – his father was an engineer – and
what he designed never fell down; and he was a wonderful craftsman
and decorator. But he was not a planner. I strongly advise you to stick
to your guide as we walk about the house or you will be lost, as I was,
in a multitude of narrow passages and spiral stairs. Also, you need a
strong heart, as there are hundreds of steps to climb to the top rooms
in the towers. I feel sorry for the servants who carried cans of water
and logs and coals and trays up this labyrinth from the basement.

We walk along a covered passage on the top of the wall to the
Clock Tower. On the threshold are the dogs I mentioned. And if you
look up, as you go into the first room, you will get a fright. A black
clawed devil with white eyes and teeth stares down on you from the
vault. Here we are in the Winter Smoking Room – coloured walls;
coloured carved chimney piece; stained-glass windows. Not an inch

is undecorated and so it is in every room we see. Everywhere there is thought and fun. Notice the bronze door, the wooden walls inlaid with mother-of-pearl, the birds carved everywhere and the door handle which is a bronze parrot. Notice the bell push which is a wooden monkey with a nut in its mouth. You push the nut and that rings the bell.

In the Batchelor's Room above there is some interesting Burges furniture: a wash stand whose basin taps are bronze idols, a chimney piece inlaid with precious stones, or glass coloured to look like precious stones and an alabaster bathroom with a deep marble bath. Bronze fish and eels and jellyfish are let into the marble so that when the bath is full of water the fish appear to be swimming in it.

And right at the top is the Summer Smoking Room, the grandest room in the tower – a riot of reds and golds and blues. The floor is tiled with an early map of the stars; the stained-glass gallery above has pictures of the four elements and different metals. The carved and coloured corbels represent the winds. The coloured tiles on the walls are of Greek legends; and from the roof hangs a chandelier made to look like the rays of the sun enclosed in a band of crystal. Look out of the windows from this great height and notice their elaborate catches, with handles designed like little church bells; see how easily the windows swing and how richly wrought are their hinges. (This is a great feature of the house: all doors and drawers and windows turn or slide or swing smoothly.) All the catches are beautifully designed in hammered metal. There is nothing shoddy. Every detail has been designed with loving care by a practical artist-craftsman. One of the chief wood carvers was Thomas John, who worked here with his son Goscombe – now Sir Goscombe John, the famous sculptor. A great brain has made this place. A great view may be seen from this Summer Smoking Room of all Cardiff and the hills beyond, and the sea and Penarth and the islands of Flat Holm and Steep Holm in the British Channel and the Somerset coast – all of which look very near when it is going to rain.

And now we go down the spiral stair – careful, that's right – and along another passage by the battlements of the old walls to the main fifteenth-century part of the Castle. There's not much that is fifteenth century: almost everything you see is mid-Victorian and by Burges.

Here is the Arab Room, where ladies will be able to imagine themselves in a harem as they look through grilled screens down into Cardiff or up at the golden dome of the ceiling. This was the place where difficult lady guests who wanted to be alone could sit in Eastern seclusion. It was the last thing Burges designed. He did it in 1881, the year before he died. He had actually left the thirteenth century and gone Moorish. Through that Gothic arch here is the Banqueting Hall, the biggest room. Over the fireplace is a model castle with ladies waving and a priest giving a farewell blessing to a knight who rides below, while a prisoner looks enviously through a grille in the wall. And notice the painted wooden roof and the painted carvings over the doors, and the stained-glass bay windows, and the view through a pointed arch to a spiral stair. On the baluster of this stair a carved alligator opens its jaws to eat a little stone cherub who is trying to slide away down the banister.

And now let's climb to the Chaucer Room, where the painted walls, the stained-glass windows and the carving are, I think, better and more spirited than anywhere else. You look up into the hollow of the lead steeple, which is coloured gold and red and blue, you look round, and everywhere is colour. You are in a world of Chaucer's stories. The figure of Chaucer watches you from the top of the carved chimney piece; you look down into the grate and there you see the letters of the alphabet done in tiles. The floor is laid out as a maze. The panelling of the walls is inlaid with representations of plants and flowers in wood twisting up through the panels amid all the colour here. Martins and starlings are carved in most lifelike positions hanging to the cresting of these panels: there must be ten thousand carved birds and animals in Cardiff Castle, all more lifelike than the stuffed ones you may see in the museum over the way. And now we come out through the Chapel and Library and so into the everyday world again.

Part of Cardiff Castle is now used as the School of Music. It was a brilliant idea to house it there for the sound of Welsh voices singing, of fiddles scraping, of woodwind and brass, suits the glittering, learned and amazing rooms. You hear music suddenly behind doors and down passages. Laughter of students goes with the jokes in the carving: a cat up a tree with a dog barking at the bottom symbolizing married life; two white mice of ivory with red eyes made with jewels climb round a bell push in the Library; there is a beaver gnawing at the Tree of Knowledge over the library door, a huge frog glaring at you beside the door of the Banqueting Room.

Though it is now five days since I was in Cardiff Castle, the spell is still over me. I don't see how anyone could fail to be impressed by its weird beauty. I did not know that architecture and decoration could be so powerful. You see people coming out blinking their eyes, awed into silence, punch-drunk as it were from the force of this Victorian dream of the Middle Ages. It may not be very Welsh, nor even mediaeval, but my goodness it's wonderful.

AUTOBIOGRAPHY

CHRISTMAS NOSTALGIA

Home Service
Thursday 25 December 1947
Producer: Eileen Molony

• • •

ANNOUNCER
'Christmas Nostalgia'. A talk by John Betjeman, in which he tells us
he is going to contrast the flavour of former Christmases with the
canned Christmas of today.

BETJEMAN
That is a lot of rot of course. I mean it's not what I've now decided
to talk about. What happened, if you must know, is this. I decided
on the title of this talk over the telephone – and who says what he
means on the telephone? And now I've changed my mind. So I apologize. And besides I don't like that word 'nostalgia': it sounds like
'neuralgia' and gives me a headache. It's smart psychological claptrap
for the more honest word 'sentimental'. And that is what I have
decided to be: thoroughly sentimental.

I hope you have had plenty to eat and drink; I hope you are feeling uncritical and kind, with all those Christmas cards on the chimney piece with their woolly, well-intentioned messages from people
you don't think about from one year's end to another. Kindness is as
catching as cruelty; friendliness is as catching as callousness. Today,
kindness and friendliness are still in the air; they are hanging about
in the tobacco smoke and in the firelight, in the still streets and
behind the lit windows of houses. The slight indigestion we may feel
from having eaten rather more than usual has not yet, I hope, induced

ill temper. So I'm wrapping up my mind in artificial snow. I imagine a robin perched on my shoulder and the announcer kindly disguised as Father Christmas to support the illusion and the new directors of the BBC dressed as elves and sitting on wooden toadstools around this microphone as I am talking. And having imagined all that, I'm going back to the two earliest events I can remember, that first gave me an idea of *lacrimae rerum* – the tears of things. One of them concerned Christmas and a Mrs Hannah Wallis when I was a small boy – a small boy with projecting teeth and yellow skin and no brothers or sisters. Spirit of the past, call up Mrs Wallis! Her address was her daughter's house, 102 Dongola Road, Philip Lane, Tottenham, and she used to work for us. And dearly I loved her. Dearly and dependently. She must have been quite seventy then, so she would be well over 100 now, if she were alive.

She was an old-fashioned person, small and dumpy, and she wore a black bonnet when we used to take the train to Philip Lane Station and walk to her daughter in Dongola Road. Mrs Wallis listened for hours while I read poetry to her. My mother recalls how once she came home and found me reading poetry aloud outside the lavatory door behind which the old girl had locked herself. She played draughts with me and always let me win. I teased her and she laughed. I crossed the bounds of decency and decorum and she didn't mind. But when I came back of an evening from my day school she had mountains of hot buttered toast waiting for me. And I never knew her angry or fussed. And then came that fatal Christmas Day. I woke up early. Heavy on my feet were the presents of my relations, presents of sympathy for an only child. I don't remember what they were. But one of them I do remember. It was one of those pieces of frosted glass in a wooden frame and behind the glass a picture in outline which one was supposed to trace on the glass with a pencil. 'To Master John with love from Hannah Wallis.' I stood up on my bed among the brown paper of the opened parcels. I stood up. I stepped a step. Crack! I had smashed the frosted glass of her present.

Hannah Wallis, you who are now undoubtedly in heaven, you know now, don't you, that I did not do that on purpose? I remember thinking then that she might think I had smashed it because I did not think it a good enough present and that it looked too cheap among the more expensive ones of my relations. But, as a matter of fact, it was just what I wanted. And now I had smashed it. I remember putting it on a shelf over my bed between some books so as to hide the accident. Guiltily I went down to breakfast. 'Did you like the slate? It was just what you wanted wasn't it? The biggest I could get!' Poor people were poor in those days and she must have saved up for it. 'Oh yes and thank you very very much. It was lovely.' Oh the guilt, the shame! I did not dare, for fear of hurting her feelings whom I loved so much, I did not dare to tell her I had smashed it. Yet that evening, when my room had been tided and the presents put away, I found the broken glass and frame put in my waste-paper basket. I think that cracked glass was the first crack in my heart, the first time I lost innocence and the first time I realized the overwhelmingly unpleasant things of the world.

And as I look back I don't seem to remember subsequent child-hood Christmases. Other things got in the way. Gangs of boys who used to waylay me as I walked back from school and throw me into a holly bush on the edge of Highgate Cemetery. Intense homesick-ness when I first went to boarding school, where there was a smell of bat oil and stale biscuits and everyone shouting 'Quis?' 'Ego.' 'Anyone seen my ruler. Anyone seen my pencil case?' 'Shut up!' 'Betjeman, you'll get unpopular if you go on like this.' Then I seem to have directed all my wits to making myself popular – siding with the majority, telling lies to get out of awkward situations. I remember one whopper. It's worth quoting as an example of how absolutely stinking small boys can be to one another. There was one immensely popular boy, good-looking, upright and I suppose rather self-righteous – he is now a prominent Labour MP and has, I expect, quite forgotten the incident. He accused me of bullying another boy. 'I'll fight you for that in the morning.' Fight me! Oh Lord – and he learned boxing. It would hurt and I wouldn't win. I should become more unpopular than ever. How could I get out of it? The next morning I hit on a brilliant lie. We received our letters at breakfast. I had one and pretended to blub. Very sober and weepy, I went up to the champion of the right who was going to fight me. 'I'm awfully sorry, Per, I can't fight you this morning. I've just had a letter from home. My mater's most frightfully ill.' 'Oh, I'm most awfully sorry. Of course we won't fight.' It makes one blush, doesn't it?

And after that the lies, the subterfuges and the indulgences increase and increase so that I cannot possibly remember them all. They get between me and Christmas. Making money, increasing my possessions, lust, sloth, self-esteem – they stand between me and that innocence now lost, so that the small boy with projecting teeth and yellow skin is as different in spirit as he is in looks from this bald-headed man with green skin sitting here and talking at this moment.

Does this seem to have nothing to do with Christmas? It has everything to do with it. My birthday, which used to seem so important in childhood, is now of no importance and passes practically unnoticed. But Christmas is the one time that becomes more and more important to me. It is the one time when the world, at any rate in England, seems to get away from the world, when my struggle to get money and possessions and to score off enemies stops.

I am really glad to think that tomorrow most people (myself included) will be doing unusual things. Fathers inconveniently large in the house will be busy at a little amateur carpentry and house repair. Children will just be beginning to grow tired of new toys. Wives will be wearing the clasp their husbands have given them although, as a matter of fact, it doesn't go with this dress. Husbands will be bravely sporting their wife's choice of tie. The answering of Christmas letters:

Dear Minnie,
How good of you to write. We never seem to see each other do we? I would have written to you for Christmas except that I was so rushed and thought you wouldn't mind my writing after Christmas . . .

(*Liar!*)

Dear Aunt Susan,
The bedsocks were exactly what Jack wanted now that his hot-water bottle leaks and he can't use it.

(*Heavens! Did my wife send those bedsocks on to Aunt Bertha, because if so, Susan is sure to get to hear of it.*)

Christmas is the one time when I feel where my roots are: at home and among my friends and family. And the unwonted silence everywhere rubs it in. For once, Time seems to merge into the Eternal and I do not think of the dead as gone for ever but as waiting for me and watching me in this wintry silence when wheels no longer spin, nor hooters hoot, nor lorries thunder down main roads, and aeroplane engines have ceased to rip the sky with noise.

I have now to speak so personally because I can think of no other way of saying why Christmas means much more to me than my birthday. The greatest reason of all will take some putting across – even to anyone who has listened so far. It is this.

I cannot believe that I am surrounded by a purposeless accident. On a clear night, I look up at the stars and, remembering amateur astronomy, know that the Milky Way is the rest of this universe and that the light from some of the stars has taken years to reach this planet. When I consider that the light from the sun ninety million* miles away takes eight-and-a-half minutes to get here, the consequent immensity of this universe seems intolerable. And then I am told that some little clusters seen beyond the edge of the Milky Way on certain nights are other whole universes in outer space. It is too much, though believable. And then on any day about now I can turn over a piece of decaying wood in our garden and see myriapods, insects and bugs startled out of sluggish winter torpor by my action. Each is perfectly formed and adapted to its life. From the immensity of the stars to the perfection of an insect – I cannot believe that I am surrounded by a purposeless accident.

But can I believe this most fantastic story of all: that the Maker of the stars and of the centipedes became a baby in Bethlehem not so long ago. No time ago at all when you reckon the age of the earth. Well, it's asking a lot. If I weren't such a highbrow it would be easier. No man of intelligence can believe such a thing. A child of Jewish parents the Creator of the universe? Absurd.

But if it is not true, why was I born? And if it is true, nothing else is of so much importance. No date in time is so important as Christmas Day, the birthday of God made man. And carol singers and Salvation Army bands and Christmas cards (yes, even Christmas cards from ardent unbelievers, who always seem to observe Christmas) and

* 'Twenty million' in Betjeman's text.

cathedrals and saints and church bells and hospitals and almshouses and towers and steeples and the silence and present-giving of Christmas Day all bear witness to its truth.

Beyond my reason, beyond my emotions, beyond my intellect I know that this peculiar story is true. Architecture brings it home to me, I suppose because architecture is, with poetry, my chief interest.

Last week I was in the most beautiful building in Britain – King's College Chapel, Cambridge. You know it. It is a forest glade of old coloured glass and between the great windows columns of shafted stone shoot up and up to fountain out into a shower of exquisite, elaborate fan vaulting. It is the swansong of Perpendicular architecture, so immense, so vast, so superbly proportioned, so mysterious that no one can enter it without gasping. All the schoolchildren of Cambridge had filed into a carol service and there they were in the candlelight of the dark oak stalls. We stood waiting for the choir to come in and as we stood there the first verse of the opening carol was sung beyond us, behind the screen, away in the mighty splendour of the nave. A treble solo fluted up to the distant vaulting 'Once in Royal David's City'. It was clear, pure, distinct. And as I heard it I knew once more – knew despite myself – that this story was the Truth. And knowing it I knew that, because of the birth of Christ, the world could not touch me and that between me and the time I smashed Mrs Wallis's Christmas present hung the figure of God become man, crucified in the great east window.

JOHN BETJEMAN READS A SELECTION OF HIS OWN POETRY

A compilation of three radio talks given by Betjeman on the Third Programme between 1949 and 1958

Producers: Noel Iliff (Saturday 20 August 1949), Paul Humphreys (Thursday 6 October 1949), Eileen Molony (Friday 26 December 1958)

• • •

I'm very pleased to be asked by the BBC to recite my verses. I shall enjoy myself very much, even though you may not, because all the verse I've written was made to be read out loud. I've shouted it out to myself time and time over, every line, hundreds of times over. I've shouted when driving motor cars, when walking in the streets or when I find myself in an empty railway carriage, and in this way I've polished and repolished stanzas and added internal rhymes to them, which you may or may not notice as I recite. So this little performance is, for me, a supreme bit of self-indulgence. I've enjoyed hearing myself read but even more, I think I'm going to enjoy reading myself. But I ought to warn you that my verse is of no interest to people who can think. It jingles for the slaves of their own passions.

First of all there's three sections into which I think my poetry falls. Topography, scenery – English scenery in particular. I'm never very happy abroad and that's why I fear that the foreign students will find me not only boring but also incomprehensible. Very English stuff it is and very local, with lots of little local jokes in it and things like that. Topography is my chief theme in my poetry, about the country and the suburbs and the seaside. Then there comes love. Oh, very strong!

And in this hot weather stronger still. And then there comes what I've discovered as I grow old becomes increasingly one of my emotions: fear of death. Not a day passes without my visualizing how I shall die and what will happen afterwards. So I've arranged the poems going from gay through the various passions to death – it gets more and more depressing as it goes on, this recital. And on that cheerful note I'm going to end my little recital, getting more and more minor as I advance.

But first I'm going to read 'Death in Leamington'. I wrote it as an undergraduate at Oxford and I don't like it very much now but as we're in Warwickshire and Leamington isn't far off, I might as well read it. I recently got greatly excited about stucco houses and that slightly overblown Georgian that you get in Leamington, and I used to go up as an undergraduate from Oxford on the luncheon car train and have lunch, and then I used to go and have the waters at Leamington; and in the cool of the evening come back down on the tea-car train and tell my tutor I had been writing an essay.

> She died in the upstairs bedroom
>   By the light of the ev'ning star
> That shone through the plate glass window
>   From over Leamington Spa.
>
> Beside her the lonely crochet
>   Lay patiently and unstirred,
> But the fingers that would have work'd it
>   Were dead as the spoken word.
>
> And Nurse came in with the tea-things
>   Breast high 'mid the stands and chairs –
> But Nurse was alone with her own little soul,
>   And the things were alone with theirs.
>
> She bolted the big round window,
>   She let the blinds unroll,
> She set a match to the mantle,
>   She covered the fire with coal.
>
> And 'Tea!' she said in a tiny voice
>   'Wake up! It's nearly *five*.'

Oh! Chintzy, chintzy cheeriness,
   Half dead and half alive!

Do you know that the stucco is peeling?
   Do you know that the heart will stop?
From those yellow Italianate arches
   Do you hear the plaster drop?

Nurse looked at the silent bedstead,
   At the gray, decaying face,
As the calm of a Leamington ev'ning
   Drifted into the place.

She moved the table of bottles
   Away from the bed to the wall;
And tiptoeing gently over the stairs
   Turned down the gas in the hall.

My own part of the country where I live myself is in Berkshire, and up on the downs we've got a wonderful training-stable area. You can always tell these places by the beautiful white posts and rails and very neat gravel along the drives and beautiful turf and Edwardian conifers, which look slightly incongruous on the downs, but one has to thank the trainers for preserving the downs – at any rate the Berkshire and most of the Wiltshire Downs – from destruction by farmers. They alone have kept the turf and this is about Upper Lambourne, a remote part, except to trainers of Berkshire.

Up the ash-tree climbs the ivy,
   Up the ivy climbs the sun,
With a twenty-thousand pattering
   Has a valley breeze begun,
Feathery ash, neglected elder,
   Shift the shade and make it run –

Shift the shade toward the nettles,
   And the nettles set it free
To streak the stained Carrara headstone
   Where, in nineteen-twenty-three,
He who trained a hundred winners
   Paid the Final Entrance Fee.

Leathery limbs of Upper Lambourne,
   Leathery skin from sun and wind,
Leathery breeches, spreading stables,
   Shining saddles left behind –
To the down the string of horses
   Moving out of sight and mind.

Feathery ash in leathery Lambourne
   Waves above the sarsen stone,
And Edwardian plantations
   So coniferously moan,
As to make the swelling downland,
   Far-surrounding, seem their own.

Do you know King's at Cambridge? I always think Cambridge really beats Oxford – its architecture – and I'm trying to do a poem on King's Chapel. Haven't finished it yet. Keep writing the last verse and it doesn't work. Sounds too grand. Sounds like a sort of state poem in the *Sunday Times* when I put the last verse on, so I'm just going to read you the first two. I've crossed out the last one. I don't know whether they are much good but King's Chapel really is such a blaze of glory and beauty, especially inside, that I've always wanted to get it into verse. If you can compose the last verse in this metre I should be very grateful and would give anybody who writes it full acknowledgement.

File you out from yellow candle light
Fair choristers of King's,
And leave to shadowy silence
These canopied Renaissance stalls.
In blazing glass above the dark
Go skies and thrones and wings,
Blue, ruby, gold and green
Between the whiteness of the walls.
And with what rich precision
The stonework soars and springs
To fountain out, to spreading vault –
A shower that never falls.

Then I've tried to give the impression of how all the colours that you see in Cambridge – and Cambridge is full of them in its

stonework and in its meadows and in all its scenery, its flint and everything outside and in its sky – become transmuted through this stained
glass just into pearl on the stone shafts that go sprouting up the walls
and bursting into the fountains I've described of fan vaulting:

> The white of windy Cambridge courts,
> The cobbles brown and dry,
> The gold of plaster Gothic
> With ivy overgrown.
> The apple red, the silver fronts
> The deep green flats, and high
> The yellowing elm trees circled out
> On islands of their own.
> Oh! Here beyond all colours change
> That catch the flying sky,
> To waves of pearly light that heave
> Along the shafted stone.

And now I don't know how to complete it, you see. One wants
to get the impression, really, that brings King's Chapel finally to life
when one's inside it, which is when the organ is going and that choir
is singing, so brilliantly conducted by Boris Ord. Then you get a sort
of fourth dimension in the place. It's absolutely that one experience,
I think, that England has got above any country in the world, in
the way of architecture and music welded together. That last verse:
I don't think I shall ever be able to write it. But I hope somebody
will one day write a poem about King's Chapel. Wordsworth's
sonnet, to me, though very wonderful, doesn't quite bring it off as I
should like to see it done, to hear it done, by some great man. It can
never be done.

Now I'm coming to the suburbs because I'm always considered a
satiric poet, because I write about suburbs and make jokes. And
I don't think the suburbs are funny particularly – well, they are funny
a bit, but I think they're also beautiful. And I was very surprised the
other day. I got a letter from the BBC saying they were doing a programme of satiric verse and they were putting in my poem
'Parliament Hill Fields', which is about the suburbs. Just tell me if you
think it's satiric. There's one line which could be said to be satiric,
which the man from the BBC quoted. I refused permission but it

struck me as odd that it should be thought satiric. Parliament Hill Fields are up in North London, you know. Hampstead Heath. The sort of slummy end of Hampstead Heath.

> Rumbling under blackened girders, Midland, bound for
>   Cricklewood,
> Puffed its sulphur to the sunset where that Land of Laundries stood.

(That was the satiric line.)

> Rumble under, thunder over, train and tram alternate go,
> Shake the floor and smudge the ledger, Charrington, Sells, Dale
>   and Co.,
> Nuts and nuggets in the window, trucks along the lines below.
>
> When the Bon Marché was shuttered, when the feet were hot and
>   tired,
> Outside Charrington's we waited, by the 'STOP HERE IF
>   REQUIRED',
> Launched aboard the shopping basket, sat precipitately down,
> Ricked past Zwanziger the baker's, and the terrace blackish brown,
> And the curious Anglo-Norman parish church of Kentish Town.
>
> Till the tram went over thirty, sighting terminus again,
> Past municipal lawn tennis and the bobble-hanging plane;
> Soft the light suburban evening caught our ashlar-speckled spire,
> Eighteen-sixty Early English, as the mighty elms retire,
> Either side of Brookfield Mansions flashing fine French-window
>   fire.
>
> Oh the after-tram-ride quiet, when we heard a mile beyond,
> Silver music from the bandstand, barking dogs by Highgate Pond;
> Up the hill where stucco houses in Virginia creeper drown –
> And my childish wave of pity, seeing children carrying down
> Sheaves of drooping dandelions to the courts of Kentish Town.

I was born in London in the borough of St Pancras and brought up in London, north of the Thames most of the time; and for my holidays I used to go down to Cornwall. There's one favourite part of mine in North Cornwall: Greenaway Beach, down near Polzeath and Trebetherick where I was brought up as a boy and which still is a lonely place – especially out of season – now. And this is a poem

which, I hope, gives some of the frightening quality of the North
Cornish coast. Greenaway.

I know so well this turfy mile,
    These clumps of sea-pink withered brown,
The breezy cliff, the awkward stile,
    The sandy path that takes me down

To crackling layers of broken slate
    Where black and flat sea-woodlice crawl
And isolated rock pools wait
    Wash from the highest tides of all.

I know the roughly blasted track
    That skirts a small and smelly bay
And over squelching bladderwrack
    Leads to the beach at Greenaway.

Down on the shingle safe at last
    I hear the slowly dragging roar
As mighty rollers mount to cast
    Small coal and seaweed on the shore,

And spurting far as it can reach·
    The shooting surf comes hissing round
To heave a line along the beach
    Of cowries waiting to be found.

Tide after tide by night and day
    The breakers battle with the land
And rounded smooth along the bay
    The faithful rocks protecting stand.

But in a dream the other night
    I saw this coastline from the sea
And felt the breakers plunging white
    Their weight of waters over me.

There were the stile, the turf, the shore,
    The safety line of shingle beach
With every stroke I struck the more
    The backwash sucked me out of reach.

Back into what a water-world
    Of waving weed and waiting claws?

Of writhing tentacles uncurled
   To drag me to what dreadful jaws?

You know that sort of agonizing feeling one has as a child when one comes back from the country and you find yourself in London again and you try to pretend everything's the sea. That's what I've tried to convey in this poem, which is a child thinking, while it lives at Harrow, about the happy time it had by the sea:

When melancholy Autumn comes to Wembley
   And electric trains are lighted after tea
The poplars near the Stadium are trembly
   With their tap and tap and whispering to me,
      Like the sound of little breakers
      Spreading out along the surf-line
When the estuary's filling
      With the sea.

Then Harrow-on-the-Hill's a rocky island
   And Harrow churchyard full of sailors' graves
And the constant click and kissing of the trolley buses hissing
   Is the level to the Wealdstone turned to waves
      And the rumble of the railway
      Is the thunder of the rollers
As they gather up for plunging
      Into caves.

There's a storm cloud to the westward over Kenton,
   There's a line of harbour lights at Perivale,
Is it rounding rough Pentire in a flood of sunset fire
   The little fleet of trawlers under sail?
      Can those boats be only roof tops
      As they stream along the skyline
In a race for port and Padstow
      With the gale?

While we're on this childhood business, there was one poem that I think combines topography and love – childhood love, you know – which was the result of the *New Stateswoman*★. The *New*

★ Betjeman's name for the *New Statesman*.

Stateswoman had a competition to write a poem on indoor games, in *my* style. I was awfully flattered and several people went in for it and I didn't think that I ought not to go in for it, but if I went in for it I might not have won, so I waited till the competition was over and then I sent them this one, which is set near Newbury. I don't much like the country round Newbury although I live near it. It's sort of conifer and card playing and catching the 10.15. You know the sort of atmosphere. And I've tried to convey that in this poem – but the nice side of it, of course, would be the children's parties, which I've also tried to convey: in among riches and children's parties and crunchy gravel drives and Lagondas and things. I'm very nineteen twentyish. I don't know what things are like now.

In among the silver birches winding ways of tarmac wander
   And the signs to Bussock Bottom, Tussock Wood and Windy
      Brake,
Gabled lodges, tile-hung churches, catch the lights of our Lagonda
   As we drive to Wendy's party, lemon curd and Christmas cake.
      Rich the makes of motor whirring,
      Past the pine-plantation purring
        Come up, Hupmobile, Delage!
      Short the way your chauffeurs travel,
      Crunching over private gravel
        Each from out his warm garáge.

Oh but Wendy, when the carpet yielded to my indoor pumps
      There you stood, your gold hair streaming,
      Handsome in the hall-light gleaming
There you looked and there you led me off into the game of clumps
      Then the new Victrola playing
      And your funny uncle saying
'Choose your partners for a fox-trot! Dance until its *tea* o'clock!
    'Come on young 'uns, foot it featly!'
      Was it chance that paired us neatly,
      I, who loved you so completely,
You, who pressed me closely to you, hard against your party frock?

(By the way, that love I think one experiences at a child's party is the deepest thing that one ever goes through. You know, when one's about nine or ten. Wonderful, self-sacrificing love.)

'Meet me when you've finishing eating!' So we met and no one
    found us.
  Oh that dark and furry cupboard while the rest played hide and
    seek!

(Interesting Freudian bit, that.)

Holding hands, our two hearts beating in the bedroom silence
    round us,
  Holding hands and hardly hearing sudden footstep, thud and shriek.
    Love that lay too deep for kissing –
    'Where *is* Wendy? Wendy's missing!'
      Love so pure it *had* to end,
    Love so strong that I was frighten'd
    When you gripped my fingers tight and
Hugging, whispered, 'I'm your friend'.

Then, that wonderful recollection afterwards:

Goodbye Wendy! Send the fairies, pinewood elf and larch tree gnome,
    Spingle-spangled stars are peeping
    At the lush Lagonda creeping
Down the winding ways of tarmac to the leaded lights of home.
    There, among the silver birches,
    All the bells of all the churches
Sounded in the bath-waste running out into the frosty air.
    Wendy speeded my undressing;
    Wendy is the sheet's caressing
    Wendy bending gives a blessing,
Holds me as I drift to dreamland, safe inside my slumber-wear.

Then from that first love one moves to the rather more conventional and, I regret to say, *lustful* poems about great strapping sports
girls that I always see as being very beautiful, and this one that I'm
going to read, called 'Pot Pourri from a Surrey Garden', is about the
beauties of Surrey – conifers and tennis courts and that kind of thing,
which has always seemed to me one of the charms of the English
countryside, especially when it's near London. And these girls displaying among the conifers:

Miles of pram in the wind and Pam in the gorse track,
  Coco-nut smell of the broom, and a packet of Weights

Press'd in the sand. The thud of a hoof on a horse-track –
    A horse-riding horse for a horse-track –
    Conifer county of Surrey approached
  Through remarkable wrought-iron gates.

Over your boundary now, I wash my face in a bird-bath,
    Then which path shall I take? that over there by the pram?
Down by the pond! or – yes, I will take the slippery third path,
    Trodden away with gym shoes,
    Beautiful fir-dry alley that leads
  To the bountiful body of Pam.

Pam, I adore you, Pam, you great big mountainous sports girl,
    Whizzing them over the net, full of the strength of five:
That old Malvernian brother, you zephyr and khaki shorts girl,
    Although he's playing for Woking,
    Can't stand up
  To your wonderful backhand drive.

See the strength of her arm, as firm and hairy as Hendren's;
    See the size of her thighs, the pout of her lips as, cross,
And full of pent-up strength, she swipes at the rhododendrons,
    Lucky the rhododendrons,
    And flings her arrogant love-lock
  Back with a petulant toss.

Over the redolent pinewoods, in at the bathroom casement,
    One fine Saturday, Windlesham bells shall call:
Up the Butterfield aisle rich with Gothic enlacement,
    Licensed now for embracement,
    Pam and I, as the organ
  Thunders over you all.

Now, oh yes, now I'm just going read a few of a more mature nature on the kind of girl I like. I ought to explain it's terrible really to be doing this stuff and calling it love because there's a good deal more of lust, I fear, in it than love. But on the other hand I think it's not indecent at all. I hope not. And this poem – I was inspired originally to write a lot of poems by my ideal: the sort of girl who would be a swimming blue and had gold hair and blue eyes and was strong and Scandinavian-looking. And Mrs Piper, the wife of my friend

John Piper, is like that, though she's Welsh. She is a swimming
blue and she has gold hair and she is strong and very beautiful-
looking, and I wrote a poem imagining her in her childhood, and
then I wrote one that John Sparrow didn't include in my selected
poems that he made, so I'm going to read it to you now, about her
at Oxford. She went up to Oxford. Do you know North Oxford
some of you? Yes.

> Pink may, double may, dead laburnum
> > Shedding an Anglo-Jackson shade,
> Shall we ever, my staunch Myfanwy,
> > Bicycle down to North Parade?
> Kant on the handle-bars, Marx in the saddle bag,
> > Light my touch on your shoulder-blade.
>
> Sancta Hilda, Myfanwyatia
> > Evansensis – I hold your heart,
> Willowy banks of a willowy Cherwell a
> > Willowy figure with lips apart,
> Strong and willowy, strong to pillow me,
> > Gold Myfanwy, kisses and art.
>
> Tubular bells of tall St Barnabas,
> > Single clatter above St Paul,
> Chasuble, acolyte, incense-offering,
> > Spectacled faces held in thrall.
> There in the nimbus and Comper tracery
> > Gold Myfanwy blesses us all.
>
> Gleam of gas upon Oxford station,
> > Gleam of gas on her straight gold hair,
> Hair flung back with an ostentation,
> > Waiting alone for a girl friend there.
> Second in Mods and a Third in Theology
> > Come to breathe again Oxford air.
>
> *Her* Myfanwy as in Cadena days,
> > *Her* Myfanwy, a schoolgirl voice,
> Tentative brush of a cheek in a cocoa crush,
> > Coffee and Ulysses, Tennyson, Joyce,
> Alpha-minded and other dimensional,
> > Freud or Calvary? Take your choice.

Her Myfanwy? *My* Myfanwy.
   Bicycle bells in a Boar's Hill Pine,
Stedman Triple from All Saints' steeple,
   Tom and his hundred and one at nine,
Bells of Butterfield, caught in Keble,
   Sally and backstroke answer '*Mine!*'

Then after that came this sense of guilt that one shouldn't write that kind of poetry, if poetry you call it, and I wrote a poem which is rather depressing called 'Senex', about the sense of horror at being so moved by physical beauty only:

Oh would I could subdue the flesh
   Which sadly troubles me!
And then perhaps could view the flesh
As though I never knew the flesh
   And merry misery.

To see the golden hiking girl
   With wind about her hair,
The tennis-playing, biking girl,
The wholly-to-my-liking girl,
   To see and not to care.

At sundown on my tricycle
   I tour the Borough's edge,
And icy as an icicle
See bicycle by bicycle
   Stacked waiting in the hedge.

Get down from me! I thunder there,
   You spaniels! Shut your jaws!
Your teeth are stuffed with underwear,
Suspenders torn asunder there
   And buttocks in your paws!

Oh whip the dogs away my Lord,
   They make me ill with lust.
Bend bare knees down to pray, my Lord,
Teach sulky lips to say, my Lord,
   That flaxen hair is dust.

After that there comes a certain amount of poetry that reflects one's feeling as one gets older that there's no chance of anyone loving one again – and love played a large part in my writings of poetry. Now you know how when you've been ill everything is more beautiful and more wonderful than when you're ordinarily quite well. Well, this was my state when I went to stay on the Beaulieu River and I rowed out in a dinghy. It was a hot day and I was lying back in the boat recovering from having rowed when suddenly a sharpie passed – a sharpie is a small sailing boat – with the most beautiful girl you can imagine in it and she asked me the time. There was a young man with her in the boat, too. She asked me the time and in order not to disappoint her, although I hadn't got a watch on me, I just made up the time so as to get a nice smile from her. And then she sailed out of my life. And I thought, Well, there'd be no chance of her ever loving me and so I shall put myself into – her name was Clemency by the way, and she was the daughter of a General Buckland – I shall put myself into the position of some old lady sitting by the lakeside, by the riverside, and seeing her go by. It's called 'Youth and Age on Beaulieu River'. And I may tell you one further point: when you're in the sailing world and messing about with small boats, everybody else who messes about with small boats is very critical of you; and along the Beaulieu River there are various houses where people look out from their houses and see sharpies passing and criticize them.

> Early sun on Beaulieu water
>   Lights the undersides of oaks,
> Clumps of leaves it floods and blanches,
> All transparent glow the branches
>   Which the double sunlight soaks;
> To her craft on Beaulieu water
> Clemency the General's daughter
>   Pulls across with even strokes.
>
> Schoolboy-sure she is this morning;
>   Soon her sharpie's rigg'd and free.
> Cool beneath a garden awning
>   Mrs Fairclough, sipping tea
> And raising large long-distance glasses
> As the little sharpie passes,
>   Sighs our sailor girl to see:

Tulip figure, so appealing,
    Oval face, so serious-eyed,
Tree-roots pass'd and muddy beaches.
On to huge and lake-like reaches,
    Soft and sun-warm, see her glide –
Slacks the slim young limbs revealing,
Sun-brown arm the tiller feeling –
    With the wind and with the tide.

Evening light will bring the water,
    Day-long sun will burst the bud,
Clemency, the General's daughter,
    Will return upon the flood.
But the older woman only
Knows the ebb-tide leaves her lonely
    With the shining fields of mud.

Then there's a poem that gives one hope – the purging effect of love – and also the fact that even the most dreary-looking people are transformed by love and raised up. It's rather, I fear, a crib of Hardy, this poem, as it's a thing I saw that happened in a Bath teashop. It's called 'In a Bath Teashop':

'Let us not speak, for the love we bear one another –
    Let us hold hands and look.'
She, such a very ordinary little woman;
    He, such a thumping crook;
But both, for a moment, little lower than the angels
    In the teashop's ingle-nook.

This is about – the final one – the fear of death. That is to me, I suppose, increasingly the one thing that motivates anything I write. Terrified of death. The loneliness of it. Anything rather than extinction. I am a practising Christian like a good many people are but of course, like all practising Christians, these moments of doubt in one's faith keep coming along and to me it's an eternal struggle whether there's an afterlife. I would rather there were an afterlife and that I should go to Hell than there should be extinction. That's how I feel about it. And I have an awful feeling too, and I expect a lot of people do who believe in an afterlife, that they will go to Hell.

I've tried to put all that into a poem that I wrote some time ago in the Ackland Home at Oxford when I was going to be operated on – not very badly, but you know how, if you are going, you get that needle put into you first. And then you have about half an hour to wait. And while I was waiting that half hour, the bells of St Giles's church were practising and the overwhelming loneliness of it rather got me and I wrote it down afterwards, when I'd recovered from the operation, lying back comfortably and happily, knowing that I wasn't going to die for a bit, in the Ackland Home. It's called 'Before the Anaesthetic'. It's the most serious one, I think, that I can read at the moment to you, though there are some manuscript ones incompleted. Can't complete anything as one gets older. Have you noticed that? Dreadful – the zest goes.

> Intolerably sad, profound
> St Giles's bells are ringing round,
> They bring the slanting summer rain
> To tap the chestnut boughs again
> Whose shadowy cave of rainy leaves
> The gusty belfry-song receives.
> Intolerably sad and true,
> Victorian red and jewel blue,

(That's cribbed from a novel of Rumer Godden. With acknowledgements.)

> The mellow bells are ringing round
> And charge the evening light with sound,
> And I look motionless from bed
> On heavy trees and purple red
> And hear the midland bricks and tiles
> Throw back the bells of stone St Giles,
> Bells, ancient now as castle walls,
> Now hard and new as pitchpine stalls,
>
> Now full with help from ages past,
> Now dull with death and hell at last.
> Swing up! and give me hope of life,
> Swing down! and plunge the surgeon's knife.
> I, breathing for a moment, see

Death wing himself away from me
And think, as on this bed I lie,
Is it extinction when I die?

I move my limbs and use my sight;
Not yet, thank God, not yet the Night.
Oh better far those echoing hells
Half-threaten'd in the pealing bells
Than that this 'I' should cease to be –
Come quickly, Lord, come quick to me.
St Giles's bells are asking now
'And hast thou known the Lord, hast thou?'

St Giles's bells, they richly ring
'And was that Lord our Christ the King?'
St. Giles's bells they hear me call
I never knew the Lord at all.
Oh not in me your Saviour dwells
You ancient, rich St Giles's bells.
Illuminated missals – spires –
Wide screens and decorated quires –

All these I loved, and on my knees
I thanked myself for knowing these
And watched the morning sunlight pass
Through richly stained Victorian glass.
And in the colour-shafted air
I, kneeling, thought the Lord was there.
Now, lying in the gathering mist
I know that Lord did not exist;

Now, less this 'I' should cease to be,
Come, real Lord, come quick to me.
With every gust the chestnut sighs,
With every breath, a mortal dies;
The man who smiled alone, alone,
And went his journey on his own
With 'Will you give my wife this letter,
In case, of course, I don't get better?'

Waits for his coffin lid to close
On waxen head and yellow toes.

Almighty Saviour, had I Faith
There'd be no fight with kindly Death.
Intolerably long and deep
St Giles's bells swing on in sleep:
'But still you go from here alone'
Say all the bells about the Throne.

COPYRIGHT ACKNOWLEDGEMENTS

The author and publisher would like to acknowledge the following for allowing usage of copyright material: Extracts from *Ancient Lights* by Ford Madox Ford (London, Chapman and Hall, 1911) are reproduced by permission of David Higham Associates Ltd on behalf of the Estate of Ford Madox Ford. References to R. M. Healey's essay 'Grigson as Broadcaster' in *My Rebellious and Imperfect Eye: Observing Geoffrey Grigson*, edited by C. C. Barfoot and R. M. Healey (Amsterdam-New York, Rodopi, 2002) have been allowed by permission of R. M. Healey and Rodopi. Extracts from *The Annihilation of Man* by Leslie Paul (London, Faber & Faber, 1944) are reproduced by kind permission of Paul Wilkinson, executor of the Estate and nephew of Leslie Paul. Extracts from the poems of Sir Henry Newbolt are reproduced by kind permission of Peter Newbolt, executor of the Estate and son of Sir Henry Newbolt. Material originating in *A Winter's Tale* by David Winter (Lion Hudson plc, 2001) is referred to by permission of David Winter and Lion Hudson plc. Part of 'On a Great Election' from *Complete Verse* by Hilaire Belloc (Pimilico, 1991), (Copyright © The Estate of Hilaire Belloc 1970) is reproduced by permission of PFD (www.pfd.co.uk) on behalf of the Estate of Hilaire Belloc.

Index

Abbotsbury, Dorset, 109, 280
Aberdeen, 20
Abney, Sir Thomas and Lady, 225
advertisement hoardings, 84
Aidé, Hamilton, 274
Albert, Prince Consort, 75, 276, 282
Alderney, Channel Islands, 281–3
Alexander, Mrs F. M., 14
Allingham, William, 178, 180, 273
Alum Bay, Isle of Wight, 257–8
Annand, Rupert, 20
'Any Questions' (radio programme), 2
Architectural Review, 4
architecture: in Victorian Wessex,
    39–45
Arnold, Matthew, 180
Arts and Crafts movement, 248
Avril, Elsie, 300n

Baldwin, Stanley (*later* 1st Earl), 51
Bampton-in-the-Bush, Oxfordshire,
    300
Baring-Gould, Revd Sabine: JB
    relates imaginative story of, 16; life
    and achievements, 35–6, 189–95;
    collects folk songs, 189–90; as
    historian of Celtic Church, 204;
    The Lives of the Saints, 190; *My Few
    Last Words*, 194; *The Vicar of
    Morwenstow*, 164
Barnby, Sir Joseph, 246n
Barnes, George, 10, 17, 19–20, 26, 28
Barnes, Julia (*née* Miles), 210

Barnes, Revd William, 209–13
Barnstaple: Holy Trinity church, 248
Barry, Sir Charles, 215–16
Bate, Mrs Julia (Toplady's aunt), 198
Bath: JB takes up Admiralty post in,
    19; Georgian architecture, 39, 79;
    Percy Chapel, 44; beauty, 57
Beardsley, Aubrey, 170
Beauchamp, William Lygon, 7th Earl
    of, 248
Beaulieu River, 338
Beer, Dorset, 109
Beerbohm, (Sir) Max, 170
bell-ringing, 130
Belloc, Hilaire: 'On a General
    Election', 141
Belt, Mrs (*née* Davenport), 174
Benson, E. F., 144
Berkshire, 327
Bernstein, Sidney (*later* Baron), 6
Betjeman, Sir John: individuality, 1, 5;
    broadcasting career, 2–3, 5–7,
    9–11, 20–1, 26–8; architectural
    interests, 4–5, 13; appearance, 5–6;
    nostalgia, 9, 13, 25, 319–24;
    populism, 10–13, 18; wartime
    employment in Ministry of
    Information, 10; on town
    planning, 13–14; missionary zeal,
    14–15; language style, 15–16; as
    wartime press attaché in Dublin,
    17, 135n; Admiralty post in Bath,
    19; earnings, 21–2, 26, 28;

Wells, A. Randall, 248
Wells, H. G., 144
Wesley, John, 196, 199–200, 202–3
Wessex: architecture in, 39–45
Westmeath, Ireland, 155–6
Weston-super-Mare, Somerset, 98,
    102, 110
Wethnoc, Cornish bishop, 205
Weyman, Stanley, 144
Weymouth, Dorset, 109
White, William, 21, 41, 44, 274
Wight, Isle of, 256–8, 275–7
Wightwick, George, 65–6
William I (the Conqueror), King, 78
William IV, King, 63
Williams, Alfred, 68
Williamson, N. and A. M., 144
Willson, Revd Martin, 26
Wimborne St Giles, Dorset, 248

Winchester College, 42
Winter, David, 6, 27
Winter Gardens, 102
'Woman's Hour' (radio programme),
    2, 13
women: slowness in paying, 88
Wood and Foster (architects), 44
Woodyer, Henry, 41, 44
Wordsworth, William, 212, 329
Wren, Sir Christopher, 231
Wright, Thomas, 200–1

Yarmouth, Isle of Wight, 256
Yealmpton, Devon: St Bartholomew
    church, 248
Yeats, W. B.: Newbolt on, 119
Yonge, Charlotte M., 36

Zealley, Mr (of Colyton, Devon), 171

John Betjeman titles available from John Murray

Collected Poems

Collected Poems made publishing history when it first appeared, and has now sold more than two million copies. This newly expanded edition incorporates all Betjeman's poems and, with a new introduction by Poet Laureate Andrew Motion, it is the definitive Betjeman companion.

9780719568503 | Paperback | £12.99

Tennis Whites and Teacakes

A treasure trove of Betjeman's poetry, journalism, radio and television programmes and private letters, revealing his lifetime love affair with England – a place of freckle-faced girls and Oxford toffs, steam trains and country churchyards.

9780719569043 | Paperback | £8.99

Trains and Buttered Toast

Broadcasting in the golden age of wireless, Betjeman was a national treasure for millions of devoted listeners. Here his eccentric, whimsical and homespun radio talks are collected in book form for the first time. From trains and buttered toast to hymn-writing vicars and Regency terraces, he teaches us how to appreciate our heritage.

9780719561276 | Paperback | £7.99

'Betjeman was an original and a star' Daily Mail

The Best Loved Poems of John Betjeman

With a new foreword by Barry Humphries, this selection is a cherished reminder for those who already know Betjeman's poetry, and the perfect gift for those who still have in store the pleasure of discovery.

9780719568343 | Hardback | £9.99

Summoned by Bells

With a new foreword by Griff Rhys Jones, Betjeman's verse autobiography tells the story of his growth to early manhood: seaside holidays; meddling aunts; school bullies; an unexpected moment of religious awakening; then Oxford, and sparkling pen-portraits of the literary greats he met there. His unabashedly musical verse is poignant, comic, reverent, defiant, devoted and – always – full of feeling.

9780719522208 | Hardback | £10

Sweet Songs of Zion

John Betjeman's radio broadcasts on the subject of hymns and hymn writers were his swansong as a broadcaster. 'Hymns are the poems of the people,' Betjeman observes in his first talk, and he shows how this insight has been borne out over generations. Rich in anecdote, these timeless talks will inspire anyone who has a fondness for hymns and delights in Betjeman's unique voice.

9780340963883 | Paperback | £8.99

Order your copies now by calling Bookpoint on 01235 827720 or by visiting your local bookshop

Read more . . .

Bevis Hillier

JOHN BETJEMAN: THE BIOGRAPHY

A masterful biography of John Betjeman, the best-loved English poet since Tennyson who became an institution

The definitive, authorized biography takes the reader from Betjeman's troubled childhood in north London, through his blossoming at Oxford; a gay fling with W. H. Auden; a clandestine marriage to a field marshal's daughter; pranks as a film critic; wartime service and espionage in Ireland; to the glory days of his later years when his *Collected Poems* became a runaway bestseller and he was Poet Laureate, a television personality and a 'teddy-bear to the nation'.

'Never have I come away from a biography with such a clear idea of what it must have been like to have been in a room with its subject . . . Hillier shows that Betjeman was as charming as his poems. It is a charm that it is fruitless to resist' Craig Brown, *Mail on Sunday*

'Bevis Hillier has tackled a lot of intricate material remarkably well, indeed brilliantly' Anthony Powell, *Daily Telegraph*

'A classic' Jad Adams, *Guardian*

Order your copy now by calling Bookpoint on 01235 827716 or visit your local bookshop quoting ISBN 978-0-7195-6444-4 www.johnmurray.co.uk